Gotthold Ephraim Lessing

By F. ANDREW BROWN

Grinnell College

Twayne Publishers, Inc.   ::   New York

Library of Congress Catalog Card Number 75–110709

To M., S., AND T.

FOR PATIENCE
AT HOME AND ABROAD

ABOUT THE AUTHOR

F. Andrew Brown is a native of up-state New York. He attended secondary schools in Lewiston and Buffalo, New York, and holds degrees from Hamilton College, Cornell University, and the University of California, Berkeley.

He has contributed numerous articles to professional journals, primarily on the subject of Anglo-German relations in the eighteenth century. He has been a member of the faculties of UCLA, the University of Michigan, and Grinnell College, where he is at present Professor and Chairman of German.

He is married and the father of two sons.

TWAYNE'S WORLD AUTHORS SERIES

A Survey of the World's Literature

Sylvia E. Bowman, Indiana University
GENERAL EDITOR

GERMANY

Ulrich Weisstein, Indiana University
EDITOR

Gotthold Ephraim Lessing

(TWAS 113)

TWAYNE'S WORLD AUTHORS SERIES (TWAS)

The purpose of TWAS is to survey the major writers —novelists, dramatists, historians, poets, philosophers, and critics—of the nations of the world. Among the national literatures covered are those of Australia, Canada, China, Eastern Europe, France, Germany, Greece, India, Italy, Japan, Latin America, New Zealand, Poland, Russia, Scandinavia, Spain, and the African nations, as well as Hebrew, Yiddish, and Latin Classical literatures. This survey is complemented by Twayne's United States Authors Series and English Authors Series.

The intent of each volume in these series is to present a critical-analytical study of the works of the writer; to include biographical and historical material that may be necessary for understanding, appreciation, and critical appraisal of the writer; and to present all material in clear, concise English—but not to vitiate the scholarly content of the work by doing so.

Preface

The first three quarters of the eighteenth century in Germany present the remarkable phenomenon of a national culture and a national literature coming of age. Immanual Kant's famous definition of Enlightenment—"man's release from his self-incurred tutelage," and his development of the courage to "make use of his understanding without direction from another"—provides in succinct phrases an outline of the German development in which Gotthold Ephraim Lessing (1729–1781) would play a key role.[1]

Lessing's career spans the crucial decades of the Enlightenment, and his principal intellectual efforts are directed to three areas in which progress toward the goal of intellectual maturity may be clearly traced: in literary creation, literary and scholarly criticism, and in those matters of theology which dominated the speculative thought of his age. It is possible to detect in Lessing's contributions to each of them the same stages traversed in theory and practice by German literature and critical thought, as well as by German theological speculation. They reveal a gradual development from marked deference to inspiration from abroad —in the earlier decades of the era the recommended models are primarily French—through an intermediate period of partially independent composition and speculation in the spirit of the accepted foreign tutors (including especially the English) to the ultimate appearance of German works bearing the unmistakable stamp of true independence and originality.

Lessing's most effective predecessor, especially in the realm of literary composition and criticism, was Johann Christoph Gottsched (1700–1760), Professor of Literature and of Logic and Metaphysics at the University of Leipzig when Lessing enrolled there as a student of theology in 1746. Gottsched's combined titles reveal a great deal about the kind of literature he advocated and condoned. As the pronouncements of the virtual literary dictator of his age, his neoclassic, prescriptive principles for literary composition, especially in the drama, stressed regularity in the manner of the French classicists, echoing Boileau, and were spread abroad by his numerous books, notably the *Versuch einer Critischen Dichtkunst für die Deutschen* (1730). Examples of approved plays were then displayed in the six volumes of his *Deutsche Schaubühne nach den Regeln der alten Griechen und Römer eingerichtet* (1740–1745). The collection featured numerous translations from the French, as well as originals by Gottsched himself, his disciples, and his faithful wife and collaborator, Luise Adelgunde Viktorie, a gifted translator with a considerable dramatic talent. Gottsched's ideas on all manner of other topics reached a wide audience through the pages of his popular weeklies, *Die Vernünftigen Tadlerinnen* (1725–1726), which passed through three editions, and *Der Biedermann* (1727–1729), as well as through the efforts of the many students and followers who emulated him in their literary careers.

Gottsched's faithful adherence to the philosophical teachings of Christian Wolff (1679–1754), the disciple of Leibniz and popularizer of the master's fundamentally optimistic view, which assumed the perfectibility of man in this best of all possible worlds, helped to maintain Wolffian rationalism as the orthodox philosophical program of the age.

It has long been a commonplace of German literary histories to deplore the influence of Gottsched, but he also has his apologists, who remind us of the salutary effects of his efforts to introduce elements of organization and restraint into the virtual anarchy then reigning, especially in the realm of drama. They point out that his strictures were by no means altogether detrimental to the cause of German literature at that stage of its development.

Opposition to Gottsched's monopolistic control over literary production and taste began to manifest itself about 1740 in a rival "school" in Zurich under the joint leadership of Johann Jakob Bodmer and Johann Jakob Breitinger. Inspired by their study of Milton, these Swiss critics began a campaign of opposition to Gottsched and his French models under the new watchwords, Imagination and Picturesque Expression, as they professed to find these qualities in Milton's work. The famous feud between Gottsched and the Swiss raged for years, punctuated by the appearance of manifestos, declarations, treatises, and attempted demonstrations of the contending views by the rivals and their followers. Much of the literary history of these years consists in tracing the gradual ascendancy of the Swiss view and the gradual eclipse of Gottsched. Without allying himself with the Swiss camp, Lessing, as a critic and playwright, was destined to play an important role in the continuation of this process.

In theology, the Enlightenment was dominated by the sharp and protracted debate between the advocates of traditional and unquestioning faith in respect to matters of religion, and the champions of reason, who argued the necessity for intellectual analysis and rational derivation of religious tenets. In this process, the English Deists played an influential role. Their ideas began to make their way into Germany in the early decades of the century, and by mid-century the orthodox could complain that the Deists were being read everywhere.

Much of the conflicting testimony was directed to the problem of revelation and the degree of reason admissible in its analysis. Here the Deists took the position that even the content of a supposed revelation must be submitted to rational examination. If it proved to be incompatible with reason's dictates, it should be rejected.[2] At the opposite extreme were the orthodox believers in a positive, revealed religion which admitted of no rational inquiry or test. Their opposition to the troublesome new ideas found reflection in a flood of polemical writings which served unwittingly to broadcast the very theories they wished to combat. (Lessing would later admit that his first urge to investigate the claims of the attackers was inspired by this wave of attempted vindications.)[3]

Between these two extremes were found the "supernatural rationalists" or practitioners of "rational orthodoxy," who would urge a compromise, permitting human reason to judge of a revelation's credentials, its claim to divine origin, but not of its content.[4] Naturally enough, the attempt to distinguish between valid and invalid revelation led to spirited controversy, and the history of theological development in the period can be recounted, in large measure, in terms of the increasingly important role assigned to human reason in arriving at such decisions. Lessing's earliest theological writings are couched in terms of this conflict, and one of his more significant early comedies deals with the ever increasing activity of the so-called "freethinkers"— a blanket term covering all those who questioned, in the name of reason, the least tenet of the orthodox canon, or exhibited unconventionality in a number of other ways. The criticism of these rebels might range from petty quibbling to confirmed atheism. Lessing's effort to come to terms with the contending claims of faith and reason informs his theological speculation from first to last.

While Germany may be said to have emulated, in its eighteenth-century development, the accomplishments of enlightened neighboring states in the realms of literature, criticism, and theological speculation, it does not share to the same degree the liberal, even revolutionary, political implications of the process of enlightenment. Though a number of Lessing's works attest a well-developed political awareness, his ultimate aim quite transcends the political realities in the age of absolutism in which his career unfolded. He advocates broad and supranational principles which direct our attention beyond the provincialism of his own era and the nationalism of the nineteenth century to an era of political tolerance still the remote dream of all men of good will.

In his contribution to the development of a German prose capable of expressing the ideas appropriate to a literature reaching its maturity, Lessing's role, especially in his own practice, but also to a degree by precept, is universally acknowledged to be vital, though still imperfectly understood in all its ramifications. In the present work, it has been possible to include only passing references to his formative influence.

The necessity to concentrate on Lessing's primary contributions to literature has also dictated the omission of detailed discussions of a number of his other interests and accomplishments, notably his early devotion to Anacreontic verse, his work in the epigram, his continued interest in the theory and practice of the fable—a form which he prized especially as a valuable educational device and a medium for ethical uplift—and his activities as a scholar and antiquarian.

After dwelling upon what is *not* to be found in the following pages, it may not be amiss to assure the reader that the subsequent discussion does contain a four-part treatment, largely chronological, of Lessing's principal contributions to the thought of his age. The first decade of his activity, from about 1746 to 1755, finds him productive in all three of the areas in which he would later excel—as dramatist, critic, and theologian. The first four chapters, therefore, analyze his early attempts in comedy to become the "German Molière," survey his writings as a budding literary critic, review his early experiments in the tragic mode, and describe his youthful exercises in coming to terms with the theological ferment of those years. A second group of chapters (5, 6, and 7) covers Lessing's activity in the years 1755–1760, largely as a critic, and the principal fruits of his subsequent Breslau interlude, the *Laokoon* (1766) and *Minna von Barnhelm* (1767). A third part, chapters 8 through 10, details Lessing's most mature dramatic criticism in the Hamburg period, discusses his most controversial play, *Emilia Galotti*, generally regarded as his demonstration of the critical principles set forth in the *Hamburg-ische Dramaturgie*, and sketches his antiquarian and theological writings in Hamburg and, thereafter, in Wolfenbüttel. Chapters 11 and 12 are devoted to the visionary Lessing of the final decade of his life; and a concluding chapter then summarizes his accomplishments and attempts to fix his position in the perspective of German literary and cultural history.

In all of this, the informed reader may well note that considerable space is devoted to the work of Lessing's earlier years, although it is admittedly of far less intrinsic literary value than his masterpieces. The explanation—it seems to me a highly defensible one—is that the works of Lessing's maturity and the degree to which they transcend the norms of his age cannot well be understood without a knowledge of the tradition in which they are grounded. For Lessing is not only a prophet but also a product of his era, seeking to transcend, by recourse to the powers of reason, the limitations imposed by reason.

The accompanying bibliography is necessarily selective, and while it includes a number of older standard works, it emphasizes, on the whole, more recent and more accessible sources as a point of departure for those who would pursue the study of Lessing beyond the introductory level. Additional specialized essays are listed in the notes. Much supplementary bibliographical information is readily available in these studies.

For similar reasons of accessibility, I have used the recent Rilla edition ("Rilla" in the notes) as the basis for references to Lessing's works, having recourse to the standard edition of Lachmann-Muncker ("LM") only where the first-named edition is deficient. (Translations in the text and notes are my own unless otherwise indicated.)

It would be remiss not to express here my gratitude to Mr. Henry Alden, Librarian of the Burling Library, Grinnell College, for cooperation quite beyond the call of duty, and to acknowledge with thanks my debt to Mr. Richard Ryan, Order Librarian, for his good-humored and untiring efforts in my behalf. Both are enthusiastic emulators of what might be called Lessing's humane Librarianism.

To the editor of this series, Professor Ulrich Weisstein of Indiana University, I am especially grateful for his patient and helpful counsel on many matters of detail.

I should like to thank the Board of Editors of the *Journal of English and Germanic Philology* and the Columbia University Press for permission to use material from articles of mine previously published in *Journal of English and Germanic Philology* and the *Review of Religion*. The University of Chicago Press has kindly consented to my using quotations from Richmond Lattimore's translation of Homer's *Iliad*. Detailed acknowledgments will be found in the notes.

F. A. B.

Contents

Contents

Chronology

1729 January 22: Lessing born in Kamenz, Saxony.

1741 June: enters St. Afra, Princes' School in Meissen.

1746 Autumn: enters University of Leipzig; student of theology; friendship with Christlob Mylius; C. F. Weisse.

1747 Publishes *Damon, oder die wahre Freundschaft*, a comedy.

1748 January: the comedy *Der junge Gelehrte* successfully performed in Leipzig. Lessing departs for Berlin, arriving in November; journalism under guidance of Mylius; *Berlinische privilegierte Zeitung*; publishes *Der Misogyn*, a comedy.

1749 *Die alte Jungfer; Die Juden; Der Freygeist*, comedies; *Samuel Henzi* (fragmentary tragedy); "An Marpurg" (verse).

1750 *Beyträge zur Historie und Aufnahme des Theaters* (with Mylius), four issues; "Gedanken über die Herrnhuter" (fragmentary essay).

1751 *Das Neueste aus dem Reiche des Witzes*, ed. Lessing, April-December; *Kleinigkeiten* (verses); *Die Religion* (verse fragment); December: to University of Wittenberg.

1752 Awarded Master's degree in April; returns to Berlin in November; *Des Herrn von Voltaire Kleinere Historische Schriften*, tr. by Lessing.

1753 *Ueber die menschliche Glückseligkeit* (verse fragment); *Das Christentum der Vernunft* (fragment).

1753– *Schrifften*, 6 vols., including *Briefe, Rettungen*, five come-
1755 dies, and *Miss Sara Sampson* (bourgeois tragedy). The latter a great success at first performance, Frankfurt/O., July, 1755; friendship with Mendelssohn (from 1753), Nicolai, Ramler.

1754 *Vade mecum für den Hrn. Sam. Gotth. Lange.*

1754– *Theatralische Bibliothek*, three issues; a fourth in 1758.
1755

15

1755   *Pope ein Metaphysiker!* (with Mendelssohn); work on a Faust-drama mentioned; other literary studies.

1756   May-August: beginning of a European tour, interrupted by outbreak of Seven Years' War. Returns to Leipzig; friendship with Ewald von Kleist; Preface to James Thomson's Tragedies.

1756–   Correspondence on tragedy with Mendelssohn and Nicolai.
1757

1757   *Hrn. Samuel Richardsons . . . Sittenlehre für die Jugend . . .* tr. by Lessing.

1758   May: Kleist leaves Leipzig; Lessing returns soon thereafter to Berlin.

1759   *Philotas* (tragedy in one act); Preface to Logau's *Sinngedichte; Briefe, die neueste Literatur betreffend;* containing many Lessing contributions, 1759–1760; *Fabeln . . . nebst Abhandlungen; Das Theater des Herrn Diderot; Sophokles.*

1760–   Lessing in Breslau; military secretary. Studies in the clas-
1765   sics, theology, and philosophy. Conception of *Minna von Barnhelm* and *Laokoon.*

1766   *Laokoon, oder über die Grenzen der Malerei und Poesie;* Lessing in Berlin.

1767   *Minna von Barnhelm;* first performance, Hamburg, September 30; Lessing as critic for the National Theater in Hamburg.

1767–   *Hamburgische Dramaturgie.*
1768

1768–   *Briefe antiquarischen Inhalts.*
1769

1769   *Wie die Alten den Tod gebildet.*

1770   May: librarian in Wolfenbüttel; *Berengarius Turonensis.*

1771   *Zerstreute Anmerkungen über das Epigramm. . . .*

1772   *Emilia Galotti;* tragedy.

1773ff. *Zur Geschichte und Literatur; aus den Schätzen der Herzoglichen Bibliothek zu Wolfenbüttel.*

1774   *Von Duldung der Deisten* (the first of the *Fragmente . . . aus den Papieren eines Ungenannten*).

1775   Italian journey as companion to Prince Leopold of Braunschweig.

1776   October: marriage to Eva König.

1777   *Ein Mehreres aus den Papieren des Ungenannten* (five additional *Fragmente*);*Ueber den Beweis des Geistes und der Kraft; Das Testament Johannis; Die Erziehung des Menschengeschlechts,* §§ 1–53.
December: death of new-born son.

1778   January 10: death of Lessing's wife; *Eine Duplik; Eine Parabel*...; *Axiomata; Anti–Goeze* (eleven pamphlets); *Von dem Zwecke Jesu und seiner Jünger* (the sixth *Fragment,* now published in full); *Nötige Antwort auf eine sehr unnötige Frage des Herrn Hauptpastor Goeze, in Hamburg; Ernst und Falk, Gespräche für Freimäurer,* Nos. 1-3; *Nathan der Weise; ein dramatisches Gedicht.*

1780   *Die Erziehung des Menschengeschlechts* (in full); *Die Religion Christi* (fragment); *Ernst und Falk,* 4–5.

1781   February 15: death of Lessing in Braunschweig.

Gotthold Ephraim Lessing

CHAPTER 1

The Early Comedies

I The Making of a Playwright

GOTTHOLD EPHRAIM LESSING was born in the little walled town of Kamenz in Saxony, not far from the city of Meissen, on January 22, 1729. As the second son and third of the twelve children born to Johann Gottfried and Justina Salome Lessing, young Gotthold was early exposed to an air of chronic financial need, as well as to that concern for the spiritual and intellectual inertia of the public at large which so frequently plagued his scholarly, orthodox, harried, and sometimes irascible father, who was then the junior Lutheran pastor in the town. Both of these concerns would periodically occupy the future playwright, critic, and theologian throughout his life. But as a descendent of a line of clergymen, the child Lessing also breathed an atmosphere of concern for religion and theology which was encouraged by his earliest education. This took place at first under the tutelage of his father, and then as a pupil in Johann Gottfried Heinitz' progressive local Latin school.[1] By the age of twelve, young Lessing was ready for St. Afra, the Princes' School in nearby Meissen.

Lessing entered the school in June, 1741, and his diligence soon earned him a scholarship. Despite a demanding schedule and a Spartan regimen—it is recorded that he was a participant in a student demonstration protesting the scanty meals served there— he proved to be an apt pupil, sometimes inclined to be cheeky, but insatiable in his appetite for knowledge; he was "a horse that required double rations" in the judgment of his teachers. Thus he not only handled the heavy required program with relative ease, but also used the opportunity for independent work to further his knowledge of mathematics, modern foreign languages, modern German literature, and the writers of classic comedy. Later he reported that, in retrospect, these seemed to him the only happy years of his life, when "Theophrastus, Plautus, and Terence were

18

my world."[2] All in all, the St. Afra years provided Lessing with a solid education unsurpassed in the Germany of his day. It is not surprising that in five years, rather than in the usual six, the young student had, in large measure, exhausted the potential of the school, and after delivering a graduation address "De Mathematica barbarorum" (On the Mathematics of the Barbarians), he was adjudged ready for the university.

At the University of Leipzig, where in the fall of 1746 he dutifully enrolled as a student of theology, he soon found the lectures in the liberal arts more to his taste, and theology was largely neglected. But in the restless, inquiring manner already typical of his intellectual bent, he also became convinced, as he later reported, that although books would make him learned, they could never make him a human being.[3] To act upon his convictions would prove characteristic of him; here this quality is apparent in the campaign he launched to acquire the skills and graces of elegant Leipzig society. "A little Paris," the young Goethe called the city two decades later when he, in turn, enrolled as a student there; and young Lessing might well have agreed, as he proceeded to learn dancing, riding, and fencing, and to be seen about town in the company of his journalistically inclined colleague, Christlob Mylius, and the group of young writers about him.[4] In this atmosphere he could extend his knowledge of contemporary literature; he soon became as adept as his friends in tossing off light and witty verses in the Anacreontic manner, then in great favor, and he joined them with enthusiasm as they patronized the performances of the local theater troupe directed by Karoline Neuber and her husband.

Since 1727, the Neuber company had held the local "privilege" in Leipzig—a theater monopoly granted by the ruling prince—and had enjoyed for years the almost equally powerful favor of Johann Christoph Gottsched (1700–60), Germany's principal arbiter in matters of literary taste as well as philosophic speculation. Lessing was thoroughly captivated by the theater, and not less so by the company of actors and actresses, with one of whom, the soubrette Christiane Friederike Lorenz, rumor linked him at the time, and legend thereafter.[5] On one occasion he even made bold to criticize a Gottsched play which had drawn much applause, and when his friends mockingly challenged him to produce a better one, he responded by retrieving the draft of a piece concocted in Meissen school days, and after revising it, he submitted it to Mrs. Neuber. She accepted it, and *Der junge Gelehrte* (*The Young Scholar*) was performed with great success in January, 1748. Since another play of Lessing's had already been printed in one of Mylius' journals, and some of his verses and narrative pieces in another, it is clear that in his first year at the university he had exhibited unmistakable and dangerous literary inclinations.

News of the prodigal's downward course had inevitably filtered back to Kamenz. His association with Mylius, a notorious freethinker and hence anathema to the orthodox, had been disturbing enough. His theater attendance had been another ominous symptom, but the revelation of his descent into playwriting was the final proof of his utter moral collapse. Periodic warnings in letters from Pastor Lessing had failed of their purpose; so the son was now summoned home on the rather unkind pretext that his mother lay at death's door. A good deal of serious discussion ensued in Kamenz before the young student was permitted to return to Leipzig for the summer term, this time as a student of medicine.

But despite his efforts to apply himself to his studies, Lessing's former habits reasserted themselves and his debts again mounted. The Neuber troupe departed from the city, Mylius left for Berlin to pursue a journalistic career, and Lessing set out to follow him, only to fall ill, enroute, at Wittenberg. After a brief interlude of convalescence there, during which he enrolled as a student of medicine at the university, he departed for Berlin, arriving in the city in November, 1748, determined to explore to the full his potential as a writer. What he had thus far produced provided some justification for hope as well as for thoughtful reservations regarding his dramatic talent. His first published work was chiefly calculated to give him pause.

II *The First Play*: Damon, oder die wahre Freundschaft

The play in question was the one-act comedy, *Damon, or True Friendship*, which in 1747 had appeared in Mylius' periodical, *Ermunterungen zum Vergnügen des Gemüts*. It is not hard to understand why the author later regretted the premature appearance of this play, as well as the publication of another early comedy, *Die alte Jungfer* (*The Old Maid*), and why he included neither in the collected editions of his works.

Damon derives from the Meissen school days, a time, as he later admitted, when he "knew people only as they appeared in books," and devoted his efforts to the delineation of "fools whose basic nature was a matter of indifference" to him.[6] Thus in his earliest work he was content to borrow liberally, alter little, and remain aloof from the fate of his characters. Not surprisingly, the result betrayed more manipulation than creative magic.

In *Damon*, the theme is friendship, an important concern in sentimental circles of that day. The play contrasts the two friends, Damon and Leander—the former a "true" friend, pathologically concerned to demonstrate a capacity for selfless devotion to this tender relationship, and the latter a "false" friend who nonetheless seems to Damon a virtuoso in the art of friendship. In reality, Leander seeks only his own advantage and would gain by trickery the hand of "The Widow" for which they are "friendly" rivals. His stratagems are eventually exposed, and although Damon has been unfortunate in his commercial exploits, The Widow nonetheless favors his suit over Leander's because Damon has demonstrated a "greatness of soul," and has been granted illumination on the falseness of his "friend." He need no longer unduly plague himself about his own capacity for true friendship; an excessive preoccupation which, in the past, has prevented him from actively pressing the claims of love. Such is her judgment, but we may be inclined to question it, for Damon, in the next breath, forgives Leander's "overhastiness," and insists that The Widow concur as a prerequisite to their marriage. An element of ambiguity thus remains, and the piece ends with a somewhat bemused Widow justifiably wondering if, after all, her principal rival for Damon's affection will not continue to be Leander, the "friend."

There is in the play much invocation of "heart" and some mention of "love," but it is clear that they are apprehended through the intellect alone. Only later will they come into their own as genuine emotional elements and anti-intellectual forces in Lessing's work.[7]

Lessing's attempts at humor in this first effort are equally rudimentary, and the motivation halting. Leander's overblown assurances of undying friendship ought to impress only by their hollowness; and the patent sophistry with which he can rational-

ize his betrayal of his dearest friend, and Damon's willingness
to forgive everything for the flimsiest reasons, together create the
effect of satire within a sentimental framework; an unconscious
satire on a favorite theme of sentimental comedy.[8]

In his next comedy, Lessing turned to overt satire, and since
the theme more accurately reflected his own intellectual bent,
the work proved to be much more satisfying, and, incidentally,
a popular success.

III   Sentiment to Satire: Der junge Gelehrte

This play in three acts, The Young Scholar, represented the
reworking of another Meissen sketch, this one supplemented by
the suggestions of Lessing's Leipzig mentor, Abraham Gotthelf
Kästner, a professor of mathematics and sometime poet, as well
as by Lessing's own broadened acquaintance with the pedants to
be found in learned circles. This was the only sort of "fool," he
later wrote (Preface to Schrifften, III and IV), about whom he
could write at this time from first-hand acquaintance.

Our pedant is Damis, who has written a treatise for a prize
contest on Leibniz' monad theory announced by the Berlin
Academy of Sciences.[9] He now impatiently awaits news of his
"inevitable" victory. In addition to the mild suspense thus generated, Lessing also makes it uncertain whether Damis or Valer
will win the hand of Juliane, the young and beautiful but supposedly penniless ward of Damis' merchant father, Chrysander.

Valer, the rival, is Damis' former friend and a one-time pedant
who has reformed, for like Lessing he has seen the danger inherent in an excessive preoccupation with books. But his romantic
prospects are dim, for Chrysander has discovered a document
which will make possible a successful suit for the recovery of
Juliane's lost fortune. This makes her a most desirable match for
his son, and her own overpowering sense of duty to her guardian
bids her renounce her true love Valer and agree to marry Damis.

To a greater extent than in Damon, the rather scanty action is
initiated and carried forward in the manner of traditional comedy
by the clever and resourceful maid Lisette; but only the arrival
of the long-awaited contest news from Berlin can resolve the
fundamentally static conflict. Damis is not the winner; indeed, his
essay could not even be considered, since it dealt only with
pedantic trifles.

Instead of being downcast, Damis is merely enraged by this mortal insult to his scholarly attainments. He resolves to forsake Germany, a land of idiots and fools, and travel abroad to more receptive intellectual climes, leaving Juliane, merely another "stupid German," to Valer. Here Damis anticipates his creator's later and more justified criticisms of the German reading public and theater audiences for their obscurantism, their lack of taste, and their excessive deference to foreign models:[10]

Though the play does not extend to the five acts recommended by Gottsched for comedies of the "higher" sort, Lessing's first performed work does conform in several essential respects to the Leipzig dictator's notions concerning the genre. Comedy, for Gottsched, was merely an intellectual exercise, aimed at perceiving, through comparison with one's own rational norm, the irrational or exaggerated aspects of human behavior as revealed by the playwright. The onlooker presumably recognizes the weakness in himself and, in consequence, is moved to self-improvement, the ultimate aim of Gottschedian comedy. But the playwright's target had to be a relatively harmless fault or quirk, neither unlawful nor subject to serious consequences. For the mood of comedy would otherwise be shattered and the audience remain unenlightened. Nor would Gottsched admit sentiment in comedy proper, for he realized that the intrusion of an emotional element was inimical to the comic spirit, which requires a temporary suspension of the power of sympathy. Plays with such an admixture should not be called comedies, Gottsched insisted, but "tragi-comedies" or even "bourgeois tragedies."[11] In short, comedy, for Gottsched, was a form of satire, and *Der junge Gelehrte* a work in fundamental accord with Gottschedian principles.

In another respect, however, Lessing's play at least approaches the limits of the prescribed system. Midway in the third act (III.ix), Damis departs after a particularly numbing display of his pedantic inhumanity. Juliane suggests that Damis is a proper object of ridicule, but Valer echoes the audience reaction when he replies: "No, Juliane, . . . it almost takes a sort of cruelty to be amused at such a deplorable fool." Sympathy or pity, or indeed any of the deeper and gentler emotions, had no place in the Gottschedian scheme. The mild hint at them here is therefore worth noticing, in light of their subsequent importance to Lessing's development as a playwright and critic.

For the most part, then, *Der junge Gelehrte* travels a well-marked pathway. And yet Lessing's natural gifts as a dramatist inject a certain liveliness, particularly in his handling of witty and pointed dialogue.[12] Despite obvious borrowings, he shows a flair for treating the foreign materials with some skill and indicates that the introduction of a "fool" with whom he could "feel involved" could result in a play which was equal to any of the German pieces then being produced.[13] Mrs. Neuber hailed the young Lessing as a national poet and the newly rising sun of the German theater. The play was a considerable success, and performances in Vienna and Hanover during Lessing's early and exceptionally lean days in Berlin brought in most welcome royalties.

IV   The Trivial Comedies

The principal themes in the two following comedies are trivial in the Gottschedian sense. The central character of *Der Misogyn* (*The Misogynist*, 1748; extended from one to three acts in the 1767 edition of Lessing's comedies as *Der Misogyne*) is as distorted and overdrawn as one might expect of one bearing the comic character name Wumshäter. His misogyny is crude and wounding, and it is remarkable that his daughter Laura withstands with relative equanimity his bluntly reiterated attacks upon her dignity as a human being; for she is sometimes ranged below the animals (I.iv). It is, therefore, not surprising that Wumshäter has forbidden his son Valer to marry his beloved Hilaria.

To demonstrate the unjustness of his father's repudiation of all women, Valer introduces into their circle as a house guest one Lelio, who is presented as Hilaria's brother, but who is really Hilaria in disguise. Her assignment is to ingratiate herself with Wumshäter and gain his confidence and respect. She can then reveal her identity and oblige the woman-hater to admit the groundlessness of his prejudice.

At first all goes well, but complications arise and eventually create a complete impasse. Lessing then causes Hilaria to appear in her own person, but Wumshäter still cannot believe that she and Lelio are identical, and stubbornly insists on the superiorty of the nonexistent "brother." As a last resort, the plotters have Lelio-Hilaria appear. (Lessing leaves the solution of this problem in costuming to the actress playing the role.) Only then, and with difficulty, Wumshäter admits his error and gives grudging assent to the marriage.

It is clear that the solutions for the manifold complications are only loosely conceived, and tensions are not so much resolved as inexpertly slackened. Perhaps in this instance Lessing's difficulty was due to a multiplicity of borrowings insufficiently assimilated, and he seems also to have missed the aid of Lisette as an impulse to action. Here she provides none, and the principal characters, left to their own devices, prove to be less than inspired.[14]

In much the same vein, Lessing's next play, *Die alte Jungfer* (*The Old Maid*), published in Berlin in 1749, also presents foolish characters with whom he reportedly could not feel involved. The piece is clearly un-Gottschedian in its derivation from the Italian tradition, notably in its introduction of an ill-concealed Hanswurst (Harlequin), a figure that Gottsched especially deplored. The satire is primarily directed at minor characters, giving the whole a somewhat unfocused quality which no doubt helps to account for Lessing's dissatisfaction with the play. Nor is the especially trivial theme congruent with the changing concept of the proper domain for comedy apparent in two other works dating from the same year.

V   *The Problem Comedies*

The first of these is *Die Juden* (*The Jews*), a play in one act completed in 1749. At the outset, two criminal types, Michel Stich and Martin Krumm (the latter is overseer of the Baron's estate), discuss the failure of their recent attempt to rob and murder the Baron. The robbers, disguised with beards suggesting that they are Jews, had been interrupted in mid-attack by a Traveler, who had driven them away. The grateful Baron had then persuaded his rescuer to interrupt his journey for a visit.

The disguise used by the robbers turns the conversation to the subject of Jews, and the Baron shows that he shares the prevalent anti-Semitism. He is more than willing to believe the worst of them. His guest quietly and without conspicuous success attempts to turn aside his sweeping condemnation: "To tell the truth, I am no friend of universal judgments upon an entire people. . . . I should think that there might be good souls and evil among all nations" (vi). And in a number of other ways, too, we are shown his acute awareness of human fallibility in matters of justice. Eventually, the Traveler's suspicions fall upon Martin and are confirmed when the false beards fall out of the man's pocket. Hesitantly he reveals his discovery to the Baron. The latter confronts Martin, who is forced to confess.

The host is now doubly indebted to his guest, who is pleased to contribute once more to the Baron's well-being. The latter now offers his benefactor his most prized possession; his daughter, in marriage. She is by no means unwilling, but the match proves to be impossible on other grounds, for the guest now reveals that he is a Jew. Consternation reigns, except in the mind of the young lady, who merely inquires: "Well, what does that matter?" But the Baron and the Traveler know that such a union is impossible in their society. Yet the Baron is now properly "ashamed" of his previous remarks and means to make amends with the unconsciously ironic exclamation: "Oh, how admirable the Jews would be if they were all like you!" But the Traveler retains his enviable equanimity and magnanimously replies: "And how amiable the Christians if they all had your qualities!" (xxii).

The Traveler's only desire is that they will henceforth judge his people justly, avoiding all sweeping condemnations. The "moral" of the piece is still largely intellectual; since it is a plea for the use of logic tied to an elevated theme with humane connotations. Choosing it, Lessing reveals a notable development in his idea of the proper province of comedy, and it is also clear that he feels personally involved. He is well aware of the plight of the Jews in mid-eighteenth-century German society, and his play urges tolerance for a much and (he clearly implies) unjustly maligned people.

In keeping with the new seriousness and the expanded ethical horizon—the theme is no longer trivial in the Gottschedian sense —the comic element is far from notable. There are occasional flashes of wit in the dialogue between the servants Christoph and Martin and the ubiquitous Lisette, but for the most part the two servants are not witty, but provoking, crude, and boorish, even to the forbearing Traveler. Though the servants stimulate the unfolding action, the ethical content of the piece is projected by the two principals—a procedure which is in keeping with the theme's increased dignity and seriousness. Lessing was to employ the same technique in more pronounced fashion in his next comedy.[15]

The young playwright was well aware of his departure from

the pattern of traditional satire, and he drew attention to the novelty (Preface to *Schrifften* III and IV) when he first published *Die Juden* in 1754. The play, he wrote, was the result of "earnest consideration" of the shameful oppression imposed upon a people whom Christians should honor and respect. Instead, they seemed incapable of imagining that a Jew could also be an upright man. "Therefore," Lessing continued, "I soon conceived the idea of attempting to discover what effect it would produce on the stage if one showed the audience virtue where they least expect it. I am eager to hear its decision."

Contemporary reviewers of his work freely acknowledged the nobility of the author's intention, but took exception with the overwhelming magnanimity and humility of his central character. To such a critique by the well-known Göttingen scholar and theologian Johann David Michaelis, writing in the *Göttingische Zeitung von gelehrten Sachen* (June 13, 1754), Lessing replied at some length in the first volume of his *Theatralische Bibliothek*, taking issue with the criticism and pointing out that he had deliberately provided his noble-minded Traveler with a background of wealth and culture which made perfectly plausible his character and his deportment. The former is admittedly exceptional. So too would be that of a Christian who resembled him. If, said Lessing, one is not willing to grant that a Jew so favored by fortune could develop the noble qualities and the magnanimous attitudes attributed to the Traveler, then one must himself share the prejudice which it was the author's intention to expose in his play.[16] Michaelis responded mildly enough (*Göttingische Zeitung*, December 7, 1754) that he would not call Lessing's exceptionally virtuous Jew an impossible phenomenon, but, for perfectly understandable reasons, merely a highly improbable one.

Since probability ranked high among the criteria for excellence in the genre, it was only natural that Lessing, too, should devote much thought and attention to it. As we shall shortly see, he had also come to consider it in his early critical writings on the theater, and in consequence he now inclined—both in theory and practice—toward departing from the notion that the sole purpose of comedy was to produce laughter. From his study of the classical as well as the contemporary theater, he would urge that both comic and serious elements, both light and shadow, are justified and commendable.

The contrast advocated, however, and that encountered in *Die Juden*, show a diversity of parallels. Characters exhibiting a single "ruling passion" may be set off against one another (the Traveler's magnanimity against the bigotry of the Baron), and the farcical scenes may alternate with serious and even tearful ones, but the contrasting elements remain discrete; they do not yet blend into an integrated and unified whole.

Despite its technical shortcomings, *Die Juden* was a milestone in Lessing's developing ideal of "humanity." Such an appeal for tolerance of the Jews was, thus far, all but unique in German literature. Since the Middle Ages, the Jews had been caricatured by playwrights and laughed to scorn by audiences. Lessing's Traveler is virtually the first educated and noble Jew in German literature, coinciding with the appearance of the first educated Jew in German life, Lessing's good friend Moses Mendelssohn.[17] At the close of his career, Lessing created, with his Nathan, an enduring monument to Mendelssohn and to the spirit of humane and exalted tolerance.

In his next play, also completed in 1749 and perhaps revised before its first publication in 1755, Lessing chose another serious theme of importance to mid-eighteenth-century German society. Again the central "message" is carried not by servants but by the principals, and it is possible to detect a considerably increased subtlety in the young playwright's treatment of character, as well as in his employment of the technique of contrast in comedy.

In a politic letter, dated April 28, 1749, to his father in Kamenz, the young Lessing sought to allay family fears that his preoccupation with the theater signaled his imminent moral collapse, and suggested that he would deal with a prevalent and troublesome class of critics of orthodoxy in a play that the clergy would not only read but praise. Lessing had in mind his five-act "problem" comedy, *Der Freigeist* (*The Freethinker*). Although we shall find an element of ambiguity in Lessing's dénouement, the letter to his father, as well as some evidence in the play itself, once led a number of Lessing scholars to range him on the side of "the angels."

The action of the piece unfolds at the home of Lisidor, the wealthy father of two attractive young daughters, Juliane and Henriette, who are engaged, respectively, to Theophan, a noble and magnanimous young clergyman, and to Adrast, who claims to be a skeptic and freethinker. Theophan has set himself the task of winning the friendship of the churlish and suspicious Adrast, and of demonstrating to him the injustice of his anti-religious and, especially, his anti-clerical views. To this end, he treats Adrast with utmost gentleness and generosity, despite the latter's rude and provocative persistence in misunderstanding the clergyman's honorable motives.

Theophan's task is complicated by the fact that in the past Adrast has encountered much misfortune at the hands of men of the cloth; we are told that one of them is even responsible for his current financial embarrassment. But another important obstacle to a friendship between the antagonists is, quite simply, Adrast's jealousy. He reveals to us, early in the play, that he really loves Theophan's fiancée, the gentle and pious Juliane. Thus Theophan's good fortune, as well as his repeated offers of friendship and financial aid, merely aggravate Adrast's resentment of him.

Adrast's decision to marry Henriette is dictated by financial necessity, but he does not look forward to the union, for the young lady is in all respects the opposite of her sister. She is rather bold and unconventional, and even inclined to a flippant and satirical approach to matters of religion; traits that Adrast finds most unbecoming. When Juliane gently suggests that Henriette is perhaps patterning her behavior after his own example, Adrast vigorously distinguishes his own "well considered" and "rationally based" attitudes on religious matters from those of thoughtless, light-minded Henriette.

Having distinguished Adrast's freethinking from Henriette's, Lessing also creates for him a position quite apart from others who qualify for the title; and it would seem that he has modified his announced intention of winning clerical approval by satirizing the freethinker in the figure of Adrast. Thus the young playwright emphasizes, from the outset, that his Adrast is "filled with virtuous propensities," and that in respect to religion he is prejudiced neither "for" nor "against." He stands uncommitted on the middle ground, "without" religion—a fact noted in the scenario and reaffirmed on various occasions in the play. As might be expected, Lessing's contemporaries found this element original and intriguing, but they scarcely knew whether to praise or condemn it.[18]

Evidently, Lessing intends his play to illustrate the sort of distinction drawn somewhat later in Adelung's dictionary, where the commonly accepted definition of freethinker is still the pejorative one. Here he is "one who divorces himself from the laws of reason, religion, and convention." In Lessing's comedy, these roles are admirably filled by Lisidor, Johann (Adrast's servant), and Henriette. But the term may also be used in quite a different sense to designate "a person who thinks and acts freely, that is, without prejudice."[19] Adrast can qualify for this favored group only after his unjustified hostility to Theophan has been dissipated. Lessing's best known biographer long ago pointed out, however, that Theophan's eventual "triumph" should not be taken to indicate a victory for orthodoxy, but for his humane and generous spirit. Most subsequent critics are inclined to agree and view the clergyman not primarily as a representative of a specifically religious attitude, but as the kind of human being that attracted Lessing's particular sympathy, that is to say, as a man of feeling.[20] Thus Lessing has created a freethinker who manages to avoid the conventional excesses of his fellows, and whose anti-clericalism may be distinguished from the usual manifestation of this trait by virtue of its unconventional basis in a feeling of jealousy and personal pique. Yet his evident dissatisfaction with these essentially negative distinctions between Adrast and the contemporary freethinker is revealed late in the play, when he indirectly ascribes to Adrast a more positive, more rational, and more sympathetically regarded motivation than jealousy for his long-continued mistrust of Theophan.

By the middle of the last act, we have learned that Theophan does not in fact love Juliane; and it has also been made clear that the two young ladies do not prefer the suitor to whom they are pledged and whose character most resembles their own. The gentle and pious Juliane really loves Adrast, while the would-be freethinker Henriette prefers Theophan.

When, at long last (V.iii), Theophan surrenders to Adrast his claim to Juliane, we naturally expect that this dissipation of the basis for Adrast's jealousy will lead to an immediate reconciliation. Yet even this gesture of apparently overwhelming generosity leaves Adrast cold, and he continues his scornful expressions of disbelief and mistrust of the clergyman, until Theophan, for the first time, loses patience with the freethinker and lashes out at him with all the anger and resentment that for so long, and in the face of ample provocation, he has kept under control.

Oddly enough, Adrast's "conversion" begins at this point. What the gentle attributes of the heart have thus far failed to bring about is now ironically accomplished by a violent outburst of temper. Adrast is now "touched" by his story, especially when he hears once more that Juliane loves him, and that Theophan will immediately surrender his claim upon her. The pact of friendship between the antagonists is then concluded, and arrangements for the happy exchange of fiancées are amicably carried out.

Adrast's deportment in this climactic scene is a puzzle not only to the audience, but also to Theophan himself. The clergyman is persuaded only with difficulty that his explosion of anger has in fact suddenly changed his opponent's attitude; and the audience is at first hardly less skeptical, for the new motivation scarcely harmonizes with Adrast's own emphasis on the part played by jealousy in his rejection of Theophan.[21] Fortunately, Lessing himself sheds some further light on the problem in a later review of a performance of the play by the Hamburg troupe. In his *Hamburgische Dramaturgie*, No. 14, he writes: "Herr Böck plays Theophan with all the friendly propriety that this part demands, in order to bring out the contrast with the eventual animosity aroused by Adrast's obstinate misunderstanding; an animosity upon which the entire dénouement is based."

It is Lessing's view, then, that the turning-point of the play comes when Theophan's apparently superhuman patience at last fails him, and it is clear that the author wishes his audience to notice this element of decisive contrast. Up to this point, we may say, Theophan's unrelieved magnanimity has made it impossible for the freethinker—who, in any case, tends to reject Theophan because of jealousy—to look upon the clergyman as a credible human being. Lessing then motivates Adrast's eventual acceptance of Theophan by "humanizing" his clergyman; by introducing the element of contrast provided by the angry outburst—in itself a natural, human, emotional reaction to Adrast's provoking behavior—quite opposed to his previous gentle demeanor.[22]

In this way, the author again permits his principal freethinker to appear in a somewhat more attractive light, and incidentally introduces a note of satire to enliven what would otherwise have been a climax of unrelieved sentimentality. Lessing's sense of irony, his awareness of the ever-present quirks and incongruities of human life, is never far beneath the surface of his thinking.

Here we see that the ironic sense may manifest itself even in the mind of a Lessing preoccupied with an essentially sentimental development, to reveal in a witty flash his intellectual awareness of the implausibility of a Theophan imbued only with the noblest human qualities. Thus the manner of Adrast's conversion involves an element of mild satire on a favorite theme of sentimental comedy: the power of friendship. As we have seen, this is not the first appearance of this rather unusual combination of elements, and we shall have occasion to return to it when Lessing's critical work comes under discussion.

In this respect, *Der Freigeist* supplies an intimation of a principle which looms large in Lessing's subsequent dramatic theory and practice, that is, his advocacy of greater realism in the figures portrayed. In serious drama and tragedy he would later brand the presentation of "perfect" characters—those dominated beyond all expectation of nature by unrelieved virtue or vice—as unnatural and hence fundamentally ineffective.[23] And in respect to comedy, as already indicated, we will soon see him advocate the contrast attained when differing character types are set off one against the other. In his *Freigeist*, however, Lessing has already extended the principle of contrast to individual figures within a comedy, creating, at least in rudimentary form, a species of "universal" character—one possessed of a variety of "passions" essential to the representation of credible human beings—and has thus anticipated a principle for which theoretical justification would later be adduced.

Lessing's *Freigeist*, and in some measure *Die Juden*, also demonstrate his pioneering efforts in the development of the problem play. In each he departs from the pattern of traditional individualized satire to dramatize a serious and important theme with broad implications, using the form of comedy not simply to ridicule the faults and foibles of selected individuals, but to demonstrate the presence of more widespread prejudices which the audience may well share. As an important corollary to such demonstration, the plays provide for the revelation, through dramatic conflict, of positive and praiseworthy character traits: a new departure for the comedy of Enlightenment.[24] (It is typical of Lessing's fundamental reluctance to accept unexamined generalizations that he chooses to demonstrate the presence of virtue where the audience might well fail to expect it.)

In *Der Freigeist,* Lessing hints at that development in the treatment of character which will make it possible for him to transcend the inherent limitations of the traditional comedy of character types. His *Minna von Barnhelm* (1767) represents the climax of this progression. In the long interval between the apprenticeship to comedy and the full flowering of his comic gift, Lessing's principal literary activities find expression in the realm of criticism and tragedy, and to these we must now turn.

CHAPTER 2

Apprenticeship in Criticism

FOR the seven years from November, 1748, until October, 1755—interrupted only by a one-year interlude beginning in December, 1751, when he returned to Wittenberg to take a Master's degree—the young Berlin free lancer tried his hand as a professional writer in a number of literary forms. Mylius, now editor of the *Berlinische privilegierte Zeitung*, a thrice-weekly newspaper, again provided a focal point for his efforts, gave him reviewing assignments, and helped in other ways to provide him with a precarious living.

Like Leipzig, Berlin under Frederick the Great, who had come to the throne of Prussia in 1740, was intellectually oriented toward France, but with an important difference. Whereas in Leipzig the atmosphere—and Lessing's youthful inclination—had tended toward elegance, the acquisition of social graces, Anacreontism in verse, and comedies in the manner of Molière, the intellectual climate of Berlin was philosophical. Here was the special domain of the Freethinkers, inclined to religious skepticism and philosophical materialism, and to the rationalism so frequently associated with the Age of Enlightenment.

In Berlin, Lessing soon formed a number of life-long friendships which reflected, in a measure, this change of emphasis. Most important among them was his association (from 1753) with Moses Mendelssohn, a Jewish merchant and self-educated scholar and writer, who came to represent for Lessing the intellectual keenness and verve and the humane understanding of this much maligned people; with Friedrich Nicolai, the man destined to provide, with his publishing house and the periodical *Allgemeine Deutsche Bibliothek*, the literary focus for the rationalistic wing of the German Enlightenment; and with Karl Wilhelm Ramler, professor-poet and later editorial collaborator with Lessing.

Lessing's literary work reflected, in turn, his own development and change. The collection of verses, *Kleinigkeiten* (*Trifles*), published in 1751, still sounded the lighter notes of the Leipzig mood, but works from the first Berlin sojourn indicate a widening range of experience. As we have seen, serious notes are to be found in the comedies *Die Juden* and *Der Freigeist*, and his criticism also reflects his broadening intellectual horizon and, especially, his concern for the improvement of the German theater. At the same time, his own dramatic and other literary production continued, so that in the period 1753–55 he could publish a six-volume collection of his best writing.

I The Early Journalism

Lessing's early reviews appeared chiefly in Voss's *Berlinische privilegierte Zeitung* and its monthly literary supplement, *Das Neueste aus dem Reiche des Witzes* (*The Latest from the Intellectual Front*), edited at first by Mylius and thereafter, beginning in April, 1751, by Lessing himself. During this demanding apprenticeship, the latter's reviews necessarily covered a broad spectrum of current publications: scholarly, theological, and scientific, as well as literary. As time went on, the growing self-confidence they reflect attests to his excellent preparation in Meissen, as well as his far-ranging private studies.

Occasionally, Lessing added to the reviews and critical discussions examples of his own verse, his fables (an interest which would persist throughout his career), and translations of short foreign pieces which had appealed to him. One can observe, from the outset, an emphasis upon the esthetic element in literature, at first, to be sure, on a rather humble level, as in an early essay in Mylius' journal, *Der Naturforscher*, in August, 1747. Here he holds forth on the theme: "What I am to read must be able to give me pleasure."[1]

Another favorite and frequently discussed topic throughout Lessing's career concerned the relation of "genius" to "the rules" of literary composition. In a contribution in verse to a Berlin journal, *Kritischer Musikus an der Spree*, for June 28, 1749, directed "An den Herrn Marpurg" ("To Marpurg"), Lessing writes that the good taste of the true genius coincides with universal good taste, so that we are all "moved" and "pleased" by whatever moves and pleases the genius:

Was ihn bewegt, bewegt; was ihm gefällt, gefällt.
Sein glücklicher Geschmack ist der Geschmack der Welt.[2]

This is a bold-sounding formulation, appearing to sanction the greatest possible originality of approach and the utmost freedom of expression for the genius. (Its author thought highly enough of the lines to quote them later when summing up his laudatory critique of Voltaire's unorthodox approach to the writing of history.) Even here, however, we see that he assumes a relation between the work of genius and a general "law," represented by universally accepted canons of taste. Thus he would not grant the genius permission to create new laws with whimsical abandon. When his taste is properly attuned (*glücklich*), however, he constitutes a kind of medium for the detection and transmission of new insights anent the prime and unchanging law.

The same idea is developed at length in a later discussion of Batteux's *Les beaux-arts réduits à un même principe* (1746).[3] Here again Lessing grants that the "rules" are derived from the work of the genius, "who never completely follows his predecessors," but he would still insist that the manifold new "rules" thus engendered must exhibit a relation to "basic principles," if they are to illuminate rather than obscure our understanding and appreciation. In subsequent critical speculation he repeatedly returns to the basic problem of reconciling first principles with the exercise of the creative spirit.[4]

Lessing's developing independence in critical matters had been aptly reflected in the introductory essay in *Das Neueste* written on his assumption of its editorship two months before, in April, 1751. Without the arts, Lessing had maintained, human society would be reduced to "the most unbearable slavery," and he defended both the arts and sciences against J. J. Rousseau's charge, preferred in the famous prize-winning essay of 1750, that their rise contributed rather to a deterioration of morality. The two phenomena might well accompany one another without being causally related. These remarks were later repeated in Lessing's critical "Briefe," where he wrote: "The arts are whatever we wish to make of them. It is our own fault if they are harmful to us."[5]

In sum, Lessing's early journalistic criticism demonstrates a notable range of competence and independence of viewpoint, together with an impressive devotion to the cause of excellence. While constantly holding up praiseworthy foreign models to his

countrymen, he did so with the ultimate aim of fostering the skills
and standards necessary to create an indigenous German literature at home. His criticism, therefore, takes increasingly sharp
issue with what he came to regard as the stultifying methods and
theories of Gottsched. What he recommended in their stead
becomes clearer as we review the larger critical works of this
earlier period.

II Beiträge zur Historie und Aufnahme des Theaters

The first of these was the ambitious project launched in
collaboration with Mylius in October, 1749, the *Contributions to
the History and Improvement of the Theater*—the first German
periodical devoted to this subject.[6] The Preface promised essays
on all facets of theatrical activity, including dramatic criticism,
translations of ancient and modern plays, and comments on acting
and stagecraft, as well as original dramatic works. The fundamental aim was to foster excellence by precept and positive
example rather than by negative criticism. The special novelty of
such a proposal lay in its broadly international and historical
perspective. No one in Europe had previously tried to do on such
a scale what was here proposed.[7]

In all of this, however, the "rules" are still recognized as
valid, and Gottsched's services to the cause of the German theater
are duly recognized. Yet even the Preface reveals the beginnings
of a tacit undermining of Gottsched's influence, for here Lessing
deplores the pejorative effect of French influence on the incipient
German drama. To help put matters in clearer perspective,
Lessing suggests an expansion of the dramatic horizon to include other foreign plays, especially Spanish and English works
embodying quite different ideals and as yet little known in
Germany. He states that among the virtually unknown English
dramatists there are many admirable men: Shakespeare, Dryden,
Wycherley, Vanbrugh, Cibber, and Congreve are in his opinion
as deserving of German attention as are the French dramatists.

Lessing's statement is something of a milestone in his critical
development. It is not only his first published reference to Shakespeare but it also reveals a fundamental inclination, destined to
continue throughout his career as a critic: to summon his countrymen to a shift of emphasis from French to English models.
Since one can best derive the "natural temper" of a people from

its dramas, Lessing adds, it is clear that if the Germans would follow their natural bent, their stage would surely resemble the English more closely than the French.

It is far from clear, at this point, how Lessing would define the German natural temper, and how it corresponded to the English. Nor does the heterogeneous list of English playwrights clarify matters. We know something of his familiarity with a number of these English writers,[8] but his first-hand acquaintance, at this early date, with the writings of Dryden or Shakespeare remains problematic. Some time will elapse before he sheds additional light on this question; his subsequent work in the *Beiträge* affords little further illumination, since the overly-ambitious project survived only through four issues, and his own contributions enlighten us rather in other areas.

At the outset, Lessing returns to Plautus, one of his favorites since the Meissen school days, and seeks to justify the Latin writer's presumed deficiencies (his "coarseness," for instance) as he would later justify Horace, by describing how Plautus was, in some measure, bound by tradition and the prescribed modes of expression: a defense already adduced by Madame Dacier in response to Horace's own criticism of Plautus.

In introducing his translation of Plautus' *The Captives*, which he calls "one of the finest plays ever presented," Lessing retreats somewhat from the position taken in his previous essay, where he had called the work without qualification "the finest play" in the history of drama. Yet he maintains that, despite certain "irregularities," this Latin play best fulfills the fundamental intent of comedy: to improve the morals of the onlookers. To do so, the author has not only made vice ridiculous, but he has also depicted virtues in an attractive light. This does not mean, however, that Lessing condones the violent shifts of mood employed by certain authors of his own day. In his Prologue Plautus had promised that there would be no such sharp contrasts; no falling into the tone of tragedy when the audience was expecting something funny. Lessing thought this a salutary suggestion for those modern playwrights who seemed determined to ignore the properties of the genres. Such excursions may be permissible to the French, who have enough examples of "normal" plays of both types, but the Germans, at the present stage of their development, would do well to avoid this practice.[9]

Less violent contrasts are permissible, however, and Plautus has provided the model in his satirical treatment of vices, together with what would later be called the "sentimental" presentation of virtues. The first procedure may amuse ("ergötzen"), but only the second can be really effective ("fruchten"). Comedy has traditionally stressed only the first of these, but Plautus has shown that by depicting virtues attractively he can involve the emotions, and the claims of the heart, in a most salutary way.[10] The continuing importance of this "discovery" for Lessing's subsequent speculation on the theory of comedy will shortly come under consideration. At this point it can be said, however, that his remarks also help to account for the admixture of comic and serious, satirical and sentimental elements in his own comedies. The same sort of contrast is understandably present in his reworking of Plautus' *Trinummus* under the title *Der Schatz*—a demonstration of the Latin writer's technique promised at the close of this discussion and completed in 1750.[11]

In the fourth issue of the *Beiträge*, Lessing translates from the French the younger Francesco Riccoboni's *L'art du théâtre* (*The Art of Acting*, 1750), and notes in a brief foreword that it is full of "excellent observations." We shall have occasion to return to this topic shortly.

III *Translator, Critic, and Master of Arts*

Lessing's early interest in history is manifested in the first of the "scholarly articles" published under his editorship in the *Berlinische privilegierte Zeitung* (February 18, 1751). Here he takes issue with the author of a long-since-forgotten *History of Learning* for providing only chronologically arranged details (to fill the memory) rather than evaluation and interpretation of the information displayed.

In similar vein, Lessing tried his hand at translating fifteen historical essays of Voltaire under the title *Kleinere Historische Schriften* (1752), warmly recommending the French author, in a preface (1751) and in a subsequent review, as a true stylist in the writing of history. Voltaire does not overwhelm us with burdensome detail, but regales us with vivid perceptions designed to illumine the mind and dispose the heart toward love of learning and knowledge of one's fellow men. Though the author has observed no special order in his account, this is no drawback; it rather enhances the reader's pleasure.[12]

When, in these early years of his apprenticeship, Lessing turns to the examination of current *belles-lettres*, he maintains a notable independence in his critical position between the warring camps of Leipzig and Zurich. He is quick to detect the shortcomings in the "unfortunate" *Hermann, oder das befreite Deutschland,* an heroic epic by Gottsched's faithful retainer, Christoph Otto von Schönaich. He recognizes the merits of the poet Klopstock, the protégé of the Swiss, as well as his defects; and Klopstock's imitators call forth some of Lessing's heavier critical artillery. Thus Bodmer's "Patriarchaden" are blasted.

A refreshing respite from three hard years spent thus in an attempt to support himself as an independent journalist arrived when Lessing returned to the University of Wittenberg in 1752. For his Master's thesis there he offered a translation of a treatise by the sixteenth-century Spanish physician and philosopher, Huarte de San Juan, entitled *Examen de ingenios para las ciencias* (1575). Lessing's translation had the title *Prüfung der Köpfe zu den Wissenschaften* and was issued in 1752. The work became a focal point for much of the discussion of the concept of genius in the second half of the eighteenth century.[13] Nor did Lessing neglect the moderns in his enthusiastic reading program. He continued especially his careful study of Klopstock and the available cantos of that poet's *Messias*—a subject to which he would later return. All in all, the Wittenberg interlude provided a mental and spiritual recharging for the busy years that followed his return to Berlin in November, 1752, as a newly-made Master of Arts.

IV   Berlin Again; the "Kritische Briefe"

In the Prussian capital, Lessing resumed his critical activities for the *Berlinische privilegierte Zeitung* and reprinted, in Volume Two of his collected *Schrifften* (1753), a number of his favorite pieces in the guise of informally styled "Briefe" ("Letters"; usually called "Critical Letters"), in which he discussed literary works and problems in the form of a fictional or actual correspondence with friends and colleagues. In his preface, Lessing disarmingly calls attention to these contributions and the expectations aroused in the reader by such a title: "Der zweite Teil enthält Briefe. Man wird ohne Zweifel galante Briefe vermuten. Allein ich muss bekennen, dass ich noch bis jetzt keine Gelegenheit gehabt habe, dergleichen zu schreiben. Mir Korrespondentinnen zu erdichten, und an Schönheiten zu schreiben, die nicht existieren, schien mir in Prosa ein wenig zu poetisch zu sein."[14] The form indicates a basic characteristic of his approach: an animated, informal, and essentially dramatic invocation of a partner in a critical dialogue.

One of the most startling of the earlier "Briefe" dealt with the long-awaited and recently published Horace translation by Samuel Gotthold Lange, pastor in Laublingen and a scholar-poet who enjoyed a considerable literary reputation at the time. Lessing was amazed to discover that the work proved to be full of errors and misconceptions of an elementary sort, and called attention to some of them in the twenty-fourth Letter. Since he found Lange's published reply provoking, he proceeded to a mercilessly ironical attack on his opponent's competence as a scholar and translator. It was published in January, 1754, as a *Vade mecum für den Hrn. Sam. Gotth. Lange*. (The title and the handy pocket format were intended to recall the well-known manuals, as well as counter Lange's slighting reference to the format in which Lessing's *Schrifften* were appearing.) The overpowering vigor and incisiveness of Lessing's attack quickly spread his name abroad in literary circles and established him as a new and authoritative critic whose voice would henceforth be heard.

Not all the "Briefe" were so startling in their effect as the one which precipitated the demolition of Pastor Lange; yet they also demonstrate Lessing's independence from received opinion. The first eight Letters, for example, defend one Simon Lemm, who had had the misfortune to incur—Lessing thought undeservedly—the displeasure of Martin Luther in sixteenth-century Wittenberg. Always a champion of the underdog, Lessing did not hesitate to condemn what he considered Luther's "mistreatment" of his opponent in this controversy.

In the Letters (Numbers 15–19) on Klopstock's *Messias*, Lessing declares his admiration for that author. For this reason, he explains, he sharply criticizes what he regards as this poet's less successful formulations. Such adverse comment is not indicative of a general disapproval, however, but rather the opposite. "There is a kind of criticism that does honor to its subject,"

Lessing points out. Each poet must be criticized in consonance with his abilities: "Einen elenden Dichter tadelt man gar nicht; mit einem mittelmässigen verfährt man gelinde; gegen einen grossen ist man unerbittlich." ("One does not criticize a miserable poet at all; a mediocre one is treated gently; but a great one is criticized inexorably").[15] Lessing has only scorn for the swarm of Klopstock imitators which had sprung up since the appearance of the first cantos of the *Messias*.

Other "Briefe" deal with topics to which with Lessing we shall later return, notably his admiration for Diderot, and the fragment of a Lessing tragedy, *Samuel Henzi*. In sum, the "Critical Letters" betray Lessing's increasing self-confidence and critical independence and incisiveness, his devotion to scholarly accuracy and excellence, and his keen interest in just criticism. The latter desire comes especially to the fore in 1754 (*Schrifften III*), where Lessing resumes his discussion of Horace, dealing with him in one of a series of *Rettungen* (*Justifications*) which he devoted to the defense of historical personalities unjustly condemned by their contemporaries or by subsequent commentators.

V   Rettungen des Horaz

Over the centuries, the poet Horace had repeatedly suffered such attacks upon his morality, his physical bravery, and his piety. Lessing, in a learned discourse, disposes of these charges by pointing out that the evidence of Horace's own admission must be tempered by the consideration that it represents concessions to convention, or a self-deprecatory modesty intended to fool no one. Nor can one adduce impiety from the "evidence" in a poem, especially in an ode. For the lyric poet borrows from here and there "the most beautiful ideas" without concern for the philosophic structure of which they are a part. (This argument will recur in *Pope ein Metaphysiker!*) The lyricist in particular must transcend the limits of personal emotional experience. Indeed, the greater the poet, the greater will be the distance between actual truth and what he says of himself. The situation, says Lessing, is paralleled when a virtuous contemporary theologian calls himself "nothing but a poor sinner."[16]

In rehabilitating Horace, Lessing is, in effect, justifying poetry in terms that were novel for that day. In his view, poetry has its own laws and values, as well as its own psychological structure and artistic existence, which differ from the poet's; and the two should not be confused when evaluating the poetic creation.

This view has been interpreted by some students as being rather arid and extreme, without meaningful relation to human existence, and even in contradiction to Lessing's own practice in his early essays in verse. And it has been said that before 1755 (at the earliest) Lessing exhibited no awareness of the value of an intimate and vital relation between the creative writer and his creation.[17] It should be remembered, however, that in the Horace essay Lessing is discussing lyric rather than didactic verse. Nor is he asserting that art and life are unrelated, but only that the work of art must not be identified with the poet's personal existence. He is declaring that the poet must not be bound by his own individual experience, and that his creative ability is measured by the degree to which he can transcend his personal limits. On the other hand, in the problem comedies of 1749 Lessing, the dramatist, had already demonstrated the values flowing from a vital interest and involvement on the part of the playwright in his creation, and had called attention to them in his remarks on these works in 1754 (Preface to *Schrifften* III and IV). In this light, Lessing's analysis does not appear to be incompatible with his earlier remarks on the nature of genius.

VI   Pope ein Metaphysiker!

A related view, and a demonstration of Lessing's penchant for making careful distinctions, emerges in the essay *Pope a Metaphysician!* which he and his friend Mendelssohn published in ironic response to a contest topic set by the Berlin Academy of Sciences, namely, an investigation of Alexander Pope's "system" and its relation to Leibnizian philosophy as contained in the Popean dictum: "Everything is good."

In a good-humored "preliminary investigation," Lessing and his friend deny that a poet, as poet, can have a system. For on the one hand, a poem is a "complete sensuous speech" (eine vollkommene sinnliche Rede).[18] A metaphysical system, on the other hand, employs language in a completely different way. The philosopher must define terms and never use them in a sense other than the one defined, while for the poet synonym, metaphor, and

even the concord of sound are sufficient reason for choosing a
term. The poet's language is characterized by a suggestive, sensuous appeal for artistic effect, and he has no need for the logical
order of the metaphysician. Inspiration, not logical inference, dictates his progress from one point to another.

The poet, therefore, cannot construct a system, nor does he
wish to. Since he desires all his ideas to be equally impressive and
effective, he chooses them from various systems, in order to present those that carry equal weight. "He speaks with the Epicurean
when he wishes to elevate pleasure, and with the Stoa when his
intention is to praise virtue." The philosopher, in constructing a
system, is content with subordinating some points to others, so
long as the whole is unified. Lessing and Mendelssohn nonetheless carry out a detailed, three-part investigation as prescribed by
the Academy, enumerating, comparing, and testing Pope's ideas.
They find only minor parallels to Leibniz. Nor do they fail to
point out that the members of the Academy, relying on the
French translation of Pope, substitute "good" for "right," since
Pope actually wrote: "Whatever is, is right." They can prove
their hypothesis that Pope's ideas are gleaned from various philosophers—an understandable procedure, for as a poet Pope was
primarily interested in collecting "the sensuously beautiful elements in all systems." In conclusion, they call attention to Pope's
letter to Swift, in which he disclaims any serious intention of
playing the philosopher.[19]

VII   Lessing as Editor: Mylius' Schriften and the Theatralische Bibliothek

The edition of Christlob Mylius' *Writings* (1754), for which
Lessing had provided a critical preface in the preceding year, had
furnished an opportunity to comment on the contemporary literary scene, emphasizing the low state of German letters and the
many obstacles to improvement. Mylius' life seemed to Lessing
a veritable case history of the difficulties plaguing a journalistic
career, where the financial necessity to write rapidly and exten-
sively worked against the attainment of excellence. (Lessing himself is sometimes called the inventor of free-lance journalism in
Germany, and the first to support himself for most of his career
by the proceeds from his writing alone.) The added burden of

Gottschedian discipleship, Lessing thought, had proved especially detrimental to his friend's literary development. Only toward the end of an unfortunately brief career had Mylius begun to turn away from the Gottschedian view, in which "wit" alone dominated the composition of comedy, and to take into account the further element of "heart." To Lessing this was a notable improvement, and we have seen that the idea had become a fundamental principle in his own approach to comedy.

The same theory comes strongly to the fore in the first number of Lessing's second venture with a theatrical periodical, the *Library of the Theater* (1754–58). Here his analysis of two "Abhandlungen von dem weinerlichen oder rührenden Lustspiele" ("Treatieses on the Tearful or Touching Comedy") illustrates his special skill in drawing distinctions and defining terms. He points out that recent innovations in dramatic technique have influenced both comedy and tragedy, the former having been somewhat elevated by the inclusion of serious passages; the latter lowered by the introduction of the "bourgeois" element. With respect to novelty and innovation, Lessing first distinguishes the true genius from the non-genius. The former wishes to accomplish more than his predecessors and departs from the traditional and the familiar because it no longer answers his needs. The "paltry spirit," the non-genius, on the other hand, merely seeks to do something *different* and leaves the beaten path only because it bores him. Of interest here is the notion that the genius works with conscious *intent*, engaging in a purposeful, creative process, and choosing original pathways with an awareness wanting in the non-genius.

The principal views of the "new" comedy technique are aptly summarized, Lessing tells his readers, by two treatises, the first by Martin de Chassiron, who opposes the tearful comedy in his *Réflexions sur le Comique-larmoyant* (1749). The second is C. F. Gellert's inaugural lecture at the University of Leipzig, *Pro Comoedia Commovente* (1751). Lessing's summary of these opposing views demonstrates his substantial agreement with the notion that the mixed comedy can and should be defended. A truly skillful admixture is not an adulteration of the form of comedy, but an approach to the ideal. Lessing now states "that only those comedies are true comedies which portray vices as well as virtues, propriety as well as absurdity, for in this very interminging they most closely approach their model, which is human life." In the element of contrast lies their resemblance to the natural order. He, therefore, rejects the exclusively "touching" comedy as described by Gellert, as well as the merely satirical or farcical comedy favored by Chassiron, and concludes: "The aim of farce is to produce only laughter; of the tearful comedy to produce only tears; whereas the aim of true comedy is to produce both."[20]

Other contributions to the *Theatralische Bibliothek* highlight Lessing's further efforts to alert his countrymen to the excellence of other literatures. Thus James Thomson's tragedies are praised, and in Part IV (1758) the gist of John Dryden's *Essay of Dramatick Poesie* (1668) is translated. The "Virginia" tragedy of the Spanish playwright Montiano is sketched—a matter of interest in the light of Lessing's own later treatment of the theme in his *Emilia Galotti*—and a considerable number of Italian comedy plots are translated as a "storehouse" for German playwrights in search of material.

On the art of acting—a subject of much interest to Lessing—he takes issue with the fundamental tenet of Rémond de Sainte-Albine's treatise *Le Comédien* (Paris, 1747), "that the outward modifications of the body are natural consequences of the inner disposition of the mind, and follow automatically" from the latter. Lessing maintains that the reverse is true. In agreement with Riccoboni, he would prefer to stress the element of conscious artistic configuration as the proper essence of the actor's performance—a principle in accord with the emphasis on conscious intent (*Absicht*) which he will later postulate as essential to all artistic creation. Yet his subsequent pronouncements are sometimes in accord with Sainte-Albine. Both advocate a certain restraint, the skillful control of the voice, the necessity for a complete knowledge of the role—tempo is especially important in comedy—and both commend actors of broad range, "who do not always insist on playing 'gallant and amiable' parts."[21]

What has been called Lessing's most original critical contribution to the four volumes of his *Theatralische Bibliothek* appeared in Part Two of the work, dated 1754, but published at Easter, 1755.[22] Here he returned to an examination of the classics, concentrating on the description, analysis, and criticism of two Seneca tragedies, the *Hercules furens* (*The Raging Hercules*) and

Thyestes. Of special interest were his suggestions regarding the emotional impact of tragedy, the necessity for an ethical element in contemporary tragedies, and his argument for a new approach to the problem of motivation.

Lessing is firm in his advocacy of an emotional appeal in tragedy: "Strong representations of emotions cannot possibly leave our own emotions entirely unaffected. And, above all, we desire these to be aroused in tragedies." In this regard, Lessing maintains, Seneca undoubtedly succeeds, despite occasional exaggerations and his inclination toward purely descriptive passages, though the latter are often extremely graphic. Thus the repeated recitals of Hercules' mighty deeds, which sometimes strike the modern reader as "senseless fairy tales," occasioned "an awesome shudder" in the ancient audience; and Lessing reiterates that we must judge a poet within the framework of his own time.

Nevertheless, Seneca's observance of the unities elicits Lessing's approval, and he judges his play technically superior to that of Euripides on the same theme, despite the beauties of the latter. The Greeks will take precedence in Lessing's later criticism, but even in this early essay he is impressed by Euripides' faithfulness to the "language of nature," and his avoidance of exaggeration. Nor was it necessary for the Greek to supply "intellectual effects" to make up for the lack of emotional impact.[23]

Lessing is far from dogmatic on the question of an ethical content for tragedy. He is concerned only that tragedy should not embody an "evil" teaching. And here, regretfully, he finds that Seneca's *Hercules* offends, for its ultimate point is either the "evil" priniciple that virtues fail to propitiate the Gods, and even provoke them, or the "tasteless" moral that one should take care not to be born the illegitimate offspring of an adventuring Zeus. In direct opposition to Gottschedian theory, Lessing concludes that the ancient writers of tragedy laid no stress on choosing a priori a moral truth which they wished to demonstrate. Then too, the requirements of tradition limited their freedom to invent and precluded their treatment of the given materials in deference to their ethical implications. The modern writer, however, is not so limited. "He can change what he wishes to change, and the responsibility is his alone if the whole work is not so instructive as its individual parts."[24] Lessing thus exhibits a curious combination of liberalism and conservatism in his view. He would condone the indifference of the ancients to an ethical "message," but would not extend the same freedom to the modern playwright.

In respect to modern adaptations of ancient materials, Lessing was much concerned with the problem of motivation. A modern dramatist reworking the Hercules theme should psychologically account for the hero's fit. In the classical version it is induced by Juno, the *dea ex machina*—a device which can no longer be plausibly invoked. A modern alternative, however, lies ready at hand, for "what is more closely allied than boldness and arrogance; than arrogance and madness?" The modern playwright could, therefore, depict his hero's all-too-prominent reliance upon his own individual powers as gradually developing into a proud scorn for the gods, and this overweening arrogance eventually passing over into megalomania. If the stages are depicted with sufficient skill, Lessing is confident that "the onlooker will finally be inclined to regard Hercules' madness as a wholly natural consequence."[25]

Lessing would revise the classical prologue in a similar fashion. In Seneca, Juno provides a "sort of prologue," and in doing so reveals too much of the specific action that follows. In a modernized *Hercules*, Lessing would recast the unacceptable appearance and speech of the goddess in the form of a priest's dream, and would blur the overly specific details, attempting to create rather a vague "oracle-like" ambiguity, calculated to engender a feeling of awe and foreboding.[26]

In his subsequent discussion of Seneca's *Thyestes*, Lessing calls attention to the spareness as well as the consummate horror of the plot, noting that modern tragedies tend to be overly complex. To Lessing this is a drawback, for he postulates an interrelation between intellect and emotion, in virtue of which the engagement of one detracts from the responsiveness of the other. "When the mind is at work [following and analyzing complexities], the heart is at rest; and when the heart is active, the mind must be able to rest." And Lessing now repeats, at the close of his discussion, that the principal aim of tragedy should be to arouse an emotional response. The extent to which Lessing anticipates such theories in his own early ventures in the tragic mode, and how he adapts them to the domestic tragedy, are the subjects to which we must now turn.

CHAPTER 3

The Early Tragedies

I   Samuel Henzi

LESSING'S earliest interest in tragedy manifested itself primarily in efforts to translate or adapt foreign models, but his most interesting early project was his attempt to treat dramatically the case of Samuel Henzi. Originating in Switzerland, reports of this contemporary *cause célèbre* began to reach Berlin in the summer of 1749 and immediately caught Lessing's attention. Lessing set to work dramatizing in rhymed Alexandrines the case of the Swiss patriot Samuel Henzi, sometime poet, supporter of Bodmer and Breitinger against Gottsched, and author of a fragmentary *Wilhelm Tell*.[1] Henzi was executed in July, 1749, for plotting to overthrow the oligarchic and tyrannical government of Berne.

Lessing's fragment (nearly two acts) was later published in his *Briefe* (1753), where it attracted much favorable critical notice. One reviewer even observed that the name "bourgeois tragedy" could be more justly applied to Lessing's work than to the *London Merchant*. Since tragedy demands heroes, the bourgeois tragedy demands bourgeois heroes, like Cato and Henzi. Whatever its proper designation, Lessing's fragment does give us the curious amalgam of contemporary figures from the middle class as principals (unlike Gottsched's *Cato*) presented in the "regular" manner. Whether the work is to be regarded as Lessing's apology for revolution and his confession of faith in republicanism is at least questionable. It would rather seem that the young playwright here espouses "non-political bourgeois liberalism."[2]

Structural obstacles may well have intervened to prevent the completion of the work. Despite some evidence that in *Henzi* the young playwright had begun to experiment with sentiment as a substitute for the comic element of wit, he was still hampered, as in an earlier fragment, by a lack of "emotional substance," the

absence of human, and especially family, complications and interrelations. In short, he lacked a medium in which to reveal, not a
mechanical progression of causality, but the inner congruence of
character and motivation which is so necessary to tragedy. The
same crux helps to explain his failure to complete such projected
dramas as *Das befreite Rom* (1756), *Kleonnis* (1758 ff.), and
Spartacus (1770/71).[3]

In 1755, however, Lessing hit upon the tragic formula he had
been seeking, and by combining a richly convoluted and complicated set of family relations with the currently popular element
of sentiment, he completed his pioneering effort in the realm of
domestic tragedy.

II   Miss Sara Sampson

"A bourgeois tragedy. Good Lord! Is there a word about such
a thing to be found in Gottsched's *Critische Dichtkunst?*" Thus
Lessing in a review of his own *Schrifften* V and VI (1755) in the
Berlinische privilegierte Zeitung. The exclamation refers to his
Miss Sara Sampson, a play written earlier that year, performed
in July, and now first published. Gottsched, says Lessing, "has
preached the three unities to his beloved Germany for more than
twenty years, and yet here the unity of place is boldly breached."
The breach was, at most, a mild one, however, and in reality more
serious departures from Gottschedian doctrine were revealed in
the play. As a matter of fact, Gottsched *had* employed the term
"bourgeois tragedy" (in the fourth edition of the *Critische Dichtkunst*, 1751) to describe "what the French call comédie larmoy-
ante." But, strictly speaking, Lessing's initial question would have
to be answered negatively, for he distinguished bourgeois tragedy
from the tearful comedy.

In Lessing's example of the genre, it is possible to perceive the
fundamental structural elements of comedy, notably the use of
the family as the basic organism, the role of chance, and the
motivation of the action by a single character—this time, however, by one deeply involved in the course of events, as the insti-
gating Lisettes of comedy were not.[4] The relation of *Sara* to the
materials and structural elements of comedy is further supported
by its close correspondence in plot, characters, and numerous details to an English Restoration comedy, Shadwell's *The Squire of*

Alsatia, with further details derived from·two English domestic tragedies, Charles Johnson's *Caelia* and Mrs. Susanna Centlivre's *The Perjur'd Husband.* Indeed, *Miss Sara Sampson* exhibits more fundamental similarities to Johnson's play than to George Lillo's *London Merchant* (1731), a drama frequently proposed as a source for *Sara.*[5]

At least one observant contemporary student of *Miss Sara* noted its similarity to comedy, and in 1756 Lessing himself asserted his belief in the close relation between comedy and tragedy, between laughter and tears. By combining these ingredients with the element of sentiment,[6] popularized in German reading circles by the novels of Samuel Richardson, and available in the English dramas Lessing is known to have studied, he created the first popular German bourgeois tragedy and, incidentally, his own first great stage success.[7]

Here tragedy afflicts not heroes and heads of state, but an unexalted family circle, a scene familiar to all onlookers. The characters speak in prose and involve themselves in psychological complexities with which the audience could and did identify with touching and tearful enthusiasm. At the première performance, Lessing's friend Ramler reports, "the audience sat listening, as still as statues, for three-and-a-half hours and wept.[8]

And well they might, for they witnessed the harrowing story of the virtuous Miss Sara, who has been seduced by Mellefont, has left her home and her loving father, Sir William, and has hidden away with Mellefont in an obscure small-town inn. Here for two months Melefont has turned aside, on both practical and psychological grounds, her repeated tearful entreaties for marriage (even for a secret marriage, the importance of which will shortly emerge). On the morning of the day on which the action begins, Sara has been especially disturbed, she tells Mellefont, by a half-waking dream, in which, as she followed him along the edge of a cliff, she heard the voice of her father, imploring her to stop. As she turned, however, she slipped and would have plunged down but for a restraining hand. Her rescuer was not her father, but a woman unknown to her, who drew a dagger, crying out: "I saved you . . . in order to destroy you!" Sara awoke in terror as the dagger struck home.

From Lessing's suggestions for the modernization of classical techniques, we know that he would seek to internalize the ele-

ment of causality and motivation, and that, as a corollary, he
suggested recasting the antique prologue in the guise of a none-
too-specific dream. Whether Sara's dream meets his criteria is
questionable, for, as we shall see, it is a rather more specific and
obvious foreshadowing of actual events than Lessing called for in
his essay on Seneca. Its intended function, however, is clearly
the creation of that aura of foreboding which Lessing desired of
a modern "prologue."

Mellefont seeks to turn her thoughts from this "senseless
dream," and from the associated guilt feelings arising from her
unmarried plight, for he cannot bring himself to accept the
"bondage" marriage represents. The economic impediment is
clear enough: by the terms of a cousin's will, he can inherit an
estate only by marriage to another distant relative. He has already
dissipated one fortune and desperately hopes to recoup by break-
ing the will. The negotiations seem promising, and in great agitation he awaits the news of their successful conclusion.

A far more important obstacle to marriage, however, is Mellefont's constitutional inability to face its reality. When the economic obstacle is removed, he still delays the irrevocable step.[9]
Yet, at the same time, he protests his undying love for Sara, and
Lessing goes to considerable lengths to establish Mellefont's good
faith and the fact that he is no mere libertine, despite numerous
affairs. (One of these, the alliance with Marwood, has continued
sporadically for ten years, and has resulted in an illegitimate
daughter, Arabella.)

Sara is, therefore, left to reflect, at what strikes us now as excessive length, upon her unhappy plight, her relation to God,
and her questionable right to the love of her father. Sir William
has learned of her whereabouts through Marwood, who has
traced them, and who hopes to create further trouble for them.
At the inn, however, the father only awaits a suitable opportunity
to welcome back daughter and seducer, forgiving all.

Into this static situation Lessing introduces the intrigue of
Marwood, who has now also arrived at the inn. Ruthless, proud,
and scheming, she confronts Mellefont, attempting first to entice
him to leave Sara and resume their alliance. When shrewd calculation fails her, she becomes enraged and attacks Mellefont with
a dagger. He disarms her, she regains her self-control, and prom-
ises to leave. But when she discovers that Sir William plans to

forgive the erring couple, she is driven once more to desperation. She persuades Mellefont to arrange a "final leave-taking" with the "victorious" Sara.

In the ensuing interview, she is presented as "Lady Solmes," a relative of Melefont's, and proceeds to defend before Sara Marwood's "claim" upon him, emphasizing his chronic inconstancy and arguing with insulting bitterness that Sara should surrender him. But Sara, in turn, bravely refuses to condemn him, and courageously rejects the parallel her opponent has drawn between Marwood and Sara. Mellefont's "fall," like her own, says Sara, can be distinguished from Marwood's, for he has not continued in his illicit relationship, but has broken away. Sara here introduces at least a faint note of relativism in the matter of ethical judgments, insisting upon the difference created by an awareness of guilt and the presence of a repentant spirit. Attitudes in some measure alter cases.[10]

Marwood is incensed at Sara's opposition and reveals her true identity, causing Sara to flee in terror. Thereupon Marwood substitutes poison for Sara's medicine and takes flight, with Arabella as a hostage whom she will horribly murder (a "new Medea") if her escape is thwarted. As Sara slowly expires from the effects of the poison, the fifth act passes, borne on a flood of Richardsonian tears of repentance and forgiveness. Sir William forgives Sara and Mellefont; Sara forgives Mellefont and even Marwood, and dies. Overcome by remorse, Mellefont stabs himself to death. Sir William sadly announces that he will grant Sara's dying wish that he seek out and adopt Arabella, the "legacy" of his daughter; and on this note the curtain falls.

One need not belabor the point that *Miss Sara Sampson* is technically "zeitgebunden"—a document, in this respect, of Lessing's age but not our own. Nor is it necessary to dwell on the several technical flaws to which critics have drawn attention over the years: the generally pale characterizations, the improbabilities of the plot (the exchange of letters, for example, in lieu of personal encounters which might well have altered the course of events), the role of chance, the verbose and watery speeches. Something of all this Lessing himself granted when he later called this "child" of his "deformed." And yet he retained an affection for it, and so did his contemporaries. It held the boards for two decades and inaugurated a form which carried over into the following era of "Storm and Stress" and beyond it, into the nineteenth century. It is worth inquiring, then, why all this came about, and how *Miss Sara* contributed to this far-reaching development.

We have already seen that the appearance of middle-class characters in tragedy is a milestone in the history of drama. Sir William's title by no means prevented the mid-eighteenth-century audience from identifying with him and others in the family-oriented cast. Here the growing sense of dignity and self-consciousness of the audience found reflection not primarily through identification with members of a particular social class, but with human beings like themselves.[11] Here the onlooker witnessed a manifold presentation of his relation to the prescriptive norms of current social and religious orthodoxy. He saw creatures like himself venturing to set themselves against these norms; in varying degrees of self-sufficiency, to be sure, and ultimately tragically. But questions had been at least tentatively posed, and the onlooker found himself fascinated by the ensuing complications.

In both *Die Juden* and *Der Freigeist,* Lessing had experimented with the presentation of virtue in characters not customarily associated with it. In *Miss Sara* that principle is elevated to the level of paradox.[12] Here he proposes to demonstrate virtue in a "fallen woman"; to present both guilt and innocence in a single character, and to develop for her that degree of sympathy with which the tragedy, in Lessing's view, should be solely concerned. The long-drawn-out theoretical justification for this view would follow, as we shall see, in the course of the next two years.

To establish the possibility of a dual standard for virtue, Lessing has recourse to a principle already notable in *Der Freigeist*: that virtue may exist quite apart from the normal orthodox religious interpretation of it. But the parallel must not be overextended. Adrast's subjectivism, his independence of orthodox norms, is almost—but only almost—entirely intellectually oriented. Miss Sara's subjectivism, however, as befits the heroine of a tragedy of sentiment, is emotion-oriented; and her distress, though spun out at great length, is intended to impress us as more intense.

In one area of her consciousness, Sara has preserved intact her belief in the religious law; she is conscious that she has "sinned," and the awareness of her "crime" occasions the keenest distress.

To this extent she is completely the child of her time. Her individualism and independence manifest themselves rather in her inclination, which gradually gains strength during the course of the action, to regard as "good" in its essence this overwhelming power of emotion, her love for Mellefont, even though it has led her "unwittingly" to this breach of God's law.

The term "unwitting" suggests a parallel to Hercules, who also incurred guilt unknowingly, during a fit originating in an external source: the jealous goddess: Sara's fall is equally involuntary, but it occurs during a suspension of normal judgment induced by a flood of emotion from within, i.e., from a part of her own nature. It was a fever which temporarily eclipsed the rational perspective of religious morality. Like Hercules, she later "comes to herself."[13] She rues the consequences of this fleeting attack, but not its cause, which is love. This faith in love's goodness also contributes to the change in her attitude toward her breach of the "law." Steadily regarded during the first three acts as a "crime" (*Verbrechen*), it is given the fleeting intermediate designation "offence" (*Vergehen*: IV. i.), and then becomes (IV. iii, and thereafter) a mere "error" (*Irrtum*). Sara herself draws our attention to this progression (IV. iii) and assures us that her father's forgiveness (announced in III.iii) is instrumental in initiating this change: the earthly father's forgiveness of his child can be regarded as a portent of the Heavenly Father's forgiveness of one of His creatures.[14] Her inward reconciliation is not unlike the experience of Hercules, whose desperate decision to die in atonement for his crime is finally turned aside by the words of encouragement and forgiveness from his stepfather, Amphitryon, whom he has so deeply wounded by his act.

In all her vicissitudes, Sara's love for Mellefont remains the prinicipal source of her strength, making it possible for her to believe with increasing firmness in her inward "innocence," despite a continued acceptance of a degree of guilt in respect to religious law. She treasures her subjective experience of love, "punishable as it is," and since she cannot bring herself to surrender it to the demands of orthodox morality, she pleads that it be sanctioned by the religious ceremony of marriage. The *social* norms concern her not at all. She would be willing to keep the marriage a secret; content, that is, to appear to be in the eyes of the world Mellefont's mistress (I.vii).[15]

In contrast to the idealistic Sara, it is the realistic Marwood who emphasizes the value of a bourgeois reputation and bitterly assails Mellefont, for whom she has sacrificed her "good name." This is a far greater sacrifice, she declares, than loss of virtue, for virtue without reputation is to her merely a "silly illusion" (II. vii).

But in the light of Mellefont's inability to accept the formal ties of marriage, Sara's dilemma is insoluble, and she is left to suffer—a state sadly pleasurable in itself, and essential to the concept of sentimentality. In these terms, the analysis of soul states can be spun out at will, and this procedure, together with the examination of the manifold psychological complications of the family-oriented interrelations, provides more than ample "emotional substance" for Lessing's requirements.[16]

By dint of such analysis, Sara can establish a degree of inward innocence, and with the strength flowing from this consciousness, she can face death, forgiving those who have contributed to her downfall and believing that her love for Mellefont, the central experience of her life, also justifies her hope of Divine forgiveness (V.v). When, at the end, she confesses, "I still love you, Mellefont, and if loving you is a crime, how guilty I shall appear in the world beyond," it is clear that Sara does *not* regard her love as a crime; indeed, she has already denied that it is. Sir William, in turn, further assures us that hers is "a spirit upon which all the blessings of heaven pour down" (V.x).

Admittedly, Sara's death at the hands of an external agent, the wildly jealous Marwood, remains stubbornly ambiguous, lacking the force of a clearly defined progression of cause and effect. Sara's acceptance of her rival's act as the manifestation of a higher power ("I die forgiving the hand that God employs to punish me" [V.x]) cannot convincingly bridge this gap.

Lessing might well agree, for there is a hint—at best a faint indication—that a potentially deeper, more genuinely tragic element has been operative, though it appears to conflict with Sara's most cherished hope that her love for Mellefont is a beneficent force. For almost in the same breath she admonishes her father, in urging him to accept Arabella: "Talk to her now and then about a friend whose example should teach her to be on guard against love in all its forms" (V.x). Despite her great expectations for the redeeming power of love, Sara is not unaware that love itself may be inherently threatening and tragic.[17]

In this respect, *Miss Sara* demonstrates that a variant of the crime of Hercules can be presented in "modern" guise, and may manifest itself in a character who is, to all appearances, the complete opposite of Herculean. Lessing here projects it into a figure of excessive meekness and gentleness, demonstrating that all are subject to the power of emotions which can have the shattering effect of Herculean strength. For, as in the case of Hercules, it can induce defiance of higher powers, leading even a Sara—at least fleetingly—to transgress the bounds of religion and the accepted moral code.[18]

Compared to Sara's dilemma, Mellefont's position is both simpler and more complex. It is simpler in that he has put aside not only the social conventions, but also religious scruples. He questions outright Sara's interpretation of orthodox morality—a daring gambit that causes her keen distress (I.vii). His independence in this respect is pronounced, yet his dilemma is more complex, for despite his freedom from externally imposed restraints, he is paralyzed by his inability to decide what his freedom is for. In a monologue protesting his eternal love for Sara, he can still recoil at the prospect of being "chained for life," and can say of the marriage that Sir William would gladly permit: "Sara Sampson, my beloved! What bliss resides in these words! Sara Sampson, my wife!—Half of the bliss has disappeared! And the other half— will disappear.—What a monster am I!—" (IV.ii).

Yet after briefly succumbing to Marwood's shrewd appeal, he is capable of resisting the urge to resume their relationship. Despite his feverish emphasis on the importance of his personal freedom, he is tormented by his love for Sara and its accompanying moral obligations, not merely to her, but to himself. Yet his inner dilemma proves to be as insoluble as Sara's. His fundamentally vacillating nature prevents his evolving a viable system of personal ethics. Indeed, both Sara and Mellefont, each in his own way, have found it impossible to conform to an existing order, but have failed to create a workable alternative.[19]

In these terms, the character of Marwood may be said to represent a third stage on this problematical scale—a stage beyond both Sara's and Mellefont's, on which the character is freed not merely of external prescriptive norms, like Mellefont, but of inner restraints as well, as Mellefont is not. Thus Marwood is fully aware of the way in which she would employ her complete free-

dom. But her cherished plan is destined to failure, despite the
fiery strength and the considerable fascination of her complex
character: a complicated amalgam of passion and intellectual
calculation, her rational perspective setting her apart from her
successors in the drama of Storm and Stress.[20] Her apparent
escape into self-imposed exile, Sara assures us, will not help her
to escape her inward fate (V.x). Complete and unrestrained
license and self-centered individualism in defiance of all norms
are, Sara implies, self-defeating. Her faith in, and deference to, the
orthodox ethical system convinces her that Marwood's punishment is inevitable. Here she manifests that same orthodox faith
which enables her to accept with equanimity, and even with
Leibnizian optimism, the judgments of Providence. ("Who would
dare to judge the dispositions of the All-highest" [V.x]?)

Such acceptance, as we have seen, is impossible for Mellefont
on his quite different and less "bourgeois" ethical ground. Yet
the result of his questioning is ultimately tragic. Lessing has as
yet no viable answer to the question he poses on the relation of
individualistic moral principles to the prevailing moral code. Sir
William's touchingly expressed faith in the "eternal goodness"
that has returned to him his daughter is sadly shaken when fate
snatches her from him, this time for all eternity. Lessing's implications here clearly call into question the foundations of the current ethical system.[21]

With all its ambiguities, the absence of viable answers, and the
generally unfocused quality of the play, it is worth emphasizing
that Lessing poses fundamental questions regarding the individual in his ethical relation to himself, his fellow men, and the Divine law. The moral order is not to be blindly accepted on authority, without examination, as Lessing had said as early as
1749.[22] He was to display a comparably critical, searching spirit
in the work of the period immediately following, in which the
theory of tragedy, and much else, would be subjected to the
same probing inquiry.

CHAPTER 4

Early Theology

I The Early Religious Verse

DESPITE his early exposure in Berlin, the Capital city of Rationalism, young Lessing's first attempts to come to grips with the conflict between faith and reason reveal no predisposition toward discarding the religious principles he had carried with him from his earliest days. But he would subject them to painstaking examination, for he was already convinced that one's religious beliefs must represent the fruit of individual thought, not the heritage of accepted authority.[1] Yet the early fragmentary poem *Ueber die menschliche Glückseligkeit* (*On Human Happiness*) is notable for its warning against the ill-considered criticisms of basic religious tenets by freethinkers who insist upon rational proof for the existence of the Divine. It may well elude demonstration, Lessing asserts, but woe to him who does not feel the divine presence, "who drives God from heaven and seeks Him only on earth."[2]

Lessing's declared, though rationally undemonstrable, religious faith was the intended theme of another unfinished poem, *Die Religion*, dating from about the same time.[3] Although Lessing assures us that the skeptical attitude pervading the first Canto was to be offset by the positive assertions in its sequels, the ultimate effect of the surviving fragment is negative. It does, however, contain a confession of faith, accompanied by the fervent hope that rational evidence for it will ultimately be forthcoming: "May thy fire, Religion, inflame my mind; already thou hast inflamed my heart."

Lessing's poem "To Marpurg" (1749), which we have already encountered in another context, deals primarily with poetry and music, but here, too, Lessing rejects as unjustified the demands sometimes made in the name of reason. Yet the orthodox could take little comfort from Lessing's reference to them: "The ortho-

dox man curses Reason; for her aim is to rob his faith, which requires blind followers, of its ancient approbation."[4]

II Theological Reviews and Early Fragments

Lessing's role as critic and reviewer frequently obliged him in
these years to deal with the numerous translations and foreign
works on the subject of freethinking, with the German works produced in emulation of the foreign models, and with the defenses
of the orthodox, who undertook to refute these attacks from
within and without. A survey of these reviews fails to establish
him either as a violent opponent or as a fellow-traveler, for he
goes his own way, judging the individual arguments on their
merits. If there is a noticeable tendency in either direction, it is
his disposition to regard as faulty the invocation of reason in the
arguments of the freethinkers. But, as we have seen in the discussion of *Der Freigeist,* Lessing does not condemn on principle
their right to pose questions and offer objections.

His own wide-ranging reading and study in quest of the hoped-
for evidence occasionally aroused in him a consuming impatience
with the sophistry sometimes encountered in theological disqui-
sitions. This discontent informs his unfinished *Gedanken über die
Herrnhuter* (*Thoughts on the Moravian Brothers,* 1750), a sect
which was then a favorite target for attacks by the orthodox.
Lessing's text in this essay is his bold declaration that "man was
created for action, not for hair-splitting." In consequence, he
characterized as misdirected the rationalizing which had over-
burdened the temple of religion. The situation was far better in
ancient times, Lessing finds, when religion was "simple, easy, and
vital." The same was true of Christianity's early stages, but after
its vigorous, militant beginnings, the Church fell to "decking out
its religion, imparting a particular arrangement to its tenets, and
propping up divine wisdom with worldly proofs," while theology
presumed "to support the proofs by means of faith." The Moravian
Brothers wished to restore the vigor and simplicity of pristine
Christian values, and should not be obliged to serve as whipping
boys for orthodox theologians in search of heresies. The Mora-
vians advocate nothing inimical to the theory of Christianity.

Yet for Lessing the claims of reason can not be denied for long.
In *Das Christentum der Vernunft* (*The Christianity of Reason*),

a fragment usually dated 1753, the rational element is again prominent. Here, in a series of twenty-seven propositions, Lessing first ambitiously attempts to account rationally for the doctrine of the Holy Trinity. By a process reminiscent of the practices criticized in the Moravian essay,[5] he postulates God, a perfect Being, to whom conceiving and creating are one. In this respect, he departs, at the outset, from Leibniz and his most popular disciple, Christian Wolff, both of whom distinguish between God's conceiving and His creative act. The result is a dualism between the world of essences—the ideas of God—and the temporal world of things. Explaining the possibility of a harmony between the two becomes a central problem in their philosophy. Lessing here employs the monistic approach, in which both the world of essences and that of things exist eternally in the mind of God.[6]

In conceiving Himself from all eternity in all His perfection, God has, in effect, created a Being who "lacked no perfection which He himself possessed" (§ 5). The Scriptures call this Being the "Son of God," or better, "God the Son" (§ 6). God and His identical image exist in perfect harmony, which the Scriptures call the Holy Spirit (§ 10). In this spirit, this harmony, "everything exists which is found in God, and hence also everything that exists in the Son; this harmony is therefore God" (§ 11), and *"all three are one"* (§ 12, Lessing's emphasis).

Continuing, Lessing assumes that God also conceives of His perfections in part, creating beings who share something of His perfection. Taken together, they constitute the world (§§ 13, 14). In contrast to Christian dogma, God and the world are thus alike in essence, and a species of Pantheism is introduced.[7] It is possible for each individual, within his limitations, to emulate God, who is aware of His perfection and can act in accord with it. The ethical law for the individual man is, therefore: "Act in accordance with your individual perfections" (§ 26).

Here the fragment breaks off, perhaps because the time had come to account for the presence of evil in the world. But if the world is assumed to be a collection of individual perfections, which are the partial concepts of God, there cannot be such *im*perfections as suffering and evil. A perfection, however divided, cannot be an imperfection, and at this juncture Lessing abandoned the attempt to rationalize Christianity from a monistic point of view.[8]

The two essays, as well as the unfinished poems, demonstrate that Lessing, in these early years, was struggling vigorously with the apparently irreconcilable claims of faith and reason. On occasion, he appears to be the anti-orthodox enemy of dogma, or again the relatively sympathetic seeker for a rationally based dogmatic substance. But in both essays, as well as in the poem, *Die Religion,* we find him advocating self-knowledge as the point of origin for knowledge of God.[9] Although viable answers elude him, it is important to notice his deep-seated desire to adduce defensible rational grounds for his religious faith. The quest begun here, at the outset of his career, will occupy him throughout his life, and, in various ways, will inform his theological speculations from first to last.

III   The Rettungen *and the Later Fragments*

Three critical essays published in Volume Three of Lessing's *Schrifften* (1754), had for their purpose the rehabilitation of scholars misjudged by their contemporaries and anathemized in history: the sort of "Justification" adduced for the poet Horace. In each instance, Lessing introduces new evidence or takes a new point of view in defense of his chosen subject. In the case of Hieronymus Cardanus (1501–1576), whom generations of scholars had charged with atheism, he shows that the accused's purpose was to vindicate Christian religious tenets by comparison with those of other religions. "What is more important," Lessing asks, "than to convince oneself of one's faith, and what is more impossible than conviction without preceding examination?" And the form suggested by Cardanus' treatise, in which representatives of contending religions defend their beliefs, will recur in striking guise in Lessing's last great poetic work, *Nathan der Weise.*[10]

A similar independent approach is apparent in the *Rettung* devoted to the author of a brief anonymous tract, *Ineptus Religiosus....*(1652), or in the one devoted to Johann Cochläus (1479–1552), a well-known enemy of the Reformation and a fanatic critic whose unjust diatribes against Luther long discouraged Lessing from coming to his rescue. Nonetheless, a "trifling matter" is worth defending. Lessing refutes the accusation, made in 1749 by the Göttingen theologian Friedrich Wilhelm Kraft, that after Luther's death in 1546 Cochläus initiated the calumny that the

Reformation came about not because of Luther's "holy zeal," but because he was envious of the Dominicans, who were profiting from the sale of indulgences. A rare volume of sixteenth-century correspondence demonstrates that such a rumor was in circulation at least as early as 1520. Cochläus is guilty of repeating the charge, but not of inventing it. Nor would the accusation bother Lessing if it were true. He reminds his readers that the Lord moves in strange ways, and that He might well have employed envy as a "tool" to set in motion the desired Reformation. "Would to God," he exclaims, "that all envy had equally fortunate consequences."[11] To Lessing, it was a common tactical error in theological disputes to impute to one's own cause all virtue and truth, and to defend it against the slightest hint to the contrary, even when the charges involved only nonessentials.

Here Lessing repeats a warning already conveyed in the first eight of the "Critical Letters" (1753), constituting a "Justification" which might well have been included among the essays so designated. In them Lessing had defended the sixteenth-century Wittenberg scholar Simon Lemm who, in his view, had been unjustly treated in a dispute with Martin Luther. Instead of explaining away Luther's unfairness in the matter, Lessing welcomes this small indication of the great reformer's human frailty, in the light of which his towering virtues stand out all the more attractively.[12]

In all of these studies, it is possible to see a three-fold significance. It is, first of all, clear that Lessing both advocates and illustrates accuracy and thoroughness in scholarly investigation. More important, these essays testify, once again, to his own independence from received opinion and demonstrate a wholly new concept of theological investigation. In effect they suggest that Christian dogma, as well as history's most venerated practitioners of Christianity, may well exhibit human fallibility. But such flaws need not be interpreted as weaknesses of Christianity itself, and much time and effort would be saved for essentials if theologians would accept this simple principle. These essential tasks are to define, foster, and practice the basic Christian virtues.

Except for a translation of William Law's *Serious Call to a Devout and Holy Life* (1728) made in Leipzig in 1756, and the theologically oriented remarks on Wieland and on the Klopstock circle in the "Literaturbriefe," only fragments of the theological work unpublished in Lessing's lifetime survive from the period between his early writing and the final decade of his life in the 1770's. They serve, however, to illustrate the continuity of his approach.

A fragment *Ueber die Entstehung der geoffenbarten Religion* (*On the Origin of Revealed Religion*), assigned to the period 1755–60,[13] contains eleven paragraphs, the first of which asserts: "To apprehend a God, to seek to form the worthiest ideas of him, and to observe these worthiest ideas in all our actions and thoughts, is the very epitome of all natural religion." Although natural religion was acceptable in a state of nature, it requires modification in a social milieu. Hence the promulgation of "positive" religion, based upon agreement to accept certain conventions, and to "*ascribe* to them the importance and indispensability which the naturally recognized religious truths *possessed in and of themselves*" (Lessing's emphasis). The esteemed founder of a positive religion testifies to the divine origin of its conventional elements.

All positive or revealed religions contain elements of both truth and falsehood. Lessing even asserts that all are "equally true and equally false," but he concludes in contradictory fashion that "the best revealed or positive religion is the one containing the fewest conventional supplements to natural religion, and least circumscribing the beneficent effects of natural religion."

This line of reasoning suggests the necessity for a thorough historical examination of religious systems, and a later fragment (ascribed to the period 1760–65) is, in effect, an outline of a large-scale history of Christianity in terms of the forces at work in its dissemination: *Von der Art und Weise der Fortpflanzung und Ausbreitung der Christlichen Religion (On the Manner of Propagation and Dissemination of the Christian Religion.)*[14] From the outline, one may conclude that Lessing would reject the familiar claim that the manner of Christianity's diffusion attested "the direct hand of God," and thus demonstrated its truth. On the other hand, he would not regard its dissemination by purely natural means as evidence *against* its validity. Once more, Lessing finds that a subject long in dispute concerns only nonessential detail. In the work of his last years, he continued not only to examine in this way the arguments and claims of his predecessors and contemporaries, but also attempted to refine his own positive concepts of religious essentials.

CHAPTER 5

The Journeyman Years:
Leipzig and Berlin, 1755-1760

IN the fall of 1755, Lessing left Berlin for Leipzig, where an offer came his way to act as traveling companion to one Johann Gottfried Winkler, a wealthy young man about to embark on a three-year grand tour of Europe. They left Leipzig in May of 1756, but in Amsterdam the news of the outbreak of what would prove to be a seven years' war arrived. Young Winkler felt obliged to abandon his plan, and the two returned to Leipzig.

Here Lessing settled down once more, turning his hand to translation as a source of income, studying and reading widely, and conducting a lively correspondence on the nature of tragedy with his friends Nicolai and Mendelssohn in Berlin. One can detect in this exchange a fundamental trait of Lessing's thinking, which also manifests itself as a characteristic of his style: the keen delight in the give and take of intellectual debate, and the stimulus he derived from the lively flow of opposing ideas—essentially a response to the underlying dramatic quality of a dialogue of conflict intelligently conducted.

Here he also enjoyed his association with Ewald von Kleist, a Prussian officer and poet of considerable skill. Kleist became Lessing's most cherished friend, to whose memory—he died of battle wounds in 1759—Lessing would erect a monument in the figure of Tellheim in the masterful comedy *Minna von Barnhelm*. When Kleist's duties took him from Leipzig in May, 1758, Lessing, too, decided to leave, and he turned once more to Berlin, where his friend Nicolai soon assumed control of the family publishing firm. At Lessing's suggestion, and with Lessing and Mendelssohn providing most of the material, they launched in January, 1759, a new critical journal, *Briefe, die neueste Literatur betreffend (Letters on Current Literature)*. In the same period,

Lessing produced a series of scholarly treatises on the fable, to accompany his own further efforts as fabulist; a one-act drama, *Philotas*, the only completed play to emerge from his long-continued attempts to encompass "modern" ideas in ancient settings; and his translation of Diderot's treatise on the domestic drama.

In November, 1760, Lessing abruptly left Berlin, telling none of his friends of his plans for the future.

I *Leipzig: 1756–1757*

In Leipzig once more, Lessing supported himself in part by translations, notably of the *System of Moral Philosophy* (1755) by Francis Hutcheson (1694–1746), published in 1756, and Samuel Richardson's *Aesop's Fables with Instructive Morals and Reflections*...published in 1757. Lessing shared the popular enthusiasm for Richardson and had already praised his novels in earlier reviews. He found the fables equally commendable, and for much the same reasons: they fostered the development of sensitivity, love of fellow-man, and every other virtue. There can be little doubt that Richardson's example helped to encourage Lessing's own work with the fable.[1]

At about the same time, letters from Lessing to Nicolai and Mendelssohn in late 1757 and early 1758 indicate that Edmund Burke's *Philosphical Enquiry into the Origin of our Ideas of the Sublime and Beautiful* (1757) had aroused his interest, and for a number of years he planned to translate it.[2]

The matter of sentiment comes to the fore in Lessing's preface to a translation, by other hands, of James Thomson's tragedies (1756). Lessing himself had once begun translating the admired English author's *Tancred and Sigismunda* (1745) and his *Agamemnon* (1738); and the *Theatralische Bibliothek* had carried a translation of Theophilus Cibber's "Life of Thomson." Lessing had been favorably impressed by Thomson's *Seasons* (1730) before he knew the tragedies, where the English author reveals genius in his "knowledge of the human heart," and in his "magic ability to cause every passion to originate, grow, and erupt before our eyes"—an encomium that recalls Lessing's earlier stress on the importance of psychological motivation. Yet Thomson's plays are also found to be completely "regular"; an unusual characteristic for English drama, though only of incidental significance. A dramatist may observe all the rules, as did Thomas Corneille, and still bring forth the equivalent of a soulless statue rather than a convincing representation of a human being.[3]

Lessing would agree that the rules are useful in maintaining a certain symmetry and proportion of the parts, but on occasion he would gladly sacrifice regularity, as Pierre Corneille had done, in order to provide "more essential perfections," that is to say, more credible representations of men. For this reason, he would rather have been the author of the *London Merchant* than of Gottsched's *Cato*, for more tears are shed at one performance of the former than will flow at all possible performances of the latter. And Lessing here insists that "only these tears of pity, of sensitive humanity, are the aim of tragedy, or it can have none."

A fuller explanation of Lessing's theory of tragedy emerged during the winter of 1756–57, when his correspondence with Mendelssohn and Nicolai in Berlin turned to this subject.[4] In August, Nicolai had sent Lessing a résumé of his *Abhandlung vom Trauerspiel* (Treatise on Tragedy) with its classification of tragedies on the basis of the "passions" aroused: terror, pity, and admiration.

Lessing in reply concedes that "tragedy is to awaken the passions," but he would dispose of "terror" (*Schrecken*) by subordinating it to pity. In agreement with Nicolai, he calls it merely "the sudden surprise of pity"; a device employed by the dramatist to catch our attention and prepare us to feel pity. Admiration, on the other hand, limits and dampens the feeling of pity and cannot be the *aim* of tragedy. Unlike Nicolai, Lessing retains a moral requirement for the form. The successful tragedy "expands our capacity to feel pity," and herein lies its ethical value, since "the most sympathetic man is the best man." That which arouses pity "makes us better and more virtuous." (It is clear that such views are especially applicable to the domestic tragedy.)[5]

Tragic characters, destined to suffer misfortune, must have good qualities, and the "best" person must also be the "unhappiest." Merit and misfortune must maintain a constant relation. Further, there must be no completely evil monster, nor may the best person be presented as a god-like paragon, comfortably surveying his virtues. Lessing, in a measure, thus accounts for the "mixed" characters in *Sara* and even in *Der Freigeist*, for the same principles apply to characters in both comedy and tragedy. The requirements are the same, whether the author chooses "to crown virtue with a happy outcome or make it even more interesting for us by an unhappy one." The point is that the persons who most attract our attention must also be the unhappiest.

In response to his friends' objections, Lessing explained that we feel great pity only for one with great "perfections." But these must always be depicted in conjunction with great misfortune, so that we feel not admiration alone, but admiration combined with pain. The blend of admiration and pain equals pity.[6]

For another reason, however, it is permissible to arouse admiration by depicting only the hero's virtues, and here it serves as the "point of rest" (*Ruhepunkt*) for pity: a necessary interlude between passages evocative of heightened emotional tension, which cannot be indefinitely sustained. But here the poet must guard against such an emphasis on virtues that the hero is transported beyond the reach of future dangers, for this would dissipate our sympathy at the point where it should be most intense—a fatal flaw in a tragedy. Here Lessing's target is obviously the classical drama of the French or of Gottsched, with its stoic tendency and its ethically "autonomous" heroes whose conflicts between reason and sensuality are confined to the plane of reality and unrelated to the realm of the transcendent.[7] It is also clear that Lessing's analysis illuminates the character of his own Sara, who maintains to the last a delicate balance between resignation and apprehension at the approach of death. She is neither indifferent to life nor so assured of Divine forgiveness that the onlooker's sympathy becomes superfluous.

On the subject of character in tragedy, Lessing grants that Aristotle's required "fault" is valid to a degree, in that character and misfortune are thus brought into harmony, forming a unified whole. To explain his own concept of pity, however, he declares that he rejects Aristotle and embraces instead a suggestion from Mendelssohn himself. He points out that in Lillo's *London Merchant* Barnwell's stabbing of the completely good (unflawed) "cousin" causes in the onlooker at first only horror, without pity, "because the blameless character of the old man contains nothing that could account for this misfortune." But as soon as the dying man is heard to pray for forgiveness for his murderer, our horror is transformed into "a most pleasurable pity, for this generous act arises out of his misfortune and has its foundation in it." We may recall here that Sara, too, "forgives the hand" that leads her to her doom. This complex has in common with Aristotle's theory only a shared element of unity or wholeness—a similarity in the abstract, but a divergence in the practical application.[8]

A final exchange of letters early in 1757 specifically dealt with the problem of pleasure derived from the artistic representation of ugliness, and revolved about Aristotle's illustration, the painted serpent. Mendelssohn took the position that our pleasure in this "ugly" object derives from our admiration for the skill and accuracy of the artist, and he would explain in the same way our pleasure when witnessing misfortunes accurately portrayed in the drama.

Lessing responds by restating two "agreed" assumptions: first that all passions are either violent desires or violent feelings of revulsion. Both make us "conscious of our reality to a higher degree, and this consciousness can be nothing but pleasurable." It follows, then, "that all passions, even the most unpleasant, are, as passions, pleasant,"[9] The revulsion accompanying our first glimpse of the painted serpent disappears as we become aware that the creature is not real. There remains only the pleasure that accompanies all excitation of the emotions. The same is true of our reaction to misfortune portrayed in drama. Our pleasure is abstract, and the emotion aroused within us is by no means identical with the one portrayed by the actor. The situation may be likened, Lessing tells his friends, to the phenomenon of sympathetic vibration. The actor in his role, directly touched by misfortune, portrays a response congruent with this unpleasant experience. As onlookers, we share his emotional disturbance, but not its specifically unpleasant quality. We have not been "touched" in the same way and vibrate only sympathetically, as it were, in the abstract. Our response can, therefore, be pleasurable. Tragic pity, Lessing concludes, is felt only by the onlooker, and only he experiences the ensuing tragic catharsis.

It is clear that Lessing's explanation of esthetic pleasure still rests upon unproved assumptions. It is important, however, that he gives such prominence to the effect of art upon the onlooker. Art is regarded as a medium which produces its own unique effects, which are not identical with those in nature. And in postulating man as the measure, Lessing serves as a guide for both Goethe and Schiller, and provides a basis on which, in the

Hamburgische Dramaturgie, he can apply the same principles to the drama.[10]

II   *Tragedies in Ancient Settings; the Fragments and* Philotas

While Lessing's theoretical pronouncements emphasized sentiment in terms of the bourgeois tragedy, the dramatic fragments of this period make it clear that he was also experimenting with tragic themes in ancient settings. It is, therefore, not suprising to learn that in January, 1758, he was planning to synthesize the two interests in a "bourgeois" version of the ancient Roman "Virginia" legend. Fourteen years were to elapse before Lessing finally completed this project, and for the time being his experiments retained the ancient framework.

The scenario of a Lucretia tragedy in three acts, *Das befreyte Rom* (Rome Liberated), indicates that he planned to retain the unities of time and place, and a certain symmetry of construction, but also wished to avail himself of a number of "freedoms" of the English stage, including mob scenes, farcical elements, and individualized dialogue.[11]

A fragmentary *Kleonnis*, probably dating from early 1758, is Lessing's first attempt at heroic drama in iambic pentameter—an experiment destined to have important consequences for German drama. The fragment employs a wartime background and martial themes, and projects with great skill the tensions in the character of Euphaes, an enlightened and humanitarian king of Messene.

A résumé of the historical background, a scenario, and a part of the first scene are preserved for a tragedy, *Der Horoscop*, which, like *Kleonnis* and a projected *Codrus*, was to treat the father-son relation and the sacrificial death of a prince. The drama shows certain overtones of the "fate tragedies" so popular in nineteenth-century German drama, but more important are Lessing's efforts to provide psychological motivation for the action. The play thus takes on the appearance of an Enlightenment character tragedy with strongly didactic overtones, demonstrating the danger to man in his drive to transcend the bounds fixed by nature to the acquisition of knowledge.[12]

A fragment of a "Fatime" tragedy, originally planned in prose, but recast in iambic pentameter, treats the theme of jealousy, and further demonstrates Lessing's grasp of characterization; his

Fatime is frequently regarded as an anticipation of the Countess Orsina in *Emilia Galotti*.

Lessing's only completed drama in the vein of *Codrus* and *Kleonnis* was the prose tragedy in one act, *Philotas* (1759). This young son of an unnamed king has been lightly wounded and captured on his first warlike mission against a rival ruler, Aridäus. Consumed by heroic ambition, Philotas bewails in captivity his broken dreams of glory. When he learns that his own forces have, in turn, captured the son of Aridäus, and that an exchange of prisoners is planned, he determines to die and thus secure to his father and his country the advantages that can flow from their sole posscsion of an important hostage. Through a subterfuge he obtains a sword, and before the horrified Aridäus and his general, Strato, Philotas stabs himself and dies.

Aridäus, like Euphaes in *Kleonnis* "more father than king," and touched with the humanitarian sentiments of the Enlightenment, thereupon puts aside all thought of war and conquest, the results of which are now ironically negated by the childish heroism of Philotas. He determines to ransom his son at any cost and to abandon his throne. His final pronouncements bitterly arraign the heroic creed as essentially pointless, conquest as vain, and over-stimulated patriotism as the domain of childlike naïveté. That Lessing shared these views seems indicated by his letters in which he writes in highly critical fashion of the exaggerated patriotism so much in evidence in the atmosphere of the Seven Years' War.[13]

III   D. Faust

In contrast to *Philotas*, Lessing's treatment of Doctor Faustus returns to the German scene and to the indigenous theme of the frustrated scholar who assigns his soul to the Devil in return for presumably limitless knowledge and power, and pays the price of eternal damnation. The story had been familiar to Germans since the sixteenth century, first as a popular narrative and then as a play, often performed with puppets. Accounts in books of magic also associated Faustus with the black arts. In England the subject had been elevated to the plane of literature by Christopher Marlowe's powerful drama not long after its first appearance in printed form in the German chapbook version of 1587.

In December, 1755, Lessing acknowledged that he was occupied with his "D. Faust," but was postponing work on the "scenes of terror" until he reached England on his contemplated tour. "If they can't be worked out there, where extreme despair is at home," Lessing wrote, "then they can't be worked out anywhere."[14] The subject still occupied him in July, 1758, yet only a single scene was published in his lifetime, and among his papers there was found in addition only a sketch of a prologue, a part of the second scene of the first act, and brief notes for three additional scenes. Recollections of the conversations of Lessing and others indicate that he also planned and perhaps, in some measure, carried through a "modernized" Faust, omitting all "the business with devils," somewhat in harmony with his suggestions for a "modern" Hercules drama; but no trace of such a text remains.[15] At one stage, Lessing seems to have contemplated a kind of phantasmagoria, in which a phantom Faust would replace the scholar in all his dealings with the infernal spirits, while the real Faust would experience, as in a dream, the evil consequences of yielding to their temptations and to his own overpowering thirst for truth, and would awaken filled with gratitude for this providential warning. One might well expect of Lessing an exposition of the essential virtue inherent in the search for knowledge, and a condemnation only of the impatient and overhasty seekers who demand ultimate truth in the here and now, failing to observe the natural limits of the knowable in a given epoch.[16]

IV   *Return to Criticism:* Theatralische Bibliothek, IV *(1758),*
        and the Literaturbriefe *(1759–60)*

A fourth (and last) volume of the Library of the Theater contains, among other Lessing contributions, his relatively complete translation of Dryden's *Essay of Dramatick Poesie* (1668), a rich mine of information on English drama and Dryden's critical thinking. Much of this, and especially the comparison of French and English drama (to the considerable advantage of the latter) could be expected to appeal to Lessing. He particularly welcomed Dryden's praise for the rich and complex texture of English drama, and would soon single out precisely this characteristic as eminently worthy of emulation. And in view of his later preoccupation with Shakespeare, it is noteworthy that he could find here, and translate for his readers, an essay in which Shakespeare's genius is lauded and his example repeatedly invoked as a touch-stone of excellence. It is probable that the Dryden essay provided the catalyst for Lessing's long-simmering outburst against "the rules," against slavish imitation of French classic models, and in favor of the English and Shakespeare that would shortly erupt in the pages of his next journalistic undertaking.[17]

This assumed the form of a new periodical, *Letters on Current Literature*, begun in January, 1759. It was Lessing who suggested both its plan and format: to limit coverage to the current scene, and to cast the discussion in the form of fictitious letters, which would permit a lively and informal tone for the whole. Of the first one hundred and twenty-seven numbers, Lessing supplied fifty-four before leaving Berlin and the project in 1760. Thereafter, only two further letters originated with him.

Lessing's most famous contribution appears early in the life of the new periodical. The seventeenth letter of February 16, 1759, is a frontal attack on Gottsched, and a clarion call to contempo-rary German writers to cast aside the Gottschedian French models which, Lessing believed, were stifling German literary develop-ment. His vivid polemical style is nowhere more aptly exemplified than in his bold opening statements, in which he again links his arguments to the pronouncements of an opponent, real or imag-ined, in order to give movement and direction to his reply. In this instance, he challenges the laudatory remarks on the Leipzig professor published in 1758 in the *Bibliothek der schönen Wissen-schaften und der freien Künste*, a Leipzig periodical initiated by Nicolai but later turned over to C. F. Weisse:

"Nobody will deny," say the authors of the "Bibliothek," "that the German stage owes a great share of its early improvement to Profes-sor Gottsched."

I am this Nobody; I deny it utterly. It would have been better if Gottsched had never meddled with the affairs of the theater. Either his alleged improvements concern superfluous trifles or they are actual aggravations.

Gottsched's detrimental aim was to substitute for the German stage a foreign one, that of the French. A study of older German drama would have shown him that the Germans, in their trage-dies, "wish to be given more to see and more to ponder than the timid French tragedy provides; that the massive, the terrible, and the melancholy are more sympathetic to the German natural temper than the agreeable, the tender, and the amorous; and that oversimplicity is more wearisome to the German spirit than over-complication." In short, German taste more closely resembles English than French taste. Hence Shakespeare, Jonson, Beaumont, Fletcher and the like— and especially Shakespeare—would have furnished better models for the Germans than Gottsched's favorites, Corneille and Racine: "For a genius can only be inspired by a genius, and most easily by one who seems to owe all things to nature alone, and does not intimidate by displaying the laborious perfections of art." Even to judge by the example of the ancients, Shakespeare is a "far greater tragic poet than Corneille." The latter resembles them more closely in mechanical dispositions, but Shakespeare more nearly approaches the tragic essence, which Lessing finds in emotional response. Shakespeare, with his *Othello, King Lear, Hamlet,* and the like, far surpasses the accomplishments of a Corneille or a Voltaire, and approaches the power of Sophocles' *Oedipus,*

And finally, in order to demonstrate the theory of English-German compatibility, Lessing introduces the theme of Doctor Faust, assuring his readers that the popular old German play reveals much of the Shakespearean spirit. In evidence he reproduces a scene purportedly from an old version of the traditional drama; but in reality the passage is drawn from Lessing's own projected *Faust,* and is, in fact, its only extant completed scene.

Lessing's announced program provides a dramatic climax to his critical development thus far, but certain ambiguities remain if one asks precisely what "English" and Shakespeare meant to him in 1759. The first term is associated with "the grand, the terrible, and the melancholy" in content and mood, and in technique with "freedom" from the mechanical restrictions of the neoclassic rules. The reference to Ben Jonson in this context must give pause, especially since Dryden, in his essay, had pointed out that his "regularity" set him apart from Shakespeare. On the other hand, this trait had not prevented Lessing from recommending the dramas of James Thomson.

Lessing's supposedly Shakespearean scene, with its witty and rationalistic Faust and his intellectualized, epigrammatic exchange with the seven infernal spirits, is of little help to us. Critical opinion from Lessing's day to our own largely agrees that it reflects neither the traditional spirit nor that of Shakespeare as Lessing himself has just represented it.[18] It seems unlikely that this was not as clear to Lessing as it has been to his critics. Perhaps this is why he later proposed to handle the material quite differently. The essential element is not Lessing's treatment of the subject, however, but rather his choice of a German theme, and his advocacy of an indigenous German drama.[19] In effect, Lessing recognizes the necessity for a transitional stage, when English models may serve as a kind of crutch for his imitation-conscious contemporaries. Eventually such aids were to be discarded. The seventeenth "Literaturbrief" is thus also a blueprint for Lessing's future development as a critic and playwright. It isolates themes that dominate his later thinking: the theory of genius, the nature and aim of tragedy, the essence of Shakespeare, and the closely allied problem of the Aristotelian "rules" and the French classical drama.

The same Letter also shares with several others one of the two characteristics that dominate Lessing's contributions, for it is part of a major housecleaning campaign in the domicile of German literature.[20] A number of other contributions are in one way or another devoted to the pernicious influence of Gottsched, the "learned charlatan"; and in the same vein there are repeated attacks upon the flood of poor translations, which posed a threat to the public, and especially to the proper education of the young, who suffered from this exposure to unsatisfactory and frequently incompetent versions of great foreign works.

On the whole, Lessing finds far less to praise than to blame as he surveys the current German literary scene (Letter No. 1), although some contemporaries, like Klopstock, survive a comparison with the ancient models (Letter No. 7). Klopstock's poetic language and his mastery of free rhythms are worth careful study, "for what such artistic masters have deemed it good to observe constitutes the rules" (Letter No. 19). Here again Lessing touches on the relation of genius to the rules in most liberal-sounding terms. And he later adds that he would welcome a similar freedom in the language of drama, where simple, emphatic, and realistic speech is preferable to the artificial declamatory style, as the example of Shakespeare clearly shows (Letter No. 52).

In further comment on Klopstock and his circle (Letters 49, 19, 111), Lessing sounds a second dominant note of his contributions: the deplorable influence on literature exerted by religious orthodoxy. Here Klopstock must be censured for his tendency, in the lyric, to depict feeling alone, neglecting to share with the reader the "rich store of clear ideas and concepts which called forth the emotional response in him." Given only emotion, Lessing finds it impossible to react to the poetry in any meaningful way. To him, it seemed that the lyrics "were so full of feeling that in reading them one often felt nothing." As he had earlier denied the title "philosopher" to Pope, so now he denied the title of "theologian" to Klopstock and deplored the poet's attempt to intermingle what he regarded as incompatible realms. In a letter to Gleim, Lessing gives the kind of ironic "choice" he so frequently offered in argument, either real or fictional, and which gives his critical and polemical style such a distinctive flavor: "What do you say to Klopstock's religious lyrics? If you judge them adversely, I will doubt your Christianity, and if you judge them favorably I'll suspect your good taste."[21]

Lessing's call for greater realism and attention to the causal relations in depicting emotions—suggestions reminiscent of his earlier remarks on the excellence of Thomson, or the "modernization" of the classics—sounds again in his related critique of the other-worldly quality in the early work of Wieland (Letters 9–11). In his remarks on education, for example, this writer neglects the *realia* and fails to recognize the importance of fundamental knowledge as a prerequisite to the higher, more abstract levels of thought. A precise use of language and accurate definitions are required for the command of an individual discipline, and the latter must, of course, precede any attempt at interdisciplinary thought, which Lessing regarded as paramount. Only the ability to rise rapidly from individual to general and fundamental truths marks the genius, the true hero in virtue, and the innovator in sciences and the arts.

Lessing's criticism takes on added severity, and his demands increase, as his concept of the nature of genius gains breadth and depth in the shadow of Shakespeare and the ancients. Here, as elsewhere during the decade of the 1750's—in 1755 Lessing had defined the genius as a combination of scholar, philosopher, mathematician, and artist—it represents either a virtually unattainable intellectual ideal or a literary capacity more or less compatible with the classic rules. These "educational" and "poetic" concepts will later combine, at least to a degree, in the assumption that the activity of both types is congruent with the world, with human nature, and with certain immutable "laws" which inform them both.[22]

In a critique of Wieland's early exercise in drama, *Lady Johanna Gray,* Lessing easily detects the English model, Nicholas Rowe's *Tragedy of the Lady Jane Gray* (1715), and faults the "ethereal" quality of the figures portrayed. Almost without exception they are "dear, pious characters" who are "morally good" but "poetically bad." They are "perfect" and, therefore, inhuman. But when Wieland has gained experience of the world as it is, and has discovered, with Homer and Euripides, that human beings are a mixture of good and evil, he will be capable of depicting the grandeur and beauty of virtue in the most touching way, through actions, according to the model of life itself (Letter No. 63).

In a programmatic statement called forth by C. F. Weisse's lament that promising young German poets were dying young or neglecting tragedy, Lessing declares that the role of tragic poet is not one to be essayed in youth. No one under the age of thirty, he maintains, will produce more than experiments in this demanding genre. (Lessing himself was only thirty-one.) A thorough knowledge of the eternal models—the ancient classics—and wide experience of human life are indispensable.

For his part, Lessing deplored the intellectual climate of mid-eighteenth-century Germany, so uncongenial to the development of a dramatic literature: "We have no theater. We have no actors. We have no audience." How different it was in ancient times, when the theater was a center of culture for entire cities! And even present-day France, despite the quoted complaint of Diderot, is more fortunate than Germany, where the theater is but the despised entertainment of the mob, completely lacking the patronage and support of the great and the influential, who justly reject the performances of miserable tailors and washerwomen turned actors (Letter No. 81).

Good drama, and indeed all good literature, should present us with a recognizable unity, a logical whole, an artistically created reflection of the world that surrounds us. This is a high standard, and the subjects of this kind of criticism sometimes protested that Lessing was unfair, and that he emphasized shortcomings while overlooking commendable traits. "The excellence of a work de-

pends not on individual beauties," Lessing replies. "These individual beauties must form a beautiful unity.... Only when the
whole is beyond reproach must the critic refrain from an adverse analysis and survey the work as the philosopher surveys
the world." Conscious planning is indispensable, and no work
can succeed when "the artist has set to work without himself
knowing what he intends to do" (Letter No. 16). This stress upon
the element of conscious intent (*Absicht*) will assume increasing
importance in Lessing's criticism, and we shall hear more about it.

Thus Lessing in the "Literaturbriefe" makes clear the principles
underlying the cogent criticism of his contemporaries. He exhorts
them all, in one way or another (seldom mildly, and sometimes
very brusquely indeed) to a thorough knowledge of the medium,
a proper appreciation of the relation of literature to human life
and, above all, to a conscious awareness of artistic intent.

V   *Past and Present: Logau, Aesop, Sophocles, and Diderot*

Lessing's interest in aspects of earlier German literature was
not confined to Faust. With his friend Ramler he planned a number of projects in this field, but the only completed product of
their collaboration was their edition in twelve Books (May,
1759) of a selection from the enormous flood of epigrams composed by the unjustly neglected seventeenth-century Silesian poet
Friedrich Logau. To this harvest Lessing provided a preface, in
which he commended Logau's unusual command of language. He
also added a glossary of Logau's vocabulary, hoping thereby to
invigorate and extend the linguistic medium of contemporary
poets.[23]

Lessing's long-continued interest in the perennially popular
fable eventually led, in the same year, to his attempt to analyze
and define the essence of the form. In the autumn, he published
his findings in a series of five *Abhandlungen über die Fabel*
(*Treatises on the Fable*), together with a new collection of his
own fables, this time in prose.

His definition derives from the example of the ancient masters
of the form, whose practice it was "to reduce to a particular case
a universal ethical principle; to ascribe reality to the particular
case, and to compose a story about it in which the universal principle is intuitively recognized."[24]

To Lessing, the fable was, at best, a semi-literary form, but from his discussion we indirectly learn something more of his literary theorizing at this time. Since the purpose of the fable is to convince the reader of a moralistic truth, its appeal is to the intellect alone. The drama or the epic, however, call forth an emotional response. The action of the fable must form a unified whole, which is achieved when the moral has been properly demonstrated, whether or not the action has reached an *inner* terminus. To stop short in this way would be completely unacceptable in the other genres. The fable action must also be consecutive, not contiguous, for a fable is none if it could be represented pictorially; it would then be an emblem. (This kind of distinction between verbal and visual form will recur as a vital tenet of the *Laokoon*.)[25]

A similar interest in the works of antiquity also seems to have inspired Lessing's broadly conceived plan for a multi-volume study of Sophocles, recognized in the seventeenth "Literaturbrief" as the supreme master of tragedy. Printing of the work actually began in 1760, with some material on hand, but came to a halt when Lessing failed to supply further copy. Despite the urgings of his friends, only a portion of Book One was completed: it contains a detailed and scholarly treatment of biographical materials borne on a flood of learned footnotes.

In the same year, Lessing turned once more to the current literary scene, erecting a monument to his admired French colleague Denis Diderot (1713–84), in the form of a two-volume work, *Das Theater des Herrn Diderot* (*The Theater of Diderot*), which included his translations of two plays, *Le Fils naturel* (1757) and *Le Père de famille* (1758), together with the dialogues and treatise on drama that had accompanied them. To his translations, Lessing added a brief but highly laudatory preface, in which he favorably compared Diderot to Aristotle and commended to his German readers the French critic's views, especially as an antidote to Gottsched's. Lessing had earlier praised Diderot's *Lettre sur les sourds et muets* ... (1751), and had called him "without question the best of the modern French critics." He found it encouraging that Diderot also censured the French theater as being far removed from "nature and truth," for he could now present this view as the opinion of a famed French critic, and hope that the Germans, who "seldom recover from the

reprehensible imitation of certain French models until the Frenchman himself begins to discard these models," would begin to
reconsider their ill-founded prejudices. It was also to be expected
that Lessing, the champion of "mixed" comedy and bourgeois
tragedy, would welcome the French writer as an ally in his campaign. Diderot illustrates in the translated plays and defends in
the critical discussions many of the characteristics that Lessing
himself had treated and exemplified in his own work.[26]

Thus Lessing had found a congenial critic to whom he was
understandably grateful. In the preface to a second edition of his
translation in 1781, he publicly expressed his gratitude to one
who had had "such a great share" in the development of his
taste. And he added that without Diderot's "models and theories"
this development would have taken a "completely different direction." Since a direct influence is difficult to substantiate, the extent
of Lessing's "debt" still remains a matter for speculation.[27] Perhaps he wished to indicate that the "influence" was a negative
one: that the views of the French critic helped to prevent him
from altering a course already fixed in broad outline, and encouraged him to continue in this chosen direction—a course which,
Lessing felt, might have been altered or attenuated but for the
encouraging support of the esteemed Frenchman.

CHAPTER 6

Breslau Interlude and Laokoon *(1766)*

I *The Breslau Productive Pause*

TO EXPLAIN, in some measure, his sudden disappearance from Berlin—as he wrote to Ramler, he devoted fifteen minutes a day to wondering at it—Lessing confided to his friend that he had again found it necessary to become more deeply involved "with people than with books."[1] The nearly five years he spent in Breslau, where he had obtained a none-too-demanding post as secretary to the Prussian commanding general, Bogislaw Friedrich von Tauentzien, constituted a decided break in the pattern followed for several years. Released from the immediate pressing need for money and surrounded by convivial companions, both military and civilian, Lessing devoted himself to the social life of the town, attended with enthusiasm the evening's gathering at an inn, and visited the theater and the gambling tables: for the latter he exhibited, in these less harried years, a decided inclination.

Despite his vow to live once more among people, it is clear that books continued to play a vital role in Lessing's life. In Breslau, he built up a remarkable private library, and made diligent use of his own and other collections in pursuit of his manifold interests. No longer obliged to read and write for deadlines, he could devote his reading time to the ancient classics. The results of this would crystallize, under the impact of Winckelmann, in the *Laokoon* and later essays. He also found time for reading the Church fathers and the philosophy of Spinoza, and maintained his interest in retrieving the work of forgotten German writers from undeserved oblivion. Of chief importance for the world of drama was his conception of a play using his own experiences and the background of the Seven Years' War to create the first modern German comedy, the masterpiece *Minna von Barnhelm.*

During the Breslau interlude, Lessing turned thirty-four and reached, as he said, the half-way point in his life; for a severe illness in 1764 had burned away, he thought, the last traces of his youth. These years afforded him a creative pause, a fallow period during which preparations for the great accomplishments to follow were made.

II   Laokoon, oder über die Grenzen der Malerei und Poesie

"Laocoon, or the Boundaries between Painting and Poetry, is one of the rare works of art produced by purely intellectual thought, and it is exciting in the extreme.... But [it] is no mere exercise in dialectics ... nor is it today chiefly valuable for its aesthetic principles, most of which have either been rejected by posterity or absorbed into the general stream of criticism and are now degraded to commonplaces.... Ostensibly, *Laocoon* is an investigation of aesthetic laws; actually both in purpose and in structure it is a drama of liberation, played out in the grand manner on a colossal stage."[2]

Thus succinctly has a gifted critic summarized the principal effects of Lessing's *Laokoon*. Determining the boundaries between literature and the plastic arts had long been of interest to Lessing. He had touched upon the distinction between genres, and between literary form and emblem in the fable essays; and as early as 1756, Mendelssohn had called his attention to a pamphlet on Greek art by Johann Joachim Winckelmann (1717–68), entitled *Von der Nachahmung der griechischen Werke in der Malerei und Bildhauerkunst (Thoughts on the Imitation of Greek Works in Painting and Sculpture*, 1755), which provided the catalyst for Lessing's quite different ideas.

"Making distinctions is his forte," Goethe says of Lessing's special genius, which is nowhere more clearly exemplified than in this delineation of the differing materials, methods, and aims of literary and plastic art. (The term "painting" in the title clearly encompasses sculpture as well, and critics have frequently censured Lessing's failure to distinguish between them.) From Lessing's day onward, the critics have also repeatedly denied him priority in these speculations, and it is clear that many authors have contributed to the ideas expressed here. Two predecessors merit immediate mention: Anne-Claude-Philippe de Tubières,

Comte de Caylus (1692–1765), with his *Tableaux tirés de l'Iliade, de l'Odyssée d'Homère et de l'Enèide de Virgile . . .* (1757), and the Reverend Joseph Spence (1699–1768) with his *Polymetis, or an Enquiry concerning the Agreement between the Works of the Roman Poets, and the Remains of the Ancient Artists* (1747). Both recognized, in essence, the distinction Lessing was to make, and he benefited also from the writings and conversations of his friend Moses Mendelssohn on the same topic. Yet it remained for Lessing to think through the implications of such a distinction, emphasizing the differences in a manner that sets him apart from his predecessors.[3]

A preface or—for those who stress the dramatic quality of Lessing's essay—a prologue, sets the scene and reminds the audience that sensitive observers have long recognized that painting and poetry share certain basic characteristics. Both create a pleasing illusion by presenting "absent things as though they were present." Such observers have recognized further that the source of this pleasure was beauty, "the concept of which we first derive from physical objects." They have also recognized that the "rules" of beauty could be applied to actions and ideas as well as to forms.

At the same time it has been clear to the more astute observers, the critics, that some of these rules were more aptly applied to poetry, and others to the plastic arts. Unfortunately, the distinction has been obscured in the intervening centuries, and now the greatest confusion reigns, induced in part by Simonides' "blinding antithesis" that painting represented "a silent poetry, and poetry a speaking painting." The moderns have come to stress only the similarities in the two arts, disregarding the fundamental differences in both the materials used and the method of their employment. The confusion is apparent in present-day plastic art, Lessing continues, where allegory dominates, i.e., the attempt to tell a story with painted or sculpted figures, while literature is afflicted with a fever of description: a completely misdirected enthusiasm for painting pictures with words.

It would appear that Lessing's criticism was aimed particularly at the currently popular idyl and the widespread inclination toward "poetic paintings," especially in imitation of Thomson's *Seasons.* Lessing found the same confusion now invading the realm of criticism, so that the standards of one art are applied to

the judgment of the other, and critics are suggesting topics fit
for the one as suitable subjects for the other. His announced
purpose was, therefore, to combat such "false taste" and "un-
founded critical principles."[4]

In the first section of his essay, Lessing takes issue with
Winckelmann, his principal antagonist, who from an analysis of
the sculpture depicting the priest Laocoön and his two young
sons enmeshed in the coils of two giant serpents, had derived the
principle that the essence of all Greek art was "noble simplicity
and quiet grandeur." Laocoön's extreme distress is manifested,
according to Winckelmann, not by unbecoming cries, like that
of the Laocoön in Virgil's poem, but rather by a controlled sigh of
anguish. Laocoön bears his inhuman suffering with restraint, like
the similarly tortured Philoctetes in Sophocles' drama.

Lessing accepts Winckelmann's analysis of the sculpture as
such, but he cannot agree to the extension of the principle of
stoic restraint to the realm of literature. He cites numerous in-
stances in which the characters of Greek literature unashamedly
vent their suffering with horrid cries, tears, and piercing laments.
Rightly so, Lessing goes on to say, for all stoicism is essentially
undramatic, and the Greeks, in their literature, were great enough
to combine stirring heroism with a natural response to all human
emotions. If, in their sculpture, they exhibit a stoic restraint, the
reason cannot be that they preferred to avoid the expression of
emotional extremes everywhere in their art. It is rather, Lessing
now contends, that the law of the plastic artist is beauty. Indeed,
for the Greeks this rule was not merely an esthetic convention,
but a political law which forbade the creation of ugly works.
Lessing would defend such a law, for the distortion of expressions
engendered by extreme physical pain or the violent stages of
emotion is ugly and, therefore, unacceptable in plastic art.

The creator of the Laocoön group has observed these limitations and softened the ugliest extremes. In further recogniton of
that characteristic of his medium which fixes the object forever
at a single moment in time, he has also avoided choosing the
climactic moment, which leaves nothing to the imagination of the
viewer, and which, as a highest stage of emotion, forever frozen
in time, cannot but produce, on repeated inspection, an unnatural
effect. (One is here reminded of Lessing's earlier observation,
made in the Correspondence on Tragedy, that a climactic emo-

tional response cannot be indefinitely maintained.) The plastic artist, limited by the characteristics of his medium to a single moment of action, must choose to depict the most fruitful one, namely, the one which suggests to the imagination of the observer what has preceded as well as what is to follow.

Is the poet limited in like fashion? Not at all, Lessing maintains, for the entire progression is his to depict, from its inception to its conclusion. Thus when Virgil's Laocoön "raises horrible cries to heaven," the harrowing effect is not forever fixed, but is transitory. It is also balanced by the previous revelations of the hero's manifold virtues, and thus our sympathy is maintained. (Again we are reminded of the Correspondence on Tragedy, where Lessing had defined tragic pity as a feeling of intermingled admiration and pain.) In his *Philoctetes* Sophocles has skillfully sustained a similar mood; and Lessing's recreation of the drama now graphically demonstrates its author's skill in maintaining our sympathy for this "rock of a man," while permitting him to surrender physically to the expression of intense pain. And though the poet has added a psychological misery to his hero's physical pain by isolating him from all human kind—a special hardship for the "sociable" Greeks—he has, at the same time, maintained Philoctetes' heroic stature and has shown us his unconquerable will. Such a combination of purely physical weakness and spiritual stamina is entirely "natural" and completely human, Lessing maintains. It, therefore, has dramatic and tragic value, for in revealing his humanity Philoctetes recalls others to the exercise of their own fundamental humanness.

Thus Lessing disposes of Winckelmann's stoic ideal as an essential trait for all Greek art. It may inform the plastic arts, for they are temporally limited. Literature, however, is, for Lessing, a completely different and essentially broader realm. Before examining its fundamental characteristics, however, Lessing injects an interlude in which he discusses Spence's *Polymetis*. The English critic here recognizes that painting and poetry are fundamentally different arts, and Lessing has been criticized for not saying that he does so. In his defense it may be stated that his English predecessor does not develop the implications of his insight, and that the principal thrust of his argument, as the subtitle of his work implies, is to establish the similarities between the two arts. To Spence, the similes of Latin poetry take their origin from representations by ancient plastic artists, and the discovery of such parallels may illuminate the accomplishments of both. Lessing agrees that this approach could be fruitful, but declares that the English critic has assumed too great a dependence of one upon the other. In Spence's view, they walked "constantly hand in hand," imitating not nature but each other, and thus reduced themselves to the role of copyists.

In like fashion, Lessing, in a third section (or a climactic "third act")[5] rejects the parallel effort of Count Caylus to encourage painters to find their subjects in descriptive poetic passages. In rebuttal, Lessing again introduces Homer, whose "whole gallery" of pictures of the coming of the plague (*Iliad*, Bk. I) would be impossible to capture on a single canvas. What could the painter show? "Dead bodies, burning pyres, the dying busy with the dead, the angry god on a cloud, launching his arrows." If Homer's account were to be lost, we could reconstruct it only thus from such a pictorial representation: "Hereupon Apollo became angry and shot his arrows among the army of the Greeks. Many died and their bodies were burned." But what in fact does Homer say? He tells us that Apollo

... strode down along the pinnacles of Olympos, angered
in his heart, carrying across his shoulders the bow and the hooded
quiver; and the shafts clashed on the shoulders of the god walking
angrily. He came down as night comes down and knelt then
apart and opposite the ships and let go an arrow.
Terrible was the clash that rose from the bow of silver.
First he went after the mules and the circling hounds, then let go
a tearing arrow against the men themselves and struck them.
The corpse fires burned everywhere and did not stop burning.[6]

Lessing concludes that here the poet is as far superior to the painter as the actual scene in nature is to its painted likeness. In the poem, everything vividly appeals to eye and ear. There are thus "paintable and unpaintable phenomena."[7] But there are likewise subjects inaccessible to the poet. "The gods in council" strikes Lessing as an eminently paintable scene; but what has Homer made of it? Four lines of verse that any mediocre poet could have written. It is, therefore, not true, as Caylus maintains, that one may judge a poet on the basis of his usefulness to the painter. If this were true, Caylus would surely have commented on the Pandarus passage, which appears to be one of the most vividly pictorial in all Homer. Here the poet tells us that Pandarus, after unwrapping and stringing his bow,

> . . . stripped away the lid of the quiver, and took out an arrow
> feathered, and never shot before, transmitter of dark pain.
> Swiftly he arranged the bitter arrow along the bowstring, . . .
> He drew, holding at once the grooves and the ox-hide bowstring
> and brought the string against his nipple, iron to the bowstave.
> But when he had pulled the great weapon till it made a circle,
> the bow groaned, and the string sang high, and the arrow, sharp-
> pointed,
> leapt away, furious, to fly through the throng before it.[8]

Why is this scene not a prime subject for the painter? Because, Lessing now declares in a climactic passage, despite certain similarities, the two arts are essentially different. Both are vivid, with elements accessible to the eye, but poetry—as we gather from the Pandarus passage—embodies a "visible progressing action . . . whose various parts occur consecutively in the course of time; [painting] on the other hand, [is] a visible static action, whose various parts develop concomitantly in space." The two arts reflect their differing materials and methods, and the proper subjects for the two are also functions of such differences. These Lessing now proceeds to reveal.

The materials of the plastic artist are "figures and colors in space"; those of the poet, "articulated sounds in time"; and "if, as is incontestable, the signs must have a proper relation to that which they signify, then coexistent signs can express only objects which coexist wholly or in part. Consecutive signs, in turn, can only express objects that follow one upon the other, or whose parts follow one upon the other. Objects that follow one upon the other, or whose parts follow one upon the other, are in general called actions. Consequently actions constitute the real object of poetry."

Thus the essential liberation is accomplished. Poetry is released from its frequently advocated subservience to painting, and each art is assigned an independent sphere in accord with its nature. But even Lessing's great admirers admit that he treats painting as something of a poor relation, and that he shows little appreciation for the subtleties of color or the secrets of plastic form. They are inclined to discount Lessing's one-sidedness, however, on the ground that exaggeration was necessary to combat the prevailing confusion regarding the similarities between the two arts.[9]

Shared elements and points of contact do exist, as Lessing freely admitted. Painting may, indeed, represent actions, but only through the medium of bodies which, of course, exist not only in space but also in time. And the chosen instant of time, Lessing reiterates, should be the most pregnant moment, in order to convey to the imagination of the onlooker both the previous and the subsequent stages of the action. Similarly, those actions which are the proper subject of poetry "cannot exist in themselves alone," but require a medium, normally a body, for their expression. In poetry this is accomplished by "dissolving," as it were, the coexistent parts into consecutive actions.

Throughout the investigation thus far, Lessing has repeatedly passed from the general to the particular and back again, and from theory to practice, testing each in terms of the other. A fourth section, therefore, turns once more from the abstraction to the concrete example, where Lessing finds his analysis of the poetic approach wholly justified by the practice of Homer. "I find," he says, that "Homer paints nothing but progressive actions, and that he paints all bodies and all individual objects only in terms of their participation in these actions, generally with a single stroke." He transforms the coexistent in space into the consecutive in time; a procedure not followed, however, by Virgil in his description of the shield of Aeneas, as Lessing then proceeds to show.

On the other hand, Homer has wisely foreborne the attempt to depict the beauty of Helen, although it is basic to his entire poem, for "painting alone can convey physical beauty." Homer, therefore, suggests it through the actions—or in this instance the reactions—of those who behold it, especially the Trojan graybeards who finds it impossible to remain indifferent in the presence of Helen's surpassing loveliness.

Since the indirect presentation of beauty is permissible in poetry, Lessing also admits the introduction of physical ugliness when presented as an ingredient, with the purpose of conveying "mixed emotional reactions" in the manner of Homer and Shakespeare. The final chapter in this section concludes that much the same thing may be said of elements that arouse horror or disgust.

Lessing introduces the final section of the *Laokoon* with a fiction. Winckelmann's *Geschichte der Kunst des Altertums (History of the Art of Antiquity,* 1764) has just appeared, he announces, and all further speculation must be suspended until it has been consulted. In fact, of course, the work had long been available to him, and subsequent critics have not failed to take Lessing to task for pretending that it was not. The procedure admittedly amounts to a theatrical ploy, but it is difficult to see that great harm results from this. In this later work, Winckelmann anticipates, to a degree, Lessing's thesis by adding to his earlier analysis the explanation that the restraint of the Laocoön group can be ascribed not only to the Greek's "great and resolute soul," but also to the law of beauty, which applies to the plastic arts but not to poetry. Yet Winckelmann never systematically developed this insight and apparently even forgot it, since his later *Versuch einer Allegorie* (1766) contains numerous examples of a confusion of the arts.[10] Lessing's comments on Winckelmann's *History* touch only on matters of minor detail and on the dating of the Laocoön group.

As it happens, neither Winckelmann nor Lessing advocated the now generally accepted date for the sculpture (ca. 50 B.C.). Nor has their detection of "noble simplicity and quiet grandeur" in the group gone unchallenged. Indeed, a modern critic is likely to see in it a vitality and a sense of motion quite the opposite of serene or statuesque.[11] But however mistaken the eighteenth-century critics may have been, the essential point is that both agreed on the interpretation of the work *as sculpture,* and Lessing's argument is not substantially affected by the misinterpretation he shared with Winckelmann.

III Laokoon: *Effect and Intent*

The liberating influence of the *Laokoon* is nowhere more vividly expressed than in Goethe's later comment:

One must be a young man in order to picture to oneself what effect Lessing's "Laokoon" exerted upon us, by transporting us with a wrench from the region of a stilted perception into the broad, open fields of thought. The *ut pictura poesis,* so long misunderstood, was suddenly put aside, the differences between plastic and verbal arts made clear; it was now apparent that the peaks of the two were separated, however closely their bases might border upon one another. . . .

All the consequences of the splendid idea were illuminated for us as in a lightning flash; all previous instructive and judicial criticism was cast aside like a worn-out cloak; we felt ourselves redeemed from all evil . . .[12]

And it is possible, though hardly demonstrable, that Lessing's essay accounts, at least in part, for the vitality and sense of motion which are such prominent and welcome characteristics of the new and powerful lyric style of Goethe's younger days.[13]

Winckelmann himself never publicly responded to Lessing's critique, although his correspondence indicates the belief that Lessing had misunderstood his primary intention. Lessing was to say much the same thing about *his* critics, for his essay by no means went unnoticed.

The most prominent among Lessing's contemporary critics was J. G. Herder, whose great respect for Lessing led him again and again to the study of his work. *Laokoon* is the subject of the first of Herder's *Kritische Wälder* (1769). Like Lessing, Herder accepted Winckelmann's interpretation as applied to the plastic arts, and he found much of Lessing's literary theorizing acceptable. But to Herder, the precursor of the age of "Storm and Stress," with its battle cries of originality and genius and its stress on the importance of folk myth and folk poetry in national literatures, Lessing's approach to the matter of literary creation seemed overly rationalistic, and his suggestions for literary composition overly intellectualized. As an enthusiastic and well-versed student of Homer, he was able to detect a number of weak points in Lessing's discussion of detail. More important, he successfully challenged the notion that poetry may represent only consecutive action. Homer does so on many occasions, but by no means exclusively. Energy, said Herder, rather than successive action, is the essential element of poetry. (Lessing had once planned to counter certain objections of Mendelssohn by employing the two terms action and movement, and to claim for poetry the province of both coexistent and successive action — a procedure which would have strengthened the similarities between his own and Herder's later definition.)[14]

No really good poet, Herder insisted, operates by consciously dissolving the coexistent in space into the successive in time. And it was also wrong of Lessing to deny to poetry all purely descriptive passages. Such a harsh limitation would rob it of many a treasured item. Herder considered it equally wrong to deny all movement to the plastic arts.

Lessing had originally planned *Laokoon* as a three-part work; and from surviving sketches and notes, as well as from his correspondence, it is clear that, among other matters, he hoped to demonstrate the inappropriateness of "morally perfect" characters in literature. Their justification had been incorrectly predicated, he believed, on a presumed parallel to the ideally beautiful figures essential to painting. And a letter to Nicolai (March 26, 1769) reveals that he planned to present the drama as the most exalted form of literature. Recalling these facts, and Lessing's later declaration that none of his critics—not even Herder—had detected his principal intention in *Laokoon*, it is possible to speculate that he regarded the work, in important measure, as a continuation of his campaign of reform and development in the drama.[15]

As early as the preface to Thomson's tragedies, ten years earlier, Lessing had distinguished between the creation of statuesque beauty and the representation of vital human beings. Here and elsewhere, as we have seen, he had campaigned against the stoic restraint of the French classical drama which, in his view, engendered only admiration without exciting the emotions. The seventeenth "Literaturbrief" had provided the climactic statement of such convictions, and he may have felt them to be threatened once more by Winckelmann's emphasis on serenity and restraint as the essence of all art. Lessing would limit these qualities to painting and reserve to literature, and more especially to the drama, the realm of action and passion. An important aspect of the *Laokoon* is thus that it "continues the work of the seventeenth 'Literaturbrief,' or rather it secures its gains against an unexpected threat from the flank which Lessing wished to forestall."[16] This campaign would continue in the *Hamburgische Dramaturgie*.

Before that, however, Lessing would provide in his *Minna von Barnhelm* an illustration of some of the theories which had occupied him—to the exclusion of practical demonstration—in the twelve-year period since 1755, a period during which his only completed drama had been the *Philotas* of 1759.

CHAPTER 7

Minna von Barnhelm, oder das Soldatenglück

A NEAR-FATAL illness that befell Lessing in Breslau in the summer of 1764 was especially irksome to him, not because of the fear of death, which he faced with an equanimity that astonished his friends, but principally because it interrupted a period of inspired work on a play that, he hoped, would surpass anything he had previously done in the realm of drama. If he was mistaken in this, he wrote to his friend Ramler, he was firmly resolved to concern himself no more with the theater.[1] Critical opinion from Lessing's day to our own generally agrees that *Minna von Barnhelm, or The Soldier's Fortune*, sketched in 1763, completed after various interruptions, published in 1767, and first performed by the Hamburg troupe on September 30 of the same year, was indeed the major accomplishment which Lessing had hoped for.

I *The First Modern German Comedy*

"The first theater piece with a specifically contemporary content based on significant life," Goethe called this work of "incalculable" significance, which lifted the eyes of the younger generation to heights of literary endeavor previously undreamed of.[2] With *Minna*, Lessing "invents" the modern German comedy and supplies the first work in the genre still playable today. Not Lessing's uncompleted *Faust* but his *Minna* represents the model for the indigenous German drama called for in his challenging seventeenth "Literaturbrief."

In *Minna*, Lessing has retained much of the external framework and a number of details characteristic of the traditional Saxon comedy. But all such elements are transformed by the vital touch of genius, and here at last the characters of drama come fully to life.[3] To a degree unattained in Lessing's own previous comedies, the traditional elements of calculation, of conscious manipulation, and of rationally formalized and "educational" satire give way to the presentation of a remarkable gallery of recognizable, fully developed human beings. They are here enmeshed in a masterfully motivated and intriguing dilemma which gives rise not only to scenes of sparkling humor, but to passages in which the deeper tones remind us of Lessing's insight into the close relation between laughter and tears, and comedy and tragedy.

The realistic background to which Goethe alludes was the recently terminated Seven Years' War (1756–63), in which the Prussia of Frederick the Great gained victory over its opponents, including Lessing's native Saxony. We have already observed that Lessing's "patriotism" transcended the narrowly provincial limits which normally circumscribed this emotion in the minds of his contemporaries. Indeed, his position above the battle had led to misunderstandings on the part of both Prussians and Saxons. Lessing later recalled that during the war he had been regarded in Leipzig as an arch-Prussian, and in Berlin as an arch-Saxon, because he was neither.[4] And now, although the active campaigning had come to an end, the feelings of hostility and suspicion between the recent antagonists persisted.

Against this backdrop, Lessing introduced as his protagonists the Baltic Major von Tellheim, who has served the cause of Prussia and Frederick with integrity, bravery, and admirable humane forbearance, and a beautiful, warm-hearted, and vivacious Saxon heiress, Minna von Barnhelm. When, after many vicissitudes, he joined them at last in happy union, the symbolically projected hope for future amity and understanding between former enemies was not lost on the audience.[5]

The contemporary German setting, the fully rounded characters, and the political overtones are notable, but they alone could not account for the immense admiration and respect for the play, nor for its inexhaustible vitality and persisting relevance, if Lessing had not, at the same time, skillfully introduced the deeper universal human problems posed by the conflict between love and duty, principle and expediency, and had he not undergirt these with a masterful reflection of the ever-present dichotomy of male and female.

II   *Minna and Tellheim: The "Great Debate"*

Lessing's Tellheim is the soul of honor, as well as the epitome of generosity and humane good will. As a Prussian officer administering occupied Saxon territory, he had been obliged to levy contributions and had agreed, without preamble (contrary to his directive), on the lowest permissible sum. In addition, he had loaned the Saxons the bulk of his own personal fortune to enable them to meet even this levy. At the close of hostilities, however, his legal claim to reimbursement is called into question by Prussian treasury officials, who regard the supposed indebtedness of the Saxons as a probable bribe; a reward for Tellheim's forbearance.

In consequence, Tellheim is dismissed from the service, his integrity clouded and his remaining funds exhausted pending the outcome of an official investigation. Yet his sense of honor which, for him, is synonymous with his very existence as an ethical being, will not permit him to accept the proffered aid of Just, his gruff but devoted servant, whom he can no longer afford to pay.[6] Nor will he accept repayment of a loan made to Marloff, a fellow soldier, now offered by the latter's widow. To Just and Marloff he had given without reservation, but he now finds it impossible to play the role of recipient. In both cases, he is made aware that the dictates of his honor infringe on their human and humane right to a reciprocal relationship—on their right to give as well as to receive in love and friendship.[7]

Equally trying for Tellheim are his relations with his old comrade-in-arms, Sergeant-Major Paul Werner, from whose canteen, in the press of battle, he had received the last sip of water, and to whom he was more than once indebted for his life. Tellheim now insists that it is "unfitting" to accept financial help from Werner, or indeed from anyone, when the prospects for repayment are so bleak. And again he is forced to recognize, in the light of Werner's evocation of their previous relationship, the curious dislocation of values now dictated by his sense of honor.[8]

Tellheim's most poignant conflict arises, however, from his determination that honor now dictates his renunciation of his beloved Minna, a Saxon girl who had originally been attracted to him by his generosity. She had sought him out, and their wartime acquaintance had resulted in their betrothal, sealed by an exchange of identical rings.

Concerned by the break in Tellheim's correspondence, Minna has followed him to Berlin, and has now arrived at the inn from which he has just been evicted for lack of funds. The inevitable meeting follows (II. viii), during which Minna at last elicits from Tellheim a most reluctant admission of his continuing love for her. She is greatly relieved, but cannot grasp his inability to disregard the purely external circumstances which have clouded his reputation. Nor can she convince him that their continuing love for each other should take precedence over everything else. Her inability to regard as serious a state of affairs which is deadly serious to him only serves to increase Tellheim's sense of unbearable strain, caused by his·awareness of the torturous dilemma which dictates either renunciation of Minna with honor or the longed-for union at the expense of his basic integrity.

After a third act primarily devoted to the interplay of subordinate characters, Lessing begins the fourth act with an episodic passage where he takes a delicious revenge on the French. He introduces a charming rogue, mercenary, and gambler, Riccaut de la Marlinière, whose rubbery ethical sense permits him to "lend fortune a hand" when the cards are not falling properly by themselves. He epitomizes all the pompousness and pretension of a variety of French "experts" so much in evidence in polite German circles of the day, and it is clear that Lessing takes a wicked pleasure in exposing them. But Minna is always kindly disposed toward anyone who knows and professes admiration for Tellheim, and she is pleased to hear from Riccaut the rumor that the Major's case will soon be decided in his favor. But since Tellheim is at the moment unavailable—and would in any event be skeptical—the unfortunate Major soon finds himself facing, once more, with great reluctance, his beloved Minna (IV.vi).

Tellheim's attempt to justify his position in the face of her continued refusal to regard it as serious again places an agonizing strain upon him. Even her evocation of the "dishonor" she will suffer if she is rejected by her fiancé fails to alter his resolve; and his mounting frustration at the savage irony of his plight causes him at length to burst forth in peals of bitter laughter.

Shocked and sobered by this palpable evidence of the depths of his disillusionment and despair, Minna now attempts not to belittle but to meet his arguments by reminding him that Saxon authorities can corroborate his testimony and thus help to effect his rehabilitation. But after the series of shocks Tellheim has experienced at the hands of officialdom, he cannot visualize such a prospect.

When it becomes clear to Minna that her arguments have only led to a complete impasse, and have forced Tellheim dangerously close to the brink of utter distraction, she sets a prearranged stratagem in motion. Feigning a cool resignation, tinged with bitterness and scorn, she returns to him the engagement ring she has been wearing. Releasing him from his vows, she departs, leaving her maid Franziska to convey the touching but fictional report that Minna, too, is "dishonored." Because of her attachment to Tellheim, the Prussian officer, she has been abandoned and disinherited by her Saxon guardian uncle. She is now alone and defenseless in the world.

As expected, Tellheim is at once consumed by protective concern. As a man of honor, and a man in love, he is eager to fulfill the obligations incurred in happier times and urges Minna to accept, once more, the ring she has returned to him. But Minna, in turn, now plays Tellheim's role, refusing to "burden" him with a dishonored and impoverished bride. His impassioned protestations that their restored "equality"—in a presumably mutual bankruptcy and dishonor—has swept aside all obstacles to their union, is now rejected by Minna, who can quote to him, with great aptness, all the objections he himself had previously raised to justify his decision to renounce her.

The humorous effect of this reversal of roles is, of course, lost on Tellheim, especially because he does not know that the ring Minna has forced him to "take back" is, in fact, the ring she had placed on his finger at their betrothal. (In his straitened circumstances, he had pawned it with the innkeeper, and Minna had recognized it and redeemed it when the innkeeper had shown it it to her.)

Even the arrival of a letter to Tellheim from the hand of the King himself, announcing the Major's complete exoneration from all charges, the restoration of his honor, and the offer of reappointment in the Prussian service, only provides Minna with further opportunity to insist, as Tellheim had previously done, that this new imbalance in their fortunes must necessarily confirm her renunciation of him.

But Minna's persistence in her deception threatens, in one final and unforeseen interlude, to drive Tellheim over the brink of tragedy, for his servant Just now reports that Tellheim's ring, which he had been sent to redeem, has already found its way to

Minna. The mistaken but shattering conviction flashes upon the Major that Minna, who he believes has already returned the ring he had given her, has now contrived to regain possession of the one she had given him. He leaps to the distracted conclusion that she has followed him to Berlin expressly in order to break with him, and that her previous protestations of continuing love were false: a cover for this wretched subterfuge. His despair, scorn, and disillusionment are acute, and he is mortally offended.

Minna now realizes that she has carried her little game too far and desperately attempts to reassure Tellheim, now on the verge of complete emotional collapse. At this tense and potentially tragic moment, the arrival of Minna's uncle is announced. Even now, as a man of honor, Tellheim would arouse himself from the depths of his disillusionment at a presumably "faithless" Minna to protect her from the "tyrannical" guardian. Minna persuades him at last, but only with the greatest difficulty, to examine his ring carefully, whereupon he discovers it to be his own, and the one presented to him by Minna. Joyful but bewildered, he can now accept Minna's glowing assurances that all has indeed ended happily.

III   *The Outcome: Lessing's Accomplishment*

It is clear that with *Minna von Barnhelm*, Lessing has come a long way since his last completed comedy, *Der Freigeist*. The later play exhibits a number of unfamiliar elements, but the novelty that remains a source of special controversy is found in the figure of Tellheim and his torturing dilemma.

It has been said that with his Tellheim Lessing introduces to the German audience the "new" man, i.e., the man of character whose integrity makes it possible for him to practice renunciation, to deny himself for the sake of a principle, and thus to anticipate a coming age of Idealism.[9] But whether his unremitting adherence to the dictates of honor emerges as a "flaw" or "virtue" is, nonetheless, still disputed. A majority of critics holds that Tellheim's sense of honor is exaggerated, and hence a traditional comic vice of which he must be "cured." But one also encounters the view that he is a "noble, good, and strong man of uncompromising ethics, asserting himself and fighting the corruption of the age."[10] One may also adopt an intermediate attitude, ascribing to him certain inconsistencies and flaws, but regarding them as mere "surface blemishes on true steel," and their possessor a representative of the "character of worth set in adversity, finding in himself the stability which in more normal times his environment would afford."[11] Or one may take up a position at the other extreme, rejecting the "seriousness" of Tellheim's expressed dilemma and viewing the portrayal of his distress as an expression of Lessing's own feelings regarding the Major's "Prussianism." In this view, Lessing, like Minna, parodies its humorless and stiffnecked stubbornness. He understands its weaknesses, but they do not blind him to its admirable and lovable qualities.[12]

If, on the other hand, one wishes to approach the problem in terms of the distressing as well as humorous implications of the total situation and accept Tellheim's sense of honor as synonymous with his "total ethical existence," one sees him confronting a genuinely tragic choice. To this extent, then, we may regard him as a potentially tragic figure, exposed to destructive pressures which even Minna's lightly bantering tone can neither conceal nor resolve. And, indeed, she herself eventually recognizes this fact, if only imperfectly. That she cannot convince Tellheim of the fundamental lightness of his various afflictions does not, however, mean that she shares Tellheim's temptation to derive from them an inclination to question the beneficence of Providence. As a representative of a transitional stage in the "Age of Reason," in which the formerly accepted rational demonstrations of God's goodness no longer suffice—and, one might add, as a woman and a Lessing heroine—Minna is incapable of *proving* the existence of a benevolent Providence. She can, however, persist in her cheerful and unshakable *faith* in its existence.[13]

Tellheim's exaggeration of the dictates of his code is, however, a fair target for ridicule and permits us to regard him, to this extent, as a comic figure. The element of absurdity comes to the fore when he overextends the code to the detriment of his fellow human beings. His ethical sense, in itself a "virtue"—indeed, the fundamental virtue in the system of the Enlightenment—overshadows his reason, the proper exercise of which, in the enlightened philosophy of the day, brings about a harmony between ethical will and the requirements of the real world. Tellheim, the "new" man who transcends this system, measures realities not in terms of his reason, but in terms of his moral feeling, and is thus enmeshed in absurdities.[14]

These we have seen develop in Tellheim's relation to the servant Just (I.viii), to Werner (III.vii), and to Minna (IV.vi). In these confrontations, it is made clear that his insistence on the code would force him to act like a "complete monster" (Tellheim in I.viii), dishonoring himself and them.[15] His much-discussed ethical sense is thus both virtue and vice, and exposes him to potential tragedy as well as ridicule.[16] Expressed in terms of the Shaftesburian ethic familiar to Lessing, Tellheim fails to achieve the proper balance between "the natural Affections, which lead to the Good of the Publick, and the Self-Affections, which lead only to the Good of the Private." Shaftesbury's corollary suggests that the exercise of principles should be subjected to the "test of ridicule," and it is Minna who tells us that Tellheim's excessive deference to his concept of honor fails to pass this test (IV.vi).[17]

Although Minna may scoff, and although we may be inclined to share her feeling that Tellheim exaggerates, our list of targets might not be identical with hers: we might omit, for example, her teasing references to Tellheim the "cripple"—he still feels some effect from a battle wound in the arm—or Tellheim the "pauper." But whichever ideas we choose to criticize, we shall elicit no agreement from the Major. To the very end, there is no clear indication (as more than one recent critic has pointed out) that he has altered his views in response to the events of the play. Ultimately, it is his love for Minna, and his sense of honor—which are inextricably interwoven—and not a change in his character or principles that dictate his enthusiastic willingness to accept at last the financial help from Werner, and inspire his exuberantly protective resolve to marry the presumably disinherited and abandoned girl.[18] Once he has learned the truth, we may be sure that the wedding would again be off.

And although we know that he feels uneasy, downcast, and even "tortured" by the inhuman necessity to deny to others their chance to express their gratitude and love, we may also be sure that he would have continued to do so had not the King's intervention resolved the dilemma. The basic conflict is thus bound to disappear, but it cannot be said to have been resolved in terms of the dramatic action.

What is resolved, however, is the development in comedy form hinted at in such earlier plays as Die Juden and Der Freigeist, where the intrigue culminates not only in the exposure of some fault or foible to general ridicule, but also in the revelation of positive values in the central characters. Minna's intrigue serves a similar purpose by revealing the full scope of Tellheim's generosity, integrity, and good will. For this reason, and despite the anguish it has occasioned, she cannot regret that her little stratagem has made possible this revelation of his "whole heart." What is exposed is not a blameworthy flaw, as in the traditional comedy, but the worthwhile character of a genuine, three-dimensional human being. With *Minna von Barnhelm,* Lessing leaves the realm of the traditional comedy of character types to create the modern comedy of character.[19]

It appears that Lessing intended no resolution of the fundamental conflict, but rather a demonstration of its inherent insolubility on the plane of reality. He would remind his audience, as he was later to remind it with *Emilia Galotti,* that the quest for absolutes is doomed to failure, and further, that men and women in their relations with one another respond in wholly different ways to the demands of reality.

This aspect of the dilemma is revealed in the "great debate" when Minna attempts to meet Tellheim on equal terms and overcome the objections derived from his analysis of "honor" (IV.vi). But here Tellheim abruptly intervenes. In all other matters she may offer a valid opinion, he admits, but not in respect to this concept. Such a double standard in Tellheim's thinking is especially provocative when we recall that with the creation of Minna, with her independent spirit, unconventional behavior, gaiety, and warm-hearted frankness in regard to her emotions — qualities which we like to think of as being especially modern—Lessing points forward to the new ideal of the equality of the sexes.

And yet the "equality", which even Tellheim has labeled the "firmest bond of love", does not extend to the debate on the nature of honor. After his rehabilitation at the hand of the King has presumably created a new imbalance between a now fortunate Tellheim and a supposedly abandoned and penniless Minna, she can turn his own words against him and insist: "It is a worthless creature who is not ashamed to owe her whole happiness to the blind tenderness of a man." To which Tellheim bluntly replies: "False, absolutely false!" He refuses to permit her to "philosophize," as he had done, and rejects as "sophistry" her attempts to stand on principle and use his own arguments. He insists that the same objections on the lips of a woman are incongruous and cannot possibly carry the weight they may have when uttered by a man. Such matters are outside a woman's area of competence. Nature has decreed it so, precisely as she has decreed that man will remain impervious to the more "feminine" appeal to the affective realm.

In listing the numerous contradictory traits with which Lessing has endowed his principal characters—the list usually includes the "northern" Tellheim, imbued with a certain severity, sternness, and, of course, inflexibility in matters of principle, and the warm-hearted, gracious, lovable, and "practical" Saxon heiress—it seems clear that Lessing also looks beyond them to the contrast that lies at the heart of the controversy: the fundamentally different approaches to life which he traces to their origins in the nature of man and woman. It would appear that a certain dichotomy existed in Lessing himself. In the figure of Minna, we are presented with a most charming and convincing advocate of equality. And yet her creator rejected the "philosophical" female as firmly as his Tellheim rejects such as "unnatural" creature. Lessing later wrote to his brother Karl: "Virginal heroines and philosophers are not at all to my taste. When Aristotle treats of the excellence of morals, he expressly excludes from it women and slaves. I know of no higher virtues in an unmarried girl than piety and obedience."[20]

It is scarcely possible to fault Lessing for failing to resolve logically the problem he has posed, since in its origin and nature it transcends the realm of logic. We can be grateful, however, for a perennially fascinating exposition of the ultimate enigma in human relations. It is a mystery which Lessing, without a trace of lugubriousness or disenchantment, assigns to the realm of the ultimately insoluble. He is convinced that the man of uncompromising principle will inevitably collide with the ever-present obstacles to the attainment of an ideal in a real and fallible world. (He himself was such a man who repeatedly experienced such collisions in his own career.) Men of this kind are bound to involve themselves in conflicts insoluble on the plane of reason and reality, and will require, like Tellheim, the intervention of a higher power, or the transfer of the action to a higher plane, in order to restore the cosmic balance.[21] In this sense, Lessing elevates *Minna von Barnhelm* above the level of pure comedy and directs

our attention to the theory of tragedy—a topic to which he returns
in the same year, when he takes on a new theater assignment in
Hamburg.

CHAPTER 8

The Hamburg Critic

AFTER resigning his Breslau position in 1765, Lessing failed to find preferment in Berlin. His hopes for appointment as Royal Librarian were disappointed when the post went to an obscure Frenchman—it is likely that Frederick still remembered Lessing's brush with Voltaire—and toward the end of 1766 he found himself at loose ends, "standing," as he said, "in the market place," when he was approached by representatives of a new theatrical venture in Hamburg. Though he did not wish to undertake the responsibility of supplying fresh dramas on demand, it was agreed that he would provide regular critical commentary on the plays and performances in a newly conceived theatrical program.

I *The National Theater and the* Hamburgische Dramaturgie

By establishing a National Theater in Hamburg, a group of "friends of the theater" hoped to elevate the German drama from the status of precarious and little admired trade and establish it on the plane of art. Instead of having an all-powerful manager, not infrequently an exploiter of his troupe, the Hamburg project was to be organized in accord with a preconceived plan agreeable and advantageous to all. In this way, it was hoped that the company could be relieved of financial and other mundane concerns and could devote itself to the development of artistic excellence.

As the official critic Lessing undertook to supply a twice-weekly commentary on current productions, intending, at first, to analyze not only the plays themselves, but the performances of the actors as well. The latter intention he was soon obliged to abandon, for the sensitive egos could not stand the strain. Indeed, the whole project soon faltered and eventually collapsed for lack of support. Performances were given in Hamburg from April to December, 1767, and struggled on through a second series from May to November, 1768, before the project was finally abandoned.[1]

103

Having, in any case, fallen far behind in his account of current productions, Lessing continued his reviews and commentary for more than a year and eventually fulfilled his obligation to subscribers with a total of one hundred and four numbers, the last of which he numbered, with tongue in cheek, "101 to 104." The entire series was published in book form at Easter, 1769, under the title *Hamburgische Dramaturgie (Hamburg Dramaturgy)*. Here his readers found not only reviews of performances and analyses of plays, but also a wide-ranging series of discussions on such topics as dramatic theory and technique, the relation of drama to history, character in drama, and the art of acting.

The principal value of the work lay not in the specific analyses and comments on the performances of plays, many of them long since forgotten, but rather in the fact that Lessing made of his *Dramaturgie* a vehicle in his long campaign to foster an indigenous German drama, independent of foreign borrowings and capable of maintaining itself in accord with the highest critical standards. To do so, Lessing understandably made use of his comprehensive historical knowledge of dramatic theory, developed ideas previously advanced in his own criticism, and frequently employed the theories of his predecessors and contemporaries.[2]

II *Aristotle and the French*

As in the past, the principal antagonist in the work is the tragedy of French classicism, and particularly that of Voltaire. But Lessing now attempts to enlist the aid and authority of Aristotle, the great law-giver, in establishing a firm basis for his opposition. As in earlier years, his venerated hero is Shakespeare.

It is frequently said that Lessing was unfair and imprecise in his analysis of French tragedy, and that the problem of reconciling Shakespeare with Aristotle was fundamentally insoluble.[3] The historical importance of the *Hamburgische Dramaturgie* remains unaffected by such claims, however, and the work constitutes an important milestone and a liberating influence in the development of German drama.

Lessing's deference to Aristotle indicates no blind acceptance of ancient authority, although he maintains that in developing standards of taste, no "true critic" would trust his personal inclinations alone, but would seek to foster them "according to the rules

which the nature of the subject demands" (No. 19). After long
study, he has concluded that Aristotle's principles for tragedy do,
in fact, constitute those required by the nature of the form, and
these he employs in his own analysis of specific plays (Nos. 101–
104). Which is not to say that Lessing had no views of his own
regarding Aristotle's announced purpose of tragedy: to bring
about a "catharsis" by arousing pity and fear. To Lessing, the fear
intended was not merely a fear for the character aroused by his
impending misfortune—a widely advocated interpretation—but
rather, according to his reading of Aristotle's *Rhetoric*, "the fear
for ourselves which arises from our resemblance to the suffering
person . . . the fear that we ourselves can become the pitied object.
In a word: this fear is pity applied to ourselves" (No. 75).

Similarly, the basic emotion of pity (the possibility of shared
suffering) can arise only when "the misfortune which is to become the object of our pity" is so constituted "that we would also
fear it for ourselves or for someone like ourselves." Pity and fear
are thus intimately interwoven, and Lessing declares that Aristotle
interprets the one in terms of the other. Everything is, therefore,
"fearful to us which, if it had happened to someone else, or was
supposed to happen to someone else, would arouse our pity: and
we find pitiable everything that we would fear if it threatened
ourselves." The victim whom we are to pity must, therefore, not
only suffer undeservedly or disproportionately in respect to his
degree of guilt, but he must not be "worse than we normally are."
Indeed, in his fundamental nature he must resemble us completely. Only then is the required identification with him possible
for us (No. 75).

Lessing interprets Aristotle's still disputed concept of "catharsis" as a "purification" of the "passions" (pity and fear) aroused
in us as spectators.[4] It is the "transformation of the passions into
virtuous accomplishments" (No. 78). This "transformation" has
been described as the generation of a classically ideal condition
in respect to these emotions of pity and fear, that is to say, the
creation of an ideal mean, in the responses of the spectator, between the extremes of too little and too much in the experience
of both. The desired result is thus not the imparting of a moral
"lesson" or the encouragement of virtuous conduct, but rather the
development of broadly virtuous propensities which make it possible to experience the potentially fearful—the idea of suffering—

not only freely (not too little) but also with a certain composure
and restraint (not too much). If one thus credits Lessing with
removing the narrowly didactic neoclassic requirement from the
aim of tragedy, he may be seen as an advocate, in some degree,
of a greater emphasis on its esthetic enjoyment: of the principle
of art for art's sake.[5]

But such accounts also collide with a number of others, notably
that of Max Kommerell, who finds Lessing mistaken in his interpretation of Aristotle's "pity" in essentially Christian terms (to
Aristotle it is not valuable but painful); as well as in his analysis
of "fear" as fear "for ourselves," and in his view of catharsis as a
transformation fostering the development of virtuous propensities
rather than a restoration of a natural balance after the disruptive
storm of pity has passed. In all of this, it is suggested, Lessing, in
his effort to advance his own strongly held views, consciously departed from Aristotle while continuing to invoke him as his authority. Yet it is granted that positive values flow from Lessing's
analysis, providing ammunition for his attack on the "stoic"
French tragedy and his championing of the drama of Diderot and
the English—salutary influences for Germany on the threshold of
the birth of its own tragic literature.[6]

In terms of Aristotle thus interpreted, Lessing examines and
largely rejects French classical tragedy and theory, particularly
as represented by Voltaire and Pierre Corneille—especially the
latter's commentary on Aristotle, composed at the conclusion of
his long career as a dramatist. It is easy to see why Lessing found
Corneille's interpretation of Aristotle unacceptable; for the French
writer condones arousing one emotion *or* the other, i.e., pity *or*
fear, thus justifying his own dramatic practice. Such French
dramas Lessing would reject. He found their analysis of unusual
"soul states" unnatural, and regarded their plots as poverty-
stricken and boring; the lyrical moods cold; the whole schematic
and intellectualized—a forced and ceremonial play, as transitory
as the ceremonial style of courtly life from which these dramas
emerged. With all of this Lessing contrasted the "natural" genius
of Shakespeare, who lacked both the impulse and the background
to strive for esthetic perfection of form, yet instinctively suc-
ceeded in projecting the essence of tragedy. As a true genius,
comparable only to Sophocles, Shakespeare exemplified what Lessing took to be the originality needed for the creative process,

freed of all temporal canons of taste, yet instinctively in accord
with "cosmic reason." In proposing Shakespeare as a model for
study, Lessing was, in effect, recognizing the philosophical orientation of the German artistic instinct, whose counterpart he found
in the tragedies of Shakespeare, but not in the psychologically
oriented tragedy of French classicism.[7]

It is clear that Lessing's "absolute" interpretation of the nature of
tragedy unfairly excluded the possibility of other approaches to the
subject. It is possible that Lessing practiced conscious oversimpli-
fication and exaggeration, defending it on historical grounds; for
he wished to combat the pervasive influence of the French models
and theories, and especially their German imitators, who still
dominated the taste of his day. Typically, forty-one of the first
forty-nine plays performed by the Hamburg company were French
in origin.[8] It is likely that Lessing would have opposed such excessive deference to *any* foreign influence in his effort to encourage independence and originality in German authors. Thus, while
recommending Shakespeare as an object of study, he advocated
neither the performance nor the imitation of Shakespeare's works
(No. 73). Indeed, his advocacy of Shakespeare was, for the most
part, couched in general and allusive terms and it nowhere led
to the sort of detailed and extensive analyses with which he buttressed his rejection of French tragedy.

As Lessing had turned to the Aristotelian concept of fear—
augmenting his previous emphasis on the element of pity in the
Correspondence on Tragedy—in order to clarify his theory of
tragedy, he now expanded his perspective in order to arrive at a
more satisfying explanation of our pleasure in tragic subjects.

In a long analysis of the contemporary German drama, *Richard
der Dritte* (*Richard the Third*), by his friend C. F. Weisse,
Lessing rejects its claim to genuine tragic stature on the ground
that the central character is a monster; an "incarnate devil" in
whom the audience could detect no single trait that would link
him to themselves. Such a figure lacks the power to generate pity
and fear and must surrender any claim to Aristotelian consideration as a tragic hero. And yet this repulsive creature was capable,
said Lessing, of arousing in the audience a certain curiosity, even
a degree of pleasure. The explanation, he now suggested, turned
on the presence of an element of *intent* (*Absicht*): "Everything
that Richard does is horror; but all these horrors occur in relation

to some intention; Richard has a plan; and our curiosity is aroused wherever we detect a plan. We are eager to discover whether it will be carried out, and how; and we are so fond of the purposeful that it gives us pleasure, quite without regard to the morality of the purpose." For different reasons, Lessing went on, the audience both wished and did not wish to see Richard's plan succeed, and this engagement of their mental energies generated pleasure. But the audience could not be "satisfied" in this way. The poet who would create true tragedy must meet very specific requirements: "It is not enough that his work produces effects upon us: it must also produce those appropriate to the genre, . . . and no others can compensate in any way for their absence . . ." (No. 79).

III   Genius, History, and the Rules

In the same vein, Lessing maintains that purely historical events are unartistic because they lack the creative and formative touch provided by the heightened perceptions of true poetic genius. Like the ultimate Creator, to whom the apparent confusion of the universe is clearly comprehensible, the true poet imparts to apparently chaotic history his own formative and interpretative vision, thus providing a comprehensible model of the universe. His creation should constantly remind us that as all things are resolved for the best in the universe of the Creator, so they will be resolved in the limited world of the creative artist, whose work supplies us with a "silhouette" of that larger whole (No. 79).[9]

Such genuine poetic insight was accessible only to the genius, to whom Lessing would grant the greatest freedom to evolve a "new" world without deference to superficial "rules" of composition. Among such freedoms, Lessing advocated release from adherence to the unities of time and place. Only the unity of action had been a principal concern to the ancients, said Lessing, and only its observance should be required of the modern dramatist (No. 46). In the world of the true poet, released from superficial restraints, the chance occurrences are "linked in a different order, yet in as precise a fashion as in this one." Causes and effects may follow in a succession different from that found in the real world, but it is the poet's intention to produce the same general effect of the Good (No. 34).

In the final analysis, the true poet of genius creates a sensible and logical world, and only he finds it possible, as the bungler does not, to dispense with the irrelevant, the distracting, the surprising, or the capricious, which are designed to titillate the curiosity and maintain the interest of the audience. "Only occurrences which are grounded one in another, only linkages of causes and effects can occupy the genius. Tracing effects to their causes, balancing causes against effects, eliminating everywhere the fortuitous, causing everything that happens to happen in such a way that it cannot happen otherwise, that is the business of the genius working in the realm of history, in order to transform the useless items of memory into nourishment for the spirit" (No. 30).

A similar consistency and universality is required of the characters in drama. "In a play, we are not supposed to learn what this or that individual man did, but rather what any man of a certain character would do under certain given conditions" (No. 19). And it is essential that the dramatist know precisely what effects he wishes to produce. "Acting with conscious intent is what elevates man above lesser creatures; to create with intent . . . is what distinguishes the genius from trivial artists . . ." (No. 34).

No true genius could be "oppressed" by the rules, Lessing elsewhere declares, for the rules are derived from the works of genius. "Not every critic is a genius, but every genius is a born critic. He has within himself a touchstone of all rules. He comprehends and preserves and follows only those which his perception expresses to him in words" (No. 96).[10]

For Lessing, the "true critic" was one who had developed his artistic taste by repeated reference to standards derived from the basic nature of the subject. The position of the genius was similar, for genius too, while acting without superficial restraint, was responsive to certain absolutes, to the dictates of an innate critical sense attuned to the basic nature of his subject. And his subject was nothing less than the whole of mankind. The difference between critic and genius lay in the fact that the former had created his standards of taste by conscious intellectual effort; and the genius had created his standards of taste by responding to mysterious dictates, the origin of which transcends reason. The foremost example of true dramatic genius since the time of Sophocles is, not surprisingly, Shakespeare.

Of his own position in the realm of drama, Lessing gives a

remarkably perceptive estimate at the close of the *Dramaturgie*:

I am neither actor nor poet. To be sure, people sometimes do me
the honor to judge me the latter. But only because they misjudge me.
They should not draw such generous conclusions from a few dramatic
efforts that I once ventured. Not everyone who takes brush in hand
and squanders colors is a painter. The earliest of those efforts were
dashed off during those years when one is so glad to consider desire
and facility synonymous with genius. Whatever is acceptable in my
later efforts is due solely to criticism, as I am well aware. I do not feel
within me the vital spring that mounts of its own power, and of its
own power shoots upward in such rich, fresh, pure streams: I must
force everything up within me by pumps and pipelines. I would be so
poverty-stricken, cold, and shortsighted if I hadn't learned, in some
measure, to borrow modestly the treasures of others, to warm myself
at their fires, and to strengthen my vision with the glass of art. For
this reason, I have always felt ashamed or annoyed when I read or
heard something detrimental to criticism. It is said that it stifles
genius: and I had the flattering notion that I got from it something
very close to genius.

As a critic, Lessing felt obliged to condemn Shakespearean
"originality" when it led to abuses (notably in the Storm and
Stress decade of the 1770's), but the general development of the
nineteenth century is in accord with the philosophical orientation
he advocated in the *Hamburgische Dramaturgie*. Here the genius
of the free individual, attuned to the basic impulses of collective
humanity, was preferred to the poet whose principal effort was
directed toward the perfection of esthetic form.[11]

IV   Audience Identification:
Martyr Drama and Middle-Class Drama

Lessing's interpretation of Aristotle's basic teaching also accounts for his rejection of the "Christian" tragedy, the popular
martyr drama which depicted the suffering and death brought
about by an enthusiastic persistence in religious conviction. For
better or worse, the eagerness of such devotees to suffer for their
faith made of them startling exceptions to the general run of
humanity. A feeling of kinship with such exalted figures was impossible, and thus the generation of tragic pity and fear was
beyond the power of these paragons, to whom torture and the
martyr's death were as easy as "drinking a glass of water" (No. 1).

In respect to bourgeois tragedy, on the other hand, Lessing was prepared to assert that identification was made easier when the "circumstances" of the tragic character linked him to the audience. The misfortunes of people on our own level "must naturally penetrate most deeply into our soul, and if we feel pity for kings, we feel it for them as human beings, and not as kings" (No. 14). Indeed, Lessing's promotion of domestic tragedy has given rise to the thesis that his analysis of tragedy was designed in large part as an apology for this genre. And in the same vein, it is suggested that we hear relatively little about Shakespeare in the *Dramaturgie*, despite Lessing's veneration of him as a "historical great," because he could recommend him as a practical model only to the extent that he could "reclaim" him for the bourgeois drama. Thus *Othello* and *Romeo and Juliet*, but not, for example, *Julius Caesar* are referred to.[12] Lessing himself, at any rate, expressly ruled out Shakespeare as a model for imitation. "Shakespeare is to be studied, not plundered," he states (No. 73), and it may well be that he consciously avoided overexposing Shakespeare in order to discourage uncritical imitation by a younger generation not yet prepared to cope with this elemental force. Perhaps he was also recalling his account of a somewhat analogous situation in his own youth, and the discouragement occasioned by a sudden "flood of masterpieces," borrowed principally from the French, which seemed to exhaust the possibilities for drama. Young Germans had been confronted with the demand "not merely to produce something good, but something better." Such a prodigious leap, however, was beyond their powers; critics could command it, but no poets were able to obey.[13]

Quite a different explanation for the relative neglect of Shakespeare's historical dramas is based on the assumption that Lessing, like his contemporaries J. E. Schlegel, Herder, and Gerstenberg, regarded these plays not as formal tragedies, but as "dramatized history." Had they known the term, it is likely that they would also have accepted them as "psychological character studies," a form for which no laws were prescribed by Aristotle. Quite naturally, therefore, such dramas would not be invoked in illustration of Lessing's analysis of tragedy in Aristotelian terms.[14]

The *Hamburgische Dramaturgie* reflects throughout Lessing's conviction that tragedy, and indeed all drama, should foster a feeling of shared humanity. Therefore, despite his great admiration for Diderot, he criticized the French playwright's emphasis, in his "serious comedies," on the "conditions" of his characters, that is, their background and their professional and social position. Lessing believed that such characters would sacrifice their universality if they were limited to a single class or "condition."[15] He found it "incontrovertible that Aristotle made no distinction at all between the characters of comedy and tragedy in respect to their universality" (No. 89).

V *In Retrospect*

Although the *Hamburgische Dramaturgie*, in its final form, fills two volumes, and ranges at will not only over the contemporary dramatic scene in Germany, but also far afield in both time and space—Spain, Italy, ancient Greece and Rome, the English drama of Shakespeare and Lillo, touching on the most diverse matters of import for the theater as a whole—its principal focal point remains France and its classical tragedy. This, too, was Lessing's view, and his own estimate of the work's chief importance turns precisely on this point. For the *Dramaturgie* took on a basic direction only after he had decided to emulate the method of Aristotle, who sought out those ideas of others with which he could take issue and developed his own views from the ensuing dialectic. Lessing found this practice especially appropriate for a critic: "Let him first find someone with whom he can disagree: in this way he will come by degrees to the heart of the matter, and the rest will take care of itself." In the *Dramaturgie*, as he frankly admitted, his choice of chief opponents had been the "French writers," and especially Voltaire (No. 70).

The failure of the National Theater naturally weighed heavily on Lessing's mind as he composed the final installment.[16] In terms reminiscent of the charges made ten years before in the "Literaturbriefe," he castigated the indifference of the public and deplored the ironic futility of attempting to erect a National Theater "when we Germans are still not a nation" in the sense of a homogeneous cultural community with a consciousness of its own individuality. "We are still the avowed imitators of everything foreign; in particular we are still the servile admirers of the never sufficiently admired French. . . ."

In the final analysis, however, Lessing could console himself and claim a modest satisfaction in having called attention not only to the shortcomings of the French, with their mistaken concept of "regularity," but also to the equally dangerous *dis*regard of *all* rules. The latter was always a threat when one recalled the false conception of the "freedoms" which certain English dramatists permitted themselves. If he had managed to introduce an element of order and control into the current "ferment in matters of taste," Lessing wrote, he would regard his work as a contribution to the cause of the German theater.

CHAPTER 9

Emilia Galotti

AFTER the collapse of the Hamburg theater venture and an ill-fated excursion into publishing—Lessing's partner in this venture, which also came to grief, was Johann Joachim Bode, a well-known translator, especially of English novels—Lessing again found himself deeply in debt. Through the good offices of the Braunschweig professor-poet Johann Arnold Ebert, he eventually secured the post as Court Librarian in Wolfenbüttel. The Court itself had been transferred, some years earlier, to the larger city of Braunschweig, and when Lessing took up his duties at the beginning of May, 1770, he found life in the sleepy little town a strong contrast to the stimulating pace of the Hamburg years. There his relation to the theater had led to friendships with the famous actors Konrad Ekhof and Friedrich Ludwig Schröder. He had become acquainted with the poets Klopstock and Matthias Claudius; Herder, on his travels, had sought him out, and Lessing had been a welcome ornament in the social and intellectual life of the city.[1]

It was not until the winter of 1771–72 that a reviving interest in the affairs of the theater led him to turn, once again, to the long-projected and slowly maturing dramatic treatment of events of the fifth century B.C. as related by Livy and other Roman historians and frequently dramatized by the playwrights of several nations. It is the legend of the ill-fated Virginia, the beautiful young daughter of the Centurion Virginius, who is slain by her father as a last resort to preserve her innocence from the lust of the tyrannical Decemvir Appius Claudius. This desperate sacrifice serves to arouse widespread opposition to the threat of despotism and makes a successful revolt against the decemvirate possible.

I Lessing's "Bourgeois Virginia"

Lessing's projected treatment was announced in his correspond-

ence of October, 1757, but it soon encountered the same difficulties that had dogged most of his previous attempts to compose
a classical tragedy. By the beginning of 1758, therefore, Lessing
decided to modernize the setting and, in harmony with his current interest in domestic tragedy, to make of his play a "bourgeois Virginia." At the same time, he determined to eliminate the
political element and concentrate on motivating in modern terms
the death of his Virginia at the hands of a father "to whom her
virtue was more precious than her life." This, he wrote, "was in
itself tragic enough, and quite capable of moving the whole
soul...."[2]

The task proved harder than Lessing at first seems to have
thought, and for ten years we hear no more of it. During the
Hamburg interlude (1767–70), he returned to the material for a
time, but again put it aside, to give it final form at last, under
the title *Emilia Galotti*, during the winter of 1771–72, working
in the cheerless quarters provided for him in the otherwise de-
serted castle in Wolfenbüttel.

In this, his most controversial drama, Lessing transfers the
scene of action to modern Italy, where we are introduced, at the
outset, to the ruling Prince of Guastalla, Hettore Gonzaga. He is
an elegant figure capable of great eloquence and charm; an
accomplished libertine, a patron of the arts, and an impulsive and
self-centered ruler who is little concerned with the welfare of his
people. We learn that at a social gathering he has met the young,
beautiful, and captivating Emilia, daughter of Odoardo Galotti,
a stern, proud, hotheaded and upright man of the middle class,
who has long since withdrawn from service to a life of retirement,
alienated by a ruler whom he regards as unworthy and disgusted
by a frivolous and licentious court.

Since the meeting with Emilia, the Prince has known no peace.
Despite his imminent marriage to the Princess of Massa, and the
recent return to court of a former favorite, the Countess Orsina,
he is consumed by a desire for Emilia. Her portrait alone, now
unexpectedly supplied by the artist Conti, provokes an impassioned apostrophe which aptly projects his burning agitation and
distraction: "Ah, beautiful work of art, is it true that I possess
you? And how fortunate the one who possesses you, too, more
beautiful masterpiece of nature! Whatever you want for her, honorable mother! Whatever you want, old grumbler! Name your price!

Name your price!—Most of all I should love to buy you from
yourself, enchantress! These eyes filled with charm and modesty!
This mouth! And when it opens to speak! When it smiles! This
mouth!"—(I.iv)

In this aroused state, the Prince learns from his Chamberlain,
Marinelli, that Count Appiani, a young nobleman of acknowledged worth—though, like Odoardo, ill-disposed toward the Prince
and his court—is destined, this very day, to marry a commoner,
one Emilia Galotti. The couple then plan to depart for Appiani's
distant estate in Piedmont.

The Prince's shock, rage, and despair at the report are made
painfully evident, and when he admits his consuming passion
for the prospective bride to Marinelli, the cynical and unprinci-
pled Chamberlain volunteers to delay the ceremony if possible.
The desperate Prince is more than willing to give him the free
hand he requests. Marinelli suggests that he dispatch Count
Appiani on an invented mission to Massa and departs, urging the
Prince to await developments at Dosalo, his country estate.
Hettore readily agrees, and in the next brief scene we see him
in a distracted fever of anticipation, "gladly" agreeing to sign
a death warrant brought in by his adviser Camillo Rota. Rota is
aghast at this display of heartless indifference and feigns inability
to locate the document. The Prince then departs, leaving Rota to
give voice to the sentiments of common humanity and to muse
in shocked solitude on his master's monstrous callousness.

The second act takes us to the house of the Galottis in Guastalla,
where Emilia and her mother Claudia had settled while the girl
completed her education. True to his principles, Odoardo has held
himself aloof by staying on his country estate. On this special day,
however, he has departed from routine to visit them and to see
that no detail of the festive arrangements has been neglected.
He is delighted at Appiani's decision to live in retirement; but
Claudia does not share his view, and cannot help voicing regret
at a prospect that seems cheerless to her. She reveals to Odoardo
their recent meeting with the Prince and recounts with pride how
thoroughly Emilia bewitched him with her youthful beauty and
verve. The father is outraged, for he sees in the Prince only a
monstrous threat to all feminine virtue. He controls himself only
with difficulty and consoles himself with the thought that circumstances will prevent further encounters of this kind. A cloud-

less future seems assured, and he departs in good spirits.

The audience, however, has no such assurance, for it has meanwhile learned that Pirro, the Galottis' servant, is linked by his criminal past to a certain Angelo. The latter has surreptitiously appeared and forced Pirro to reveal the detailed wedding plans, which include a relatively unprotected journey by coach for the mother, the bride, and the bridegroom to Sabionetta, the Galotti country home where the ceremony is to take place.

Emilia now makes her first appearance, returning in great agitation from the Mass, where the Prince has approached her with protestations of love, intermingled with sighs of regret at her imminent marriage. Deeply shocked at such blasphemous conduct, she had attempted to flee, but he had followed and detained her. She can no longer remember what either of them said and only recalls thinking that she could not break away without alerting others to a shockingly improper situation. She can no longer say how the encounter ended, since she remembers only a desperate flight and the terrifying impression that the Prince followed her through the streets to her very door. With difficulty Claudia calms her and assures her that she has mistaken courtly gallantry and idle flattery for serious declarations. With relief, Emilia permits herself to be dissuaded from disclosing the news to her fiancé.

In the following scene (II.vii), the couple reveal a deep regard for each other, despite a certain reserve that characterizes their exchange. Emilia is moved to tell Appiani of a recurring dream in which the jewels he has given her are transformed into pearls, and she recalls the popular superstition that "pearls mean tears" —a somewhat melancholy reflection which casts a faint shadow of foreboding and aggravates Appiani's innate tendency to brooding introspection. He admits that this predilection is especially and unaccountably in evidence this day, and when Emilia leaves to make final preparations for their journey, he cryptically muses on the relativity of time ("... if only time were independent of our consciousness!—If only a minute measured by the clock were unable to extend itself within us to a span of years!—") and admits to Claudia his vague fears that he may never attain his long-cherished goals, although their attainment appears imminent (II.viii). (In a fashion far subtler than in the account of Sara's dream, Lessing projects the "modern" essence of the classical prologue as suggested in his Seneca essay.)

Nor are Appiani's spirits notably lifted in a subsequent interview with Marinelli (II.x), who arrives to put his plan in motion.
The ill-will between the two reaches a climax when Appiani
loses patience with the transparent, fawning schemer and goads
him into a challenge to a duel. The cowardly and blustering
courtier evades the immediate satisfaction that Appiani offers
and departs, vowing vengeance.

The revenge soon follows, for the coach bearing the wedding
party is attacked near Dosalo by Marinelli's hirelings disguised
as highwaymen. Appiani is slain and Emilia led to the Prince's
castle by Marinelli's agent who is posing as her rescuer. She is
understandably distraught at this eruption of violence, and especially so when the sudden entrance of the Prince reveals to
her where she is. But by exerting all his charm and apologizing
especially for his "unjustifiable" deportment at the religious service, Hettore is, in a measure, able to calm Emilia's fears for her
mother and Appiani, whose fate remains unknown to her. The
Prince leads her away, and Marinelli is obliged to cope with
Claudia, who has been directed to the castle by neighboring
peasants. Discovering, in turn, that she is at Dosalo, she realizes
that Marinelli is the instigator of the attack, for Appiani has
uttered his name with his dying breath. The full import of the
day's events is now clear to her, and in a fit of rage, shame, and
disgust she bursts forth at their perpetrator. Her shrill accusations are overheard by Emilia, who cries out from an inner
chamber, and Marinelli cannot prevent the distraught mother
from rushing to rejoin her daughter.

 When the Prince learns from Marinelli of Appiani's death, he
is at first shocked and repelled by the crime of murder; but when
the courtier feigns great indignation at his master's "ingratitude,"
and threatens to withhold further advice and cooperation, the
Prince gives in weakly.

Hettore is now more than ever in need of Marinelli's aid, for
their colloquy is interrupted by the arrival of Countess Orsina, the
rejected favorite. Her presence, like Claudia's, is a most unwel-
come obstacle to the plan to isolate Emilia. The Prince avoids
an encounter by taking refuge in an adjoining room, but Marinelli's attempts to persuade the strong-willed and emotionally distracted Orsina to leave, and his evasive replies to her insistent
requests for an audience with the Prince, succeed only in arous-

ing her suspicions. She soon elicits from him the story of the day's events. When she learns of Emilia's presence in the castle, the plot seems clear to her, too, for her agents have been following the Prince. They have observed his encounter with Emilia at the service, and have even overheard his passionate declarations. Orsina now assumes that the attack was carried out with Emilia's foreknowledge and connivance. Alternately enraged and crushed by despair, the Countess is convinced that the Prince has found a new and pliant mistress, and she prepares to leave, boldly threatening to make public the whole sordid story.

Her departure is interrupted by the arrival of Odoardo, who has learned of the day's violence. Marinelli reluctantly leaves the two together when he goes to inform the Prince of this latest complication. Orsina thereupon reveals to Odoardo the details of the plot. He is inclined to reject her suggestion of Emilia's complicity, but he is understandably enraged at the Prince and gladly accepts from Orsina the dagger she has brought with the intention to murder her faithless lover. With great effort, Odoardo contains himself while escorting Orsina and Claudia to the former's coach. Claudia is to send the Galotti coach for Odoardo and Emilia.

On his return to the castle, Odoardo has had time to compose himself and has decided that nothing can be gained by murdering the Prince. To avenge the enraged Orsina is beneath him; while to avenge Appiani is the prerogative of a higher power. His only duty, he now persuades himself, is to his daughter, and her rescue from the Prince his only responsibility. And yet his resolve to maintain his composure is badly shaken when Marinelli announces that Emilia will remain in custody of the Prince, pending an investigation of the day's violent happenings. The possibility of her complicity in a plot to rid herself of Appiani cannot be overlooked, as he suavely points out. Odoardo rages bitterly and even fumbles for his dagger, and the Prince, who is aware of the father's agitation, but not of his desperate intention, casually admonishes him: "Get a grip on yourself, my dear Galotti." The remark is sufficient to recall Odoardo to his feverish resolve to remain calm. He subsides, accepting the helpless role thus thrust upon him.

Ostensibly in order to reassure Odoardo, the Prince now declares that Emilia will not be imprisoned while awaiting the

investigation, but will be established in the home of his Chan-
cellor, Grimaldi. Hereupon Odorardo's despair deepens, for he
knows only too well this creature of the Prince and his notoriously
licentious household. But when his protests are blandly ignored,
he gives in and asks merely to see his daughter and explain to
her this new turn of events. The Prince grants his request, and
father and daughter confront each other in the play's most crucial
and controversial scene (V.vii).

Odoardo's explanation of events confirms Emilia's worst fears
for Appiani and her own hopeless plight. Rising to surprising
heights of scorn for the Prince and his physical power over her,
she pleads for the dagger Odoardo has shown her, so that she may
assert her will in proud opposition to the Prince. Odoardo hesi-
tates, reminding her that she has "but *one* life to lose." "And but
one honor," she replies. "Which is exalted beyond all force,"
Odoardo declares. "But not beyond all power of seduction,"
Emilia cries, and continues in embittered and passionate tones:
"Verführung ist die wahre Gewalt.—Ich habe Blut, mein Vater,
so jugendliches, so warmes Blut als eine. Auch meine Sinne sind
Sinne. Ich stehe für nichts. Ich bin für nichts gut." ("Seduction
is the real force.—My blood, father, flows as youthfully, as warmly
as in any girl. My senses are senses too. I will vouch for nothing.
I will be responsible for nothing.")

And she reveals to him now the tumult of feeling that welled
up within her on her previous visit to the house of Grimaldi,
that "house of pleasure"—a storm of feeling "which the severest
exercises of religion could scarcely quiet for weeks afterward."
Hesitantly Odoardo hands her the dagger, but as she is about to
stab herself, he impulsively wrenches it from her, exclaiming:
"No, that is not for your hand." Sadly she agrees, and her hand
strays to her hair, in quest of the bodkin of Hamlet's soliloquy.
Her fingers encounter the rose entwined there, and she withdraws
it, for it "does not belong in the hair of a girl—like the one my
father wants me to become." And then, bitterly she says, as she
plucks the petals from the rose: "Once there was a father, who
to save his daughter from shame plunged into her heart the first
steel that came to hand—gave her life a second time. But all
such deeds belong to a past age. There are no such fathers any
more!" "There are, my daughter, there are!" Odoardo exclaims
and stabs her. Immediately overcome by remorse, he cries out:

"God, what have I done!" And the dying Emilia murmurs: "Plucked a rose, before the storm could tear away its petals."

To the Prince and Marinelli, who now reenter, Odoardo can bitterly and fearlessly declare himself Emilia's murderer, though with her last breath Emilia had taken the responsibility for her death upon herself. Odoardo will deliver himself to the Prince's judgment and await a confrontation with him before a Higher Judge.

The shocked and frustrated Hettore exiles Marinelli, contemplates with despair the fact that Princes, too, are subject to human weakness that brings misfortune to many, and faces with horror the realization that "devils conceal themselves in the guise of their friends."

II *The Political-Social* Emilia: *Odoardo*

With such a wealth of themes and viewpoints, and with characters appearing on various political, social, and ethical levels, it cannot surprise us that *Emilia Galotti* has remained, from Lessing's day to our own, his most controversial drama. More or less plausible readings have been offered, as, for example, those that designate it as a play of political protest or a drama of social conflict in which the virtuous bourgeoisie is pitted against the morally bankrupt nobility. Others regard it as a sharp warning to a middle class sadly lacking in initiative in times of great provocation and stress; and still others view it as a psychological character study, a collection of such studies, or a modern demonstration of Aristotelian theorems.

Nor do the authorities agree on the identity of the central character or the placing of the tragic focus of the play, which is sometimes ascribed to Emilia, sometimes to the Prince, or to Odoardo, or again to a combination of father and daughter. With such latitude for conflicting views, it is not surprising that a recent critic denies the presence of any central character at all. Lessing himself has contributed to this confusion by giving a certain sanction to those who would seek the central character elsewhere than in the title. To his brother Karl he wrote: "Because the play is called "Emilia" was it my intention to make her the most prominent character, or even one of the prominent characters? By no means. The ancients named their plays after persons who did not even appear on the stage."[3]

122   GOTTHOLD EPHRAIM LESSING

We know that Lessing disclaimed any political intent in the play, and there is certainly no overt call for revolution. Implications of protest lie not far beneath the surface, however, and a number of Lessing's contemporaries of the younger generation chose to regard them as paramount. These they welcomed and proceeded to emulate in their own dramas of protest against the abuses of a cynical and egotistic despotism. Schiller's *Kabale und Liebe* (*Love and Intrigue*, 1784) is the most famous, but by no means the only play to evince a feeling of kinship with Lessing's work. And there has been no dearth of students in the intervening two centuries who have read Lessing's play primarily in these terms.[4]

As a social document, the play is in some degree amenable to interpretations quite different from those just recounted. Just as Lessing's *Sara* may be viewed as a domestic tragedy exhibiting an initial stage in the questioning of dominant theological tenets of the "enlightened" middle class of the day, so, too, *Emilia* is sometimes read as an analysis and critique of the prevailing bourgeois social ethic in a period of awakening self-consciousness and self-confidence. In this view, the socio-political ethic which enjoined the middle class to resignation in all relations with its rulers, is epitomized in Odoardo.[5] His "retirement," his repeated, and successful, self-administered admonitions to retain his composure at all costs, and his ultimate renunciation of the role of avenger to a "higher power," all establish him as typical of his time and class. The ultimate tragedy, then, exposes the bankruptcy of such a moral code. In the same vein, the dutiful Emilia, whom her mother characterizes as "compliant in all things and prepared for them all" (IV.viii), condemns in great agitation her father's fleeting impulse to turn the dagger against the Prince: "In Heaven's name, no, father!—This life is all that the wicked have—" (V.vii). As a child of her time and station, she can rise to heights of self-assertion only when the choices have been reduced to dishonor or self-annihilation.

Among the Prince's victims it is, in this view, significant that only Orsina, the first completely subjective character in German drama, departs from the pattern of passivity. She is by no means resigned to the role assigned to her by the Prince and determines to take fate violently into her own hands. Equally significantly, Lessing prescribes such a role not for a member of the middle class, but for an "outsider." And though she, too, is an "episodic" character, she is much more intimately allied to the action than the figure of Riccaut in *Minna*. She provides for Odoardo the information and some part of the spur he requires to reach a decision; she illuminates, by contrast, the character of Emilia and by revelation that of the Prince, and she supplies to the falling action a vital element of passion. She is thus important alike to the action, the characterization, and the technique of the drama.[6]

Most striking in this figure is the unalloyed passion she projects in both language and deportment, the violence of which actually threatens the reflective restraint, the ever-purposeful preservation of perspective which Lessing had recommended to the tragic poet. To a greater degree than in the case of Marwood in *Sara*— who always manages a certain rational perspective, despite her agitation—Orsina's individuality and passion break through the recommended rational structure and thus provide a link with the generation of "Storm and Stress."[7]

If one finds the focus of the play to lie in Odoardo's paralyzing bourgeois vice of passivity, it is possible to take another step, seeing its "inner meaning" in something very akin to incitement to revolution. The "shrill note of injustice, shame, and despair" at the end of the play is, in this view, not simply an outcry against specific abuses of a corrupt nobility. Its implication is "broad and philosophical" and is primarily directed at the entire middle class, aiming "at the whole spiritual regeneration and awakening of a sleeping giant."[8]

III   *The Logical* Emilia

In contrast to those who interpret the play in socio-political terms, placing Odoardo in the central position, there are others who continue to regard it as an "Emilia tragedy." They may grant that the play resounds with political and social overtones, but these are held to be incidental to the main theme. For these critics, the play turns on the character of Emilia, and the motivation of her death is the central problem. This approach may also claim a certain sanction from the playwright himself, for we know it to be his announced intention when he determined to create a "bourgeois Virginia."

Estimates of Lessing's success in solving the problem of motivation, not merely for the character of Emilia, but for the course of the action as a whole, have been as varied as the views on other aspects of the play. As a critic, Lessing had evolved and set down in the *Hamburgische Dramaturgie* certain meticulous standards for the dramatist in this regard. There he had demanded the creation of an immutable logic of cause and effect; a chain of events linked firmly one to another, and leading purposefully to a single, inevitable conclusion. The characters of drama were to exhibit a similar consistency and universality.

On this score, a number of critics from Goethe to the present day have detected an overemphasis on this "logical" aspect of motivation in *Emilia*. They share the judgment of the Romantic critic Friedrich Schlegel, who called the play a demonstration of "dramatic algebra." They see mechanical manipulation and a puppet-like response to external forces rather than a natural and inexorable flow of events originating within the characters themselves. On the other hand, Lessing's defenders describe how admirably he has fulfilled the requirements he had postulated as a critic. Lessing himself expressed reservations on certain matters of detail, but would be content if the play as a whole were to prove effective. He looked to an outstanding performance on stage to overcome the difficulties that might occur to the reader or the viewer of a routine performance.[9]

We know that Lessing rejected the narrowly moralistic aim for tragedy, while enjoining the dramatist to create, in essence, his own world with its own inner logic. ("The laws which govern the conduct of his characters, and the elaboration and resolution of the conflicts in which these characters are involved, are the laws, not of life, but of drama, of an aesthetic category.")[10] The dramatist's world must nonetheless provide a "silhouette" of the real world, and the reactions of his characters must carry the stamp of universality.

To account for the fate of Emilia in these terms has been a problem ever since the first performance of the play in 1772. Most critics are inclined to accept at face value Emilia's own admission of susceptibility to the seductive charms of the Prince, and they account such a lapse from the accepted moral code quite sufficient to constitute tragic guilt. Others find a stronger and more plausible motivation for the catastrophe when Emilia's susceptibility is combined with Odoardo's innate impetuosity and his extreme sensitivity in matters of family honor.[11]

IV   *The Innocent Emilia*

A number of recent critics have chosen to view the play, however, as a demonstration of bourgeois virtue rather than as a condemnation of courtly corruption. Its primary implication is thus
found to be social rather than political. But if the play is to demonstrate the virtue of the middle class, it cannot condone an
Emilia susceptible to seduction; and yet the heroine cannot be
completely free of fault. The *Hamburgische Dramaturgie* assures
us that the misfortunes of the completely innocent are not truly
tragic, but only "horrible" (No. 82). It is argued, therefore, that
Emilia's senses are momentarily "inflamed" and her emotions cast
into confusion by the approach of the Prince during Mass. By
confessing this only to her mother, who turns the whole matter
aside, Emilia has contributed to the ensuing fateful events. Her
"silence" has led indirectly to the death of her bridegroom. Added
to her awareness of this guilty omission is her subsequent sense
of outrage that the Prince, by detaining her, seems to assume
that his seductive campaign can succeed. To her excitable father
she, therefore, feigns a susceptibility which she has long since
overcome. Only such a fiction can incite him to kill her, and her
death is suicide in all but name.[12]

To another critic, equally interested in exonerating Emilia from
the charge of susceptibility, this kind of rehabilitation does not go
far enough. One cannot impute bourgeois virtue to one who responds, however fleetingly, to the notorious libertine. A virtue
which persists only so long as it remains untested is none. Emilia's
confusion at Mass is, therefore, ascribed not to aroused passion,
but to fear and awe in the presence of the all-powerful ruler of
the State. Emilia's guilt is still her silence, but it is induced by a
"wrong-headed respect for the divinity that hedges royalty."
Emilia's flaw is not related to questions of right and wrong; it
consists in her showing respect—in itself a good thing—"at the
expense of human dignity." Each of these elements is right in its
own way, and the conflict points forward to the nineteenth-
century attempt to strike a viable balance in the manner of
Hegel–Hebbel–Ibsen–Shaw.

Here the prospect of seduction conjured up by Emilia is labeled
a "fiction," invented to induce her father to kill her, and we
should not regard her description of inner turmoil as a revelation

of a blameworthy response to the Prince's charms. It refers merely
to the great distress occasioned by this exposure to licentious-
ness.[13] Emilia emerges as the embodiment of bourgeois virtue
and the play as a sketch of the evolution of bourgeois self-
consciousness. At the outset, Emilia is discovered on a stage
between the lower level represented by Claudia, an impression-
able social climber, and the pinnacle of bourgeois virtue and
pride occupied by Odoardo. Tragic events then transform her
into the "heroic woman" who "becomes what her father has
always been."[14]

The principal obstacle to the assumption that Emilia fears but
does not feel attracted to the Prince is raised by her mother
(II.iv). For Claudia tells us that at the Grimaldi's, Emilia had
completely captivated the Prince with her charm and vivacity;
and there is no hint in this "eye-witness" account that her daughter was overcome by fear and awe in his presence.[15] And at
Dosalo, once her initial shock has passed, she resolutely obliges
the Prince to keep his distance (IV.viii).

An equally "innocent" but similarly "flawed" Emilia emerges
when one shifts the focus from her failure to achieve a balance
between opposing social norms to the inner problem posed by a
sharply conflicting combination of character traits. Claudia tells
us that Emilia is at once "the most timid and most resolute of
our sex" (IV.viii). Excessive timidity enjoins her silence respect-
ing the encounter with the Prince at Mass; when this silence contributes to the death of Appiani, she determines to pay the highest penalty for her lapse. Here, too, the revelation of a supposed
affinity for the Prince is regarded as a mere stratagem—"debater's
points" to convince her father that her death is required. In her
character, the extremes of weakness and strength cause her to
miss the Aristotelian mean between them; first through excessive
timidity, "then through the nobler error of excessive resolution."[16]

V   The Irrational Emilia

Still others find in such interpretations an overemphasis on the
formal or intellectual elements. They remind us that although
Lessing possessed in abundance those powers highly prized in a
so-called age of Reason, he also transcended such limits in his
awareness of the strength of the "non-rational and non-intellec-

tual factors in determining the course of human existence." Thus
Emilia's often-criticized dying evocation of rose and storm is
seen as the real key to Lessing's fundamental intention. Her
death at the hand of her father preserves her from the plunge
"without hope of rescue into the dark undercurrent of non-
rational vital powers. For even before her father destroyed the
'rose,' the storm of natural passion had begun to tear it asunder."
Emilia testifies to Lessing's recognition of the "inherent tragedy
of a character striving for fulfillment as a biological being."[17]

The idea that irrational elements account for the catastrophe
takes a different form if one detects in Emilia's character an echo
of the impetuosity so apparent in her father's nature, and when
in addition one ascribes to her that "eccentric strength of moral
feeling" sometimes imputed to him. In this view, Odoardo appears as a hollow man; his much-discussed integrity and strength
of character are in fact a sham; his will to assert himself is repeatedly paralyzed, and the resulting image of him is a "carica-
ture" of the bourgeois virtue of reticent self-control. When his
complete collapse becomes clear to Emilia, and when she discovers that the hope of rescue at his hands is vain, the psychic shock
completely overpowers her, and the subsequent determination to
die is impulsive and irrational, arising from vague fears that have
no real foundation. Her admission of sensual susceptibility cannot, therefore, be taken at face value, for Claudia has already
assured us that even as a virtual prisoner of the Prince, Emilia
has demonstrated her ability to repulse him with a cold dignity
(IV.viii).

The feeling of "degradation" dictating her impulse to suicide
is therefore not a projection of her own possible seduction, but
rather a measure of her despair in contemplating a father whose
apparent moral strength has proved illusory. This is made clear
in her evocation of the Virginia motif which triggers Odoardo's
impulsive and fatal act—a deed which immediately fills him with
bitterest remorse. Only in his determination to submit to the law
does he demonstrate real strength of character.

In thus shifting the emphasis to Odoardo's collapse, one must
necessarily neglect Emilia's own assumption of complicity in the
death of Appiani, as well as the fact that she has herself rejected,
in great agitation, her father's suggestion that he might still
"rescue" her by killing the Prince. In this light, it is difficult to

grant that she believes for a moment that her father has "willingly" abandoned her, or "ignominiously surrendered her to the enemy."[18] With her dying breath, she assumes full responsibility for the catastrophe and would gratefully kiss the hand of her father which, at her own urging, has released her from the further threat of the "dark powers."

VI   Emilia *and Lessing's Theory of Tragedy*

In the final analysis, it seems clear that the attempts to exonerate Emilia from the charge of responsive reaction to the power of passion involve us in strained readings and even, at times, in contradictions. Nor would it appear necessary to declare her innocent of such impulses in order to maintain her stature as a suitable tragic heroine, and even a bourgeois heroine. Clearly, Lessing did not regard such innocence a necessity in *Miss Sara Sampson,* and there is no compelling reason to suppose that he expected us to ascribe it to Emilia. The manifold differences between the two heroines, and the notable technical advances Lessing the dramatist has made in the intervening years—tighter organization and motivation; "epigrammatic" dialogue;[19] action arising from character—should not obscure the fact that Sara and Emilia are sisters, and subject to the same fundamental urges. To these Sara has succumbed, but her own subsequent inner development makes it possible for her to gain a perspective on her action which permits her to defend it while, at the same time, acknowledging it as blameworthy. She can, therefore, "forgive the hand" that transmits her punishment and thus in terms of Lessing's Correspondence on Tragedy, beget a genuine tragic sympathy for herself.

In many respects, Emilia's predicament is subtler, more harrowing, and certainly fraught with more pervasive overtones. But the social and political implications, spreading like waves from the storm center in Emilia, need not obscure our awareness of her all-too-human kinship with Sara. The potentially disruptive and tragic power of "all manifestations of love," to which Sara alludes, reveals itself in Emilia not as an element of conscious desire, or of will, but as a force of nature to which all are subject. Her impassioned acknowledgment of her sensual awareness need not alienate us. On the contrary, in this way Lessing links his heroine more firmly to the family of fallible humanity.[20] And in doing so, he enhances our sense of identification with her, and thus opens the way to our sharing in her heightened fear of impending evil: the climax of that vaguer but more pervasive wave of fear set in motion by the earlier melancholy presentiments of Emilia herself, with her dream of pearls, and especially of Appiani, with his apprehensive expansions on this theme. (From the *Hamburgische Dramaturgie*, No. 75, we know that Lessing's reading of Aristotle led him to regard the fear of evil impending for someone like ourselves a paramount requirement for tragedy.)

In goading her father to a final, irrevocable act, Emilia establishes the connection with the legend required for a "bourgeois Virginia," and whatever the motivation we ascribe to her, it is more important to notice that by causing her to forgive the hand that has struck the fatal blow, Lessing would again transform our horror at a monstrous act into genuine tragic pity.

Thus Lessing has attempted to fulfill the basic requirements he himself postulates for tragedy. Pity and fear flow from our contemplation of Emilia's temporal misfortunes and ultimate fate. (It was Appiani who earlier alerted us to the fateful quality of the dimension of time.) And the larger context in which these temporal events have their link with the transcendent realm of the "Creator of us all"—a further requirement set forth in the *Hamburgische Dramaturgie*—is specifically established in Odoardo's final lines. He will surrender himself to the Prince's "justice," but will then await the later confrontation with the Prince before the "Judge of us all."[21]

The "silhouette" of the universe presented to us in the necessarily selective recreation of the dramatist cannot, by its very nature, convey to us the details of the higher reality in which the tragedies of the finite realm find their solution. But it is Orsina who assures us in the play: "The word chance is blasphemy. Nothing under the sun happens by chance" (IV.iii). And in Lessing's view the successful tragic poet must convey to us the shape, the outline, and the presence, however dimly perceived, of an ordered, universal structure existing beyond the apparently aimless, whimsical, or enigmatic alarms and confusions on the temporal plane. Such a vision cannot, in the nature of things, assume the character of demonstration, and *Emilia Galotti* is at best a vague and elusive indication of Lessing's hope for the eventual resolution of these tragic mysteries. As we have seen, its ambiguities have led a number of students to diagnose its principal import as a questioning, or even a denial, of the essentially optimistic world view whose demonstration Lessing, in the *Hamburgische Dramaturgie*, postulated as the principal task of the tragic poet.

Lessing's hope takes on the quality of faith only when, in the final decade of his life, he traverses the pathway of theological struggles leading to the final visions projected in the *Erziehung des Menschengeschlechts* and *Nathan der Weise*.[22]

CHAPTER 10

Antiquarian and Theologian

LESSING'S interests during the Hamburg period had not been exclusively confined to affairs of the theater, and it will be convenient here to sketch briefly his scholarly activities, as well as the theological polemics of the subsequent Wolfenbüttel years.

I *Lessing contra Klotz*

One of the many published critiques of Lessing's *Laokoon* was a rather condescending review, in 1766, by Christian Adolf Klotz, Professor in Halle, editor of the journals *Acta Literaria* and *Deutsche Bibliothek der schönen Wissenschaften*, and an avowed rival of Lessing's friend Nicolai and the Berlin circle. Lessing ignored the review, but a later work of Klotz betrayed such a misunderstanding of passages in the *Laokoon* that its author felt obliged to expose them. Klotz replied, and a thoroughly aroused Lessing then proceeded to defend himself ably and to reveal the shortcomings of his opponent in a series of fifty-seven *Briefe antiquarischen Inhalts* (*Antiquarian Letters*), published first in Hamburg periodicals and thereafter in a two-part book edition (1768–69). Certain related materials remained unpublished in Lessing's lifetime.

Lessing's *Briefe* reveal, in addition to his great erudition, a pronounced impatience with Klotz's penchant for personal criticism: "As soon as a critic betrays that he knows more about the author than the author's works can tell him; as soon as he draws upon this further knowledge in the slightest way to the discredit of the author, his criticism at once turns into personal affront. He ceases to be a critic and becomes the most despicable object that a rational creature can become: blabbermouth, slanderer, lampooner."[1]

Spurred by his opponent's ill-considered critique, Lessing was also induced to the composition of separate essays, the most important of which was his study, *Wie die Alten den Tod gebildet* (*How the Ancients Represented Death*, 1769), an elaboration of his statement in *Laokoon* "that the ancient artists had not depicted death as a skeleton." Klotz, in "refutation," could point to numerous representations of skeletons in ancient art, but Lessing began his reply with an apt figure vividly illustrating the irrelevance of Klotz's critique. "Mr. Klotz constantly thinks he's right on my heels. But as I turn around to him when he hails me, I see him always far off to the side, in a cloud of dust, following a pathway I have never trod."[2] In short, Lessing reminds his critic that he had not denied the obvious fact that ancient art depicts skeletons, but only the assumption that such images were intended to represent death or the god of death. On the basis of his wide-ranging study of classical literature and of pictorial representations of classical tombs, Lessing now contended that the ancient artists, like Homer, regarded death as the "twin brother of sleep" and pictured it as an angel, never in the horrid guise of a skeleton. The latter represented not death but the departed spirit.[3]

The idea that the Greeks never symbolized death as a skeleton —confirmed by subsequent research—came as a welcome revelation to Lessing's contemporaries. Both Goethe and Schiller adopted the idea, for it fostered the development of a more serene view of death—"the triumph of the beautiful," Goethe called it—in sharp contrast to the feelings of dread, disgust, or horror usually associated with the skeletal image.[4]

II *Language, Literature, and the "Wolfenbüttler Beiträge"*

In other essays and notes, which reflect his special concern for the nature and limits of literary forms as well as of individual lexicographical items, and for retrieving the literary products of a past age from undeserved obscurity, Lessing treated the epigram in a manner reminiscent of his earlier examination of the fable; he discovered and presented to the reading public some long-neglected works of the seventeenth-century Silesian poet Andreas Scultetus, and added to his notes on grammar and usage in preparation for a long-planned dictionary.[5]

Although this hope was never realized, the years Lessing spent as a librarian did provide the opportunity to draw upon the excellent Wolfenbüttel collection in further pursuit of other favorite interests, as well as to explore new fields and avenues of investigation. As a vehicle for the retrieval of neglected works, the analysis of treasured items, and for commentary on diverse philosophical, philological, and theological subjects, Lessing began, in 1773, to publish the series *Zur Geschichte und Literatur; aus den Schätzen der Herzoglichen Bibliothek zu Wolfenbüttel* (*On History and Literature; from the Treasures of the Ducal Library in Wolfenbüttel*), usually called "Wolfenbüttler Beiträge" (*Wolfenbüttel Contributions*).

The range of subjects covered in the *Contributions* is extensive, for Lessing's intellectual curiosity was virtually boundless, and the library rich in all manner of rare and unusual items. From this treasury, Lessing could appreciably add to current information on the history of the fable, supply additions and corrections to the contemporary knowledge of Marco Polo's travels, and supplement the accepted printed text of the fourteenth-century *Chronikon Flandriae*. A separate essay, *Vom Alter der Oelmalerei* (*On the Antiquity of Painting in Oil*, 1774), dealt with his discovery of a description of this process by one Theophilus Presbyter in a manuscript which Lessing dated back to the eleventh century. He, therefore, rejected the ascription of the invention of oil painting to the Flemish artist Jan van Eyck, in the first half of the fifteenth century, although he considered it likely that van Eyck had discovered a more suitable type of oil as a mixing medium and had thus "reintroduced" a mode of artistic expression that had been largely abandoned for technical reasons. In the manner typical of scholarly writing of that day, Lessing's twelve-page text was buttressed by nearly twenty-seven pages of notes.[6]

A *Contribution* of 1773, *Von dem Schickard-Marchtalerschen Tarich Beni Adam*, took Lessing even farther afield, as he published a report of his chance discovery of a Turkish genealogical table in manuscript of the Ottoman rulers. Since the publication of Wilhelm Schickard's partial analysis of the work (Tübingen, 1628), it had disappeared from view, and Lessing now wished to make his accidental discovery available to Orientalists, since, as he wrote disarmingly in his concluding remarks: "I hope people will believe that for my part I understand as little Turkish as any of my readers. I have spoken here merely as a librarian, and a librarian is permitted to speak about works which he does not understand."[7]

With these and many other *Contributions*, as well as with his faithful attention to the time-consuming duties of his office, including responses to many a scholarly inquiry, Lessing, the conscientious librarian, fulfilled his official obligations.[8] Not all of it was appealing work. It is clear that he sometimes wrote only from a sense of duty; and being thus obliged to interrupt or postpone more congenial work sometimes provoked him to an impatient outburst. The ultimate result was that many a plan was never carried out. His wide-ranging antiquarian and philological interests are broadly reflected, for example, in a volume of *Collectanea zur Literatur*—the harvest of many years of intensive reading and thinking. They were probably not intended as background material alone, for they contain the germ of many a likely project.[9] The most important *Contributions*, however, deal with Lessing's preoccupation, in the last decade of his life, with theological problems; and to these we now turn.

III   *Theological Controversy*

In Wolfenbüttel it appeared for a time that fate would look at last with favor upon Lessing. After many delays, including the interruption occasioned by an Italian journey in 1775 as the companion of Prince Leopold of Braunschweig—a journey to which Lessing, in earlier days, had eagerly looked forward, but which in the circumstances meant little to him—he and Eva König, the widow of a Hamburg friend, were able to marry in October, 1776. After only one year of happiness, Eva bore him a son on Christmas day, 1777. The child died two days later, and Eva succumbed on January 10, 1778. To his friend and sometime collaborator, the Braunschweig Professor Johann Joachim Eschenburg, Lessing wrote on December 31, 1777, about the death of his son: "My joy was only short-lived. And I was so reluctant to lose him; this son! For he had such understanding. . . . I know what I'm saying.— Wasn't it understanding that he noticed so soon that something was amiss, when he had to be drawn into the world with iron forceps?—Wasn't it a sign of understanding when he seized the first opportunity to make off again?" And to the same friend Lessing wrote, with a deeply moving display of fortitude on the day of his wife's death: "Meine Frau ist tot: und diese Erfahrung habe ich nun auch gemacht. Ich freue mich, dass mir viel dergleichen Erfahrungen nicht mehr übrig sein können zu machen; und bin ganz leicht—Auch tut es mir wohl, dass ich mich Ihres, und unsrer übrigen Freunde in Braunschweig, Beileids versichert halten darf." ("My wife is dead: and now I have had this experience too. I am glad that there cannot be many more such experiences for me, and my mind is quite at ease.—It is also comforting to know that I may count on your condolence and that of our other friends in Braunschweig.")

Thereafter Lessing's own health continued to decline; he survived for only three years and died in Braunschweig on one of his frequent visits to friends on February 15, 1781. The bitter experiences of this harrowing period, as well as his triumphs over them, inevitably find reflection in the controversial theological writings of his final years.

The work which reintroduces Lessing to the theological scene in 1770 is strongly reminiscent of the earlier *Justifications*. At the outset of his tenure as a librarian, he was able to startle the scholarly world of theologians with a reappraisal of the controversy revolving about the eleventh-century cleric Berengar of Tours, who had been condemned for heretical views on the doctrine of transubstantiation.[10] But the term "heretic" did not unduly alarm Lessing, for he defined it as "a person who has desired at least to see with his own eyes." Yet theologians had maintained for centuries that this bold truth-seeker, after recanting, had remained silent in the face of triumphant, thunderous criticism by his chief opponent, Lanfranc.

Lessing's *Berengarius Turonensis* (1770) is a beautifully organized, closely argued, and conclusive demonstration of his opposite view, for he has unearthed Berengar's own detailed refutation of Lanfranc's accusations in the library. It is altogether the most elaborate of Lessing's essays of vindication and the work whose writing, according to his own admission, gave him the most pleasure. Although the work attracted widespread attention in learned circles and contained a number of thrusts at the shortcomings of certain theologians, ancient and modern, it provoked no controversy, for the Protestant clergy preferred to welcome Lessing's justification of one who had so successfully disputed orthodox Catholic dogma. For once Lessing found himself, as he wrote to Eva König, bathed in the "lovely aura of orthodoxy," and he warned her to expect to hear him mentioned abroad as a pillar of the church. At the same time, he hinted that he might soon lose this reputation again.[11]

The predicted fall from grace did occur when Lessing turned to the publication of excerpts from a work on theology by Hermann Samuel Reimarus (1694–1768), one-time Professor of Oriental Languages in Hamburg. Lessing had been acquainted with the family, and after the death of their father, the son and daughter entrusted the manuscript of his work to Lessing. This extensive *Apologie oder Schutzschrift für die vernünftigen Verehrer Gottes* (*Apologia for the Rational Worshipers of God*) set forth the negative element in Reimarus' thinking, wherein the importance of revelation was entirely denied.[12] Twenty years in the making, the work revealed the strong influence of the English Deists, and contained such vigorous criticism of favorite orthodox tenets that its author had never ventured to publish it. As a firm advocate of informed public discussion of controversial views, Lessing felt that the work should be published, at least in part.

Promising Reimarus' heirs to preserve the incognito of the author, he, therefore, reports in the *Beiträge* the discovery of this "anonymous" work, and forthwith prints the first of these *Fragmente . . . aus den Papieren eines Ungenannten* (*Fragments . . . by an Unknown Author*), entitled *Von Duldung der Deisten* (*On the Toleration of Deists*, 1774).

In general, Lessing agrees with the ideas on toleration advanced by Reimarus, although he finds them somewhat outmoded, for the toleration advocated thirty years before by his anonymous essayist was now in effect, "at least in Protestant Germany." It is a phenomenon which Lessing would gladly see extended. Why suppress the writings of freethinkers? "They can only increase the triumph of *our* religion." Why continue the long-drawn-out quarrel between "biblical Christians" and "rational Christians"? Cannot and should not the simple designation "Christian" encompass both? As Lessing puts it: "We would like to see the man who can adduce the least contradiction between *our* Christianity and sound human reason."[13]

Despite Lessing's challenge, the publication of this first *Fragment* created no furor and, indeed, attracted little notice of any kind—a fact which attests the correctness of Lessing's analysis. Three years later, however, his publication of five additional fragments under the title *Ein Mehreres aus den Papieren des Unge-*

nannten, die Offenbarung betreffend (*Something Further on Revelation from the Papers of the Anonymous Author,* 1777) brought on the not unexpected storm of criticism and involved Lessing in one of the bitterest controversies of his frequently controversial career. The wrath of the orthodox descended upon his efforts, despite the fact that he carefully appended to these five new excerpts his own "Gegensätze" ("Antitheses"), in which he took issue with Reimarus and set forth his own contrasting views.

In these published *Fragments,* Reimarus had protested the "decrying" of reason from the pulpit; denied the possibility of a revelation acceptable to all men on demonstrable grounds, and criticized the story of the passage of the Israelites through the Red Sea. He had declared that the Old Testament had not been written with the purpose of revealing a religion, and had branded the Biblical accounts of the Resurrection as contradictory.

Lessing's blanket response to all these charges reflects the thought traceable in a number of his earlier theological essays: "The letter is not the spirit; and the Bible is not religion." He also stated that "Religion is not true because the Evangelists and Apostles taught it: but rather they taught it because it is true." Religion is thus a matter of "inner truth," and written records must be interpreted in this light.[14]

On the relation of reason to revelation, Lessing admittedly took up an intermediate position between the extremes just described. Like others in this position, he would not only permit but require the exercise of reason in judging the authenticity of a revelation. Reason must rule on its "probability," but having done so, it "surrenders." From a revelation found to be genuine it may not reject those elements which transcend the power of reason. A completely explicable revelation, Lessing points out, would be none. Reason's capitulation is "nothing but the acknowledgment of its limits, as soon as it is convinced of the reality of the revelation."[15] In these terms, Lessing takes issue with the "anonymous" author's further criticisms. Although he had expected that such a publication would strike fire, he had anticipated that the principal flames of opposition would spring up in the camp of the rationalists. Instead, it was the orthodox who objected most heatedly. In reply to the arguments of Johann Daniel Schumann, Director of the Hanover Lyceum, Lessing, in an essay *Ueber den Beweis des Geistes und der Kraft: I Cor. II.4 (On the Proof of the Spirit and of Power,* 1777), reiterated and developed the argument of his fifth antithesis. Although the accounts of miracles and prophecies were as dependable as other historical reports, they were not more so: *"Accidental truths of history can never serve as proof of necessary truths of reason."*[16]

The position of an eighteenth-century observer, Lessing reminds his readers, is, after all, fundamentally different from that of Jesus' contemporaries. Modern man has been granted neither the direct experience of prophecies fulfilled (proof of the spirit) nor of miracles performed (proof of power). He has only the historical reports of Jesus' claim to be the Son of God, and only historical reports that those who echoed this assertion were divinely inspired and could not err. Therefore, these declarations lie in a wholly different category from the necessary truths of reason, and Lessing views this discrepancy as a "horrid gulf" which he cannot cross, however often and earnestly he has essayed the leap. He would not deny "that prophecies were fulfilled in Christ," or that He performed miracles. He would deny, however, "that these miracles, since their truth has wholly ceased to be demonstrated by currently wrought miracles," can oblige one to acknowledge "the least faith in Christ's further teachings." These must stand or fall on their own merits. At the time of their promulgation, the attendant miracles facilitated the acceptance of such new and unfamiliar doctrines. What human reason has accomplished through its preoccupation with them in the intervening centuries constitutes the real "fruits" of the miracles and fulfilled prophecies, and, Lessing adds, "the fruits are excellent."[17]

One of these "further doctrines" was the admonition of John in his apocryphal Testament, as reported in Jerome's commentary on Galatians. Lessing heartily recommended it, for its observation could well unite in brotherhood those who had been separated by their differing interpretations of the Gospel of John. In a pendant to his reply to Schumann, Lessing, therefore, in a wittily conducted "conversation" under the title *Das Testament Johannis* (*The Testament of John;* published anonymously in 1777) developed the implications to be drawn from the relatively obscure account of the aged disciple's last days in Ephesus. Though scarcely capable of logical discourse, John continually repeated to his congregation the words: "Little children, love one another." When asked by his impatient followers why he reiterated this single admonition, he replied: "Because it is the command of the Master, and if only this is done, it is sufficient."[18] To Lessing, the real "proof of the spirit and of power" should rest not upon un-demonstrable historical accounts, but upon the ethical conduct of a religion's practitioners. In this instance, a "proof" would be demonstrated if all professed Christians observed in their own lives the admonition to "love one another."

In January, 1778, Lessing published *Eine Duplik,* a rather sharply worded *Rejoinder* to a second critic of the *Fragments,* the Wolfenbüttel Superintendent Johann Heinrich Ress, who objected especially to the assertion, in the sixth *Fragment,* that the Gospel accounts of the Resurrection betrayed discrepancies. In reply, Lessing repeated and expanded his view of the Gospels as "historical" reports, defended Reimarus against Ress's imputa-tions of bad faith, and praised his honest effort to arrive at truth. For Lessing, this was the principal criterion for judging the worth of individual men: "It is not the truth which any man possesses, or thinks he possesses, which is the measure of his worth, but rather the honest effort he has put forth to discover the truth." And he goes on to make explicit a principle long implied in his own theological investigations: the preference for the *stimulus* to seek the truth—a human capability—to the *possession* of truth, which he declared to be the prerogative of a higher power. "If God held in His right hand all truth, and in His left hand the unique and ever active impulse to seek the truth—even with the added condition that I be eternally in error—and said to me: Choose! I would humbly seize His left hand, saying: Father, give me this! Pure truth is surely for Thee alone."[19]

In sum, Lessing's *Rejoinder* reasserts, in clearest terms, his independence of both extremes: that of his "anonymous" ration-alist, who asserts that the discrepancies in the accounts of the Evangelists provide "further" evidence against the credibility of the Resurrection of Christ, as well as that of the orthodox, that the story of the Resurrection must be accepted, since the accounts of it do not contradict one another. Lessing replies to both: "The Resurrection of Christ can be perfectly true, *even though* the accounts of the Evangelists are contradictory."[20]

The year 1778 also marked Lessing's involvement in the bitter-est and most extensive controversy arising from his publication of the *Fragments.* Late in 1777, the senior Lutheran pastor in

Hamburg, Johann Melchior Goeze, with whom Lessing had once been on relatively friendly terms, attacked the work in two published articles. Other essays followed as Lessing took up the challenge, and the exchange became ever more bitter, for the Hamburg pastor persistently failed to distinguish between the positions taken up by Reimarus and those defended by Lessing. This sort of campaign seemed to Lessing not only a clear challenge to the right of theological inquiry, but a frontal attack on the principle of intellectual freedom itself. To the defense of both, Lessing dedicated all his skill, enthusiasm, and intellectual acuity.

His first response, in March, 1778, bore the title *Eine Parabel. Nebst einer kleinen Bitte, und einem eventualen Absagungsschreiben an den Herrn Pastor Goeze, in Hamburg* (*A Parable, Accompanied by a Small Request, and finally a Declaration of Hostility* . . .), and was immediately followed by the *Axiomata* (*Axioms*), where Lessing analyzed and expanded his "Antitheses," especially his contention that Christianity had long existed independently of its written records; that its "whole truth" was not dependent upon the Scriptures, and that the disappearance of the records of the Apostles and Evangelists need not imply the disappearance of the Christian religion. In short, he would "divorce religion from the history of religion"—a distinction which would release the friends of religion from the necessity to defend those frequently embarrassing and illogical aspects of the historical record.[21] But the orthodox were far from convinced, least of all Pastor Goeze, whose continued attacks led to Lessing's publication of a series of eleven pamphlets under the title *Anti-Goeze* (April–June, 1778).

During the course of composition, Lessing felt it necessary to return to the much-attacked sixth Fragment, which dealt with the Resurrection, and in May, 1778, he published in full Reimarus' chapter *Von dem Zwecke Jesu und seiner Jünger* (*On the Intention of Jesus and His Disciples*). Lessing's brief preface explains that objections to the previous fragmentary version had necessarily missed the mark, since Reimarus' principal argument was not the "simple-minded" one that doubts of the authenticity of the Resurrection accounts constituted a sufficient reason to reject the Christian religion. His real point had been much more serious, for he had asserted that "the religion based on the Resurrection is false;" that the Resurrection is likewise false, and that the accounts of it will reveal themselves as fabrications, as, in fact, they do.[22] In order to explain his substitution of a greater provocation for a lesser one, Lessing declared that the work merited publication in full, so that public refutations could be directed to the heart of the matter. He warned his readers that the complete text of Reimarus was circulating secretly in a number of copies "from hand to hand" and from "province to province," and in this way it was surely gaining more followers than such a work could command in the face of widespread and informed public refutation.

The publication only served to inflame the orthodox, however, and by intervening with authorities of both church and state, they brought about the cancellation in July, 1778, of Lessing's official freedom from censorship and the prohibition of further controversial publication. Lessing was understandably angered and frustrated by this turn of events, and the record of his reaction, unpublished during his lifetime, dramatically reveals the depths of his enthusiastic involvement, as well as his keen powers of self-analysis:

"Well, come on, my good old irascibility! Where are you? Where are you hiding? You have a clear field. Break loose! Have a good romp!

Tricky little rogue! You want only to take me by surprise, eh? And because you can't take me by surprise this time, because I'm baiting you and spurring you on myself, you'll play lazy to spite me.

Go on, hurry up, do what you want to do, grind my teeth, strike my brow, bite my underlip.

And as I actually find myself doing the latter, he is suddenly there before me, as he was in life—my late father. That was his habit, when something began to vex him, and any time I want to recall him vividly to mind, I need only bite my underlip in the same way.

All right, old boy, all right. I understand you. You were such a good man, and at the same time such a choleric man. How often you yourself complained to me . . . that you so easily became excited, and overhasty in your excitement. How often you said to me: 'Gotthold, I beg you, take an example from me: be on your guard. For I fear me, I fear me—. . .' All right, old boy. All right. I still feel it often enough—"[23]

But in· this instance at least, Lessing tells us, he maintained a cold self-control. His further work in theology necessarily took other forms, and by no means unfortunately so, for we are indebted to this enforced change for his remarkable dramatic poem *Nathan der Weise.*

As a postscript to the controversy with Goeze, we have Lessing's response to his opponent's demand that he make clear what he understood by the Christian religion. His *Nötige Antwort auf eine sehr unnötige Frage des Herrn Hauptpastor Goeze, in Hamburg (Necessary Answer to a Very Unnecessary Question of Senior Pastor Goeze in Hamburg,* 1778) is his explanation that by "the Christian religion" he understood "all those articles of faith . . . which are contained in the symbolic books of the first four centuries of the Christian church."[24] This response is in perfect accord with his long-continued efforts to establish fundamentals and liberate the friends of religion from the necessity to defend *in toto* the later, more complicated (and complicating) interpretations and explanations of the sort found in the Biblical canon.

It is possible that a number of planned but unfinished responses to other critics might have helped to clarify Lessing's theological position, both for his contemporaries and for posterity. In their absence, we may now leave the area of largely negatively oriented polemics and turn to those works of the later years which indicate, in some measure, his own final attitude toward fundamental problems.

CHAPTER 11

Lessing's Religious Testament

I Die Erziehung des Menschengeschlechts

LESSING'S commentary on the fourth Reimarus Fragment had included the first half of a work not published in full until Easter, 1780, under the title *The Education of the Human Race*. In a series of one hundred numbered paragraphs it sets forth Lessing's final published position on the central problem of the relation between human reason and Divine revelation.[1] His ultimate "solution," based, in part, on ideas long current in theological speculation, describes his interpretation of human history as a process of spiritual evolution, and of progressive education of the human race.

Like his German predecessor, Leibniz, and his English predecessor, the philosopher John Locke, Lessing at the outset affirms his belief in the efficacy of revelation as a quicker and easier means of introducing necessary truths to man.[2] Indeed, revelation and education are but different aspects of the same process: "What education is to individual men, revelation is to the whole race of men (§ 1). . . . Education gives man nothing that he could not derive from himself: it merely gives him more quickly and easily that which he could have from himself." Serving the same purpose for all men, revelation gives him "nothing which human reason, left to itself, would not discover: but it merely gave and gives him the most important of these things earlier" (§ 4). In such a definition, the supernatural element in revelation virtually disappears, and a number of Lessing scholars regard it as evidence that Lessing the rationalist altogether rejected the theory of Divine revelation.[3]

Preserving the metaphor of the progressive education of child and youth, paralleled by the ethical instruction imparted in the childhood and youth of the race, Lessing points out that in the

143

first stage of development, the children chosen by God to receive this instruction (the Hebrew people) had been given a "primer." This elementary work, the Old Testament, set forth an ethical system appropriate to a people still on the child's intellectual level, and amenable to education "through direct sensuous punishments and rewards" (§ 16); a system related to earthly life, without reference to the prospect of a future life on another plane (§ 17). By trial and error, the chosen people, in the course of centuries, had mastered the principles of their primer and, above all, a doctrine from which they had repeatedly strayed, namely that of the One God (§§ 39–40). They finally proved themselves ready for a more advanced level of instruction. "A better teacher must come to tear from their hands the outmoded primer—Christ came" (§ 53). To men on a youthful stage of awareness he brought a second text, the New Testament, with its nobler and worthier ethical principles. These Christ illustrated in his teaching of the immortality of the soul. He was the first "dependable, practical teacher" of this tenet (§ 58).

As, in the course of centuries, man had fulfilled the requirements for admission to a second stage of ethical development, he might justly hope, in the subsequent course of his historical development, to make further progress, eventually mastering, with his reason, those dictates at present accepted as revelation:

Just as we can now dispense with the Old Testament in understanding the doctrine of the oneness of God; and just as we are gradually beginning to be able to dispense with the New Testament in understanding the doctrine of the immortality of the soul: could not, in this process, a number of similar truths be prefigured, truths that we are destined to marvel at as revelations until our reason has learned to derive them from its other settled truths and combine the two? (§ 72)

Lessing was aware that the goal is distant, and that revelations had been necessary in the past to keep man's striving properly directed. At the time of their disclosure, they were not "truths of reason; but they were revealed in order that they might become so" (§ 76). Lessing then suggests that revelation also gives us "more precise and better concepts of the divine essence, of our own nature, and of our relation to God" than human reason would ever develop by itself (§ 77). Such a statement stands in apparent contradiction to the rationalistic implications of § 4, and the critics have long pondered a possible resolution of the difficulty. Many of those who find Lessing's "true" position reflected in the earlier statement interpret § 77 exoterically, viewing its inclusion as a prudent tactic on the part of Lessing to conceal from the naive and uninitiated the real impact of his argument, which they see directed toward the dissolution of the orthodox concept of revelation.[4] These critics remind us that Lessing was now operating under a ban on polemical writing, and that he published the *Erziehung* anonymously. The anonymity, the supposed contradiction, and other considerations have occasionally given rise to doubt as to the work's authenticity.[5]

Another explanation is possible if one sees a "dualism" in Lessing's concept of reason and finds him postulating both a limited, "historical" concept and a "transcendental" reason in terms of his principle of progressive development—a "transcendental" reason which merges with the concept of revelation.[6] With exemplary patience, Lessing would await that future time when the dictates of reason and revelation are finally united, and the distinction between rationally demonstrable truths and undemonstrable revelation is dissolved. Meanwhile, he would avoid the temptation to discard all doctrines not capable of present demonstration, and would caution his more "advanced" colleagues against introducing their ideas prematurely to a society not yet prepared to receive them. A better course for these "more capable individuals" might well be to re-examine their own arguments (§§ 68–69).[7] Revelation could lead the way, but the exercise of reason was unavoidable if man were to attain the exalted state in which he no longer practiced virtue for the reasons appropriate to the first two stages of spiritual development: external compulsion and the hope of future reward. Anticipating the ethical teachings of Kant, Lessing foresees man's highest development at that level on which he will practice virtue for love of virtue itself (§§ 80, 85).[8]

Lessing was well aware that progress was painfully slow and often so gradual as to be undetectable by mere mortals, to whom the course might sometimes even appear to be reversed. Since each man must sooner or later traverse each of the stages (§§ 90–93), and since one human life-span was clearly insufficient to complete such a journey, Lessing did not recoil from the implication of metempsychosis, i.e., from the theory that the soul could reappear whenever it was "prepared for new insights and accomplishments" (§ 98). In the very antiquity of this hypothesis he would see good evidence for its validity, since human reason in an earlier and purer state, unclouded by the "sophistry of the school," had hit upon the idea at once (§ 95). Lessing would welcome a principle which makes available for man's development "the whole of eternity" (§ 100). The theory thus envisions the preservation and further development in a historical context of all that is truly great and noble in the spirit of man. Such a view of immortality provides an important link between Lessing and the subsequent classical age of German Idealism.[9]

Thus Lessing transcends the systems of his day to provide a glimpse of a mysterious, and even mystical, vision of the nature and purpose of man and his history, the complete import of which eludes a final determination.[10] As he himself wrote when introducing, in editorial guise, the complete text of the "anonymous" *Erziehung*: "In it the author has taken a position upon a hilltop, from which he believes he has surveyed something more than the prescribed pathway of the present day." From this vantage point, bathed in a "gentle sunset glow," the author's gaze into the "measureless distance" is understandably limited, and Lessing will be content if in his visionary report he has detected and made clear that all positive religions represent merely the diverse pathways along which human reason has everywhere developed in the past and will continue to develop in the future. All of them merit our respect and toleration, despite the mistakes men have made along the way. Why should we assume that the guiding hand of God is present in all things except our errors?

II Theological Fragments, Leibniz, and Spinoza

Along the pathway of man's development, there is vital need for a strong faith, even in the mysteries that now elude analysis. Indeed, for Lessing the very essence of faith lies in its inaccessibility to reason, and he expresses surprise that this fundamental principle is so frequently ignored in theological discussion. Thus in the second of the Wolfenbüttel *Beiträge* in 1773, he allied himself with Leibniz and defended the doctrine of the Trinity in his essay *Des Andreas Wissowatius Einwürfe wider die Dreieinigkeit* (*Andrew Wiszowaty's Objections to the Doctrine of the Trinity*) against the attack of Wiszowaty, a seventeenth-century Polish nobleman and supporter of the Socinian heresy. To Lessing, this Christian tenet is a basic mystery not subject to rational investigation. He would accept—and in the light of the *Erziehung* we can add: at the present stage of human development—"a two-fold basis for the truth of our religion; human and divine, . . . that is to say . . . explicable and inexplicable."[11]

Such comments puzzled not only the orthodox but also his circle of rationalistic friends in Berlin. In clarification, Lessing wrote in a letter to his brother Karl (February 2, 1774) of his long-cherished desire to keep the areas of religion and philosophy, or faith and reason, separate and distinct, for only confusion could result from the effort to combine them. In the light of the evolutionary principles of the *Erziehung*, and the associated warnings against prematurely abandoning the tenets at present undemonstrable, Lessing's fundamental assumption is clearer to the later reader than it was to his contemporaries in the 1770's when he compared the "newfangled theology" of that day to orthodoxy in terms of the contrast between "liquid manure" and "impure water." Formerly, Lessing continued, a salutary barrier was maintained between philosophy and the old orthodoxy, behind which each could develop without interference from the other. "But what are they doing now? They are tearing down the barrier, and, under the pretext of making us rational Christians, they are turning us into extremely irrational philosophers." Lessing freely acknowledged his dissatisfaction with the orthodox canon; it is "impure," certainly, but preferable to the alternative offered by modern rationalistic theology.[12]

The evolutionary motif of the *Education* also informed Lessing's contention *Dass Mehr als Fünf Sinne für den Menschen sein können* (*That More Than Five Senses are Possible for Man*).[13] According to this fragment, the soul exists before being related to a specific body, and it may also migrate from one physical body to another. In the course of its development, it has acquired the present five senses and may well accumulate others, whose nature we cannot describe on our present level of awareness. Again the very antiquity of such a theory seemed to argue for its validity; and we are reminded that Lessing's explanation of his "understanding" of the Christian religion was keyed not to the Scriptural canon but to the oldest available sources of Christian doctrine.[14]

Certain ideas expressed in the *Education* also help to explain Lessing's readiness to surrender the notion of free will; for in the view of history as a progressive revelation of a developmental course predetermined by God, the individual must necessarily play a preordained role. In his editorial comments on Karl Wilhelm Jerusalem's *Philosophische Aufsätze* (*Philosophical Essays*), which Lessing published in 1776, he heartily agrees when Jerusalem follows Leibniz in postulating in man a predetermined inclination to the Good. Lessing would inquire "what . . . we lose, if freedom is denied to us. Something—if it is something—that we do not need; that we need neither for our activity here nor for our happiness in the next world. . . . Force and necessity, according to which the concept of the Best brings about its effects, how much more welcome they are to me than the arid ability to act now in one way, now in another, in the same circumstances. I thank the Creator that I am *compelled;* compelled to do what is best."[15]

Despite apparent areas of agreement with Leibniz, Lessing reportedly embraced the philosophy of Spinoza. His friend Friedrich Heinrich Jacobi attests that in conversations with him during the summer of 1780 Lessing declared: "There is no other philosophy than Spinoza's."[16] The report especially distressed Lessing's old friend Moses Mendelssohn, who rejected it and asserted angrily its implausibility.

We have seen evidence of Lessing's early interest in Spinoza; and it is known that he deepened his understanding of the latter's thought during the Breslau period. His correspondence with Mendelssohn, as well as unfinished essays dating from about this time, also touch directly or indirectly on the problem. The fragment *Ueber die Wirklichkeit der Dinge ausser Gott* (*On the Reality of Things Outside of God*) attests to Lessing's inability to form any such concept. In correspondence and in another fragmentary essay, *Durch Spinoza ist Leibniz nur auf die Spur der vorherbestimmten Harmonie gekommen,* he clearly distinguishes Spinoza's concept of the harmony between body and soul (an identity which Lessing is inclined to dismiss as "word play") from Leibniz' much more difficult, and, it is implied, more useful attempt to harmonize "two such different essences." Strictly speaking, however, Lessing expresses no preference for one or the other.[17] Despite his reportedly wholehearted support of the teachings of Spinoza, the authorities continue to express reservations, and no one has proposed a generally accepted answer to the question of Lessing's "Spinozism."[18]

III *The Final Word*

Lessing's fundamental inclination to draw distinctions reaches something of an abbreviated climax in one of his last fragmentary writings on religion. It was apparently intended as an orderly summation of his views, but stops short after only eight numbered paragraphs under the title *Die Religion Christi* (*The Religion of Christ*). Reportedly set down in 1780, it was first published in the Theological Posthuma of 1784.[19]

Lessing begins by distinguishing between the religion of Christ and the Christian religion (§ 2). The former he defined as the religion Christ himself "accepted and practiced as a man"; the religion "which every man can have in common with Him; which every man must necessarily wish all the more to share with Him, the more exalted and attractive the image he has of Christ as a mere mortal" (§ 3). The Christian religion, on the other hand, accepts the idea that Christ was "more than man, and as such makes Him an object of its veneration" (§ 4).

At this point, Lessing makes no explicit commitment to either view, asserting that the two religions were "utterly incompatible" (§5). To him it seemed "obvious" that the religion of Christ, as set forth in the Gospels, was "totally different" from the Christian religion to be found in them (§ 6). "The religion of Christ is contained therein in the clearest and plainest terms; the Christian religion, on the other hand, so uncertainly and ambiguously that it would be difficult to find a single passage of which two men have had the same conception in the whole history of the world" (§§ 7–8). Here the fragment breaks off, but it is clear that the effort to distinguish religious essence from dogmatic accretion continues to the end.

The fragment reveals not a firmly fixed position, but rather an indication of direction in Lessing's religious thinking. We are again reminded that the essential element in the *Erziehung* was not static, but evolutionary and progressive. We must also recall that much of Lessing's writing on the subject comes to us in fragmentary form, and that it is usually shaped to a particular polemical purpose. Although the *Education* can illuminate, it also exemplifies, in its elusiveness, that element which makes of "Lessing's religion" one of the most controversial chapters in his story.[20] It is nonetheless clear that Lessing advocated not only constant intellectual analysis and refinement of theory, but also unceasing attention to the parallel development of viable rules for ethical conduct. The same emphasis on practice as well as precept informs such late works as *Ernst und Falk* and especially his last great literary achievement, the "dramatic poem" *Nathan der Weise*.

CHAPTER 12

Politics and Ethics: Ernst und Falk and Nathan der Weise

I   Ernst und Falk; Gespräche für Freimäurer (*1778; 1780*)

THE five dialogues comprising *Ernst and Falk*, subtitled *Conversations for Freemasons*, dealt ostensibly with the aims and purposes of the Masonic order, but in reality their content far transcended a discussion of Masonry, by whose current state and practices Lessing was much intrigued, but after admission to membership, considerably disappointed.[1] In his view, the organization was not making notable progress toward its avowed goals. These goals he declared to be general, humanitarian, and laudable, but scarcely the discovery of the Masons. Such ideas had existed quite apart from the Order, and in fact had antedated it, in so far as enlightened and far-seeing men of all eras had entertained similar goals. The Masons had merely codified such ideas, and Lessing suggested, at the outset, a parallel to the situation in Christianity, where the "systematic texts" had followed long after the promulgation of Christianity's essence, and had added little or nothing to it. Thus "Freemasonry is not an arbitrary thing, nor is it superfluous: it is, rather, a necessary element in the essential nature of man and society. Consequently one must be able to hit upon its principles by dint of one's own contemplation, as well as by being led to them." This is a clear parallel to Lessing's view of the nature of Christian principles and the role of reason and revelation as set forth in the *Education*.

Society, like religion, involves fundamental principles which men have corrupted in the course of history. Deplorable political and social barriers have arisen between nations and classes, as well as between religious sects. To their removal, every enlightened man should dedicate himself, not merely by announcing principles or dogmas, but by exemplary deeds. A parallel to

Lessing's emphasis on ethical action in the Testament of John suggests itself. The ultimate purpose of such action is thus to render the necessity for "what are commonly called good deeds" increasingly "superfluous."

Turning to politics, Lessing declares that the State exists only for the greater happiness of its members. "The sum total of the individual happiness of all members makes up the happiness of the State. Other than this there is none." Anything that brings harm to even the smallest minority is an expression of tyranny. The duty of every enlightened man, in turn, is to transcend considerations of state or religion in deference to the higher claims of humanity as a whole. There is a need for men who know "where patriotism ceases to be a virtue," as well as for men "who are not subject to the prejudices of their native religion, who do not believe that everything they consider good and true must necessarily be good and true."[2]

Lessing had no illusions about the attainment of such far-reaching political and social goals, just as he had expressed none in describing the hard road to ethical autonomy in the *Education*. Following Leibniz, he accepted the principle of diversity as fixed in the nature of things. Therefore he would not expect its complete eradication from the affairs of men, but he felt that it could at least be minimized. Complete unity and universal brotherhood might well be impossible on the human level, just as ultimate truth might be unattainable for mortal man.[3] Yet we recall that for Lessing, the *search* for truth remained a fundamental duty as well as the test of man's ultimate worth.

Thus in the final Masonic dialogues we find not only the counsel of patience offered in the *Education*, but also a reiteration of the suggestion in its preface that even the erroneous pathways which men follow may serve a useful purpose. However mistaken these courses may be, they still signify the urge to continue the search for truth, which Lessing looks upon as the best augury for its ultimate attainment.

II   Nathan der Weise

Following the invocation of censorship, Lessing wrote to his brother Karl (August 11, 1778) that he proposed now in his time of need to publish a play based on an old sketch whose situation

represented a "kind of analogy" to his own. And in a letter to
Elise Reimarus, written not long thereafter, he ventured to express the hope that he would at least be permitted to preach from
his "old pulpit, the theater." With each letter, he included a copy
of an "Announcement," offering to publish "Nathan the Wise, in
Five Acts" at public subscription. According to Lessing's notes,
he completed his work between mid-November, 1778, and March
7, 1779. It was published in May of the latter year with the subtitle "a dramatic poem."[4]

As its subtitle implies, the structure of *Nathan* is not strictly
dramatic. For his theological and philosophical purpose, Lessing
"invented" a remarkably suitable form: a series of loosely con-
nected scenes providing ample opportunity for the characters to
reveal themselves primarily through the dialectical exchange of
ideas rather than through actions. It also constitutes an elevated
version of Lessing's most successful formula for the theater: the
domestic drama. Here, however, the family interrelations are
meant to symbolize those of all men, and the work not unexpectedly exhibits a number of parallels to Lessing's *Education of the
Human Race,* the first half of which had preceded *Nathan.*[5]

In consonance with its exalted theme—an ideal representation
of human and humane brotherhood and religious tolerance—the
"poem" is in verse, using the five-foot unrhymed iambic line
which the following age of Classicism would adopt as its principal dramatic meter. *Nathan* further anticipates the age of Classicism in its presentation of an idealized humanity in a scene far
removed in time and place—twelfth-century Jerusalem—where the
figures may move in a kind of utopian dream world. Here they
work out their salvation on an elevated plane, beyond the demands of ordinary reality. Having introduced the modern comedy
of character with *Minna,* and advanced the domestic tragedy
with *Emilia,* Lessing now moves in still another direction, toward
the age of Idealism and the resolution of the tragic potential on
an exalted plane. As we have seen, this problem in *Emilia* eluded
a solution in the finite world of ordinary men.[6]

This is not to say that the principal characters in *Nathan* lack
psychological substance. The impetuous young Templar, the
worldly Sultan, Saladin, and the old, wise, and immensely
wealthy Jew, Nathan, are personalities in their own right, as well
as representatives of three revealed world religions (Christianity,

Mohammedanism, and Judaism) and of three stages of human life (idealistic and impulsive youth, world-weary and somewhat cynical maturity, and wise and tolerant old age).[7]

Immediately popular with the reading public,[8] the work failed for twenty years to establish itself as a successful stage piece—it was sometimes also subject to the censor's ban—but Schiller's adaptation for the Weimar theater in 1801 eventually rescued it for the German classical repertoire.

At the outset of the play, Nathan returns from a commercial expedition to discover that in his absence a white-cloaked young Templar has rescued his young daughter, Recha, from death in their burning house. Thereafter, the young man has spurned the persuasive efforts of Nathan's Christian servant, Daja, and the desire of the smitten girl herself, and has refused to accept thanks for saving one whom he calls scornfully "only a Jewess."

We learn that the Templar is the sole survivor of a band of Crusaders captured by the Sultan's forces. His life has been spared by the Sultan for reasons unknown to him. Nathan seeks him out and by his overpowering nobility of spirit converts the bigoted young hothead from scornful intolerance of the Jews to warmhearted admiration and friendship. Yet when Nathan learns from the knight that his name is Curd von Stauffen, he becomes unaccountably cool to his clear intimations that he actually has a deep regard for Recha.

Nathan is now summoned by Saladin, whose treasury is sadly depleted, in good part because of his generosity. He has been alerted to Nathan as a source of revenue by his sister, Sittah, who persuades the basically blunt and direct Saladin to play craftily with his visitor, securing an advantage over him that will make it easier to extract large loans or contributions. The Sultan's agreement to this stratagem is rather ill-motivated and dubious on the whole, but it is necessary for what is to follow.

Nathan arrives, forewarned of the financial emergency by his friend, Al-Hafi, who has become the Sultan's treasurer. Yet Nathan is more than willing to cooperate with Saladin, the savior of the Templar, who in turn has rescued his Recha. Saladin first seeks to confuse and compromise him by posing the question: Which of the three great religions is the true one? Surprised and puzzled, Nathan quickly collects his thoughts and responds by relating the parable of the three rings—an ancient story which

Lessing adapted from the version found in Boccaccio's *Decamerone.*

Lessing's parable explains that an opal ring of mysterious origin had passed down from father to son for countless generations until it was finally supplemented by two identical copies, commissioned by a father who could not decide which of his three sons to favor. No one can now distinguish the original ring, which confers upon the bearer who has faith in it the favor of God and man. The judge to whom the sons turn for a settlement of their quarrel suggests first that perhaps none of the rings is genuine; that the original ring has disappeared, since no two of the sons love a third more than themselves. If one of the rings is genuine, however, and if its owner can summon the proper faith, its power will eventually manifest itself.

The judge's advice to the three is, therefore, to live exemplary lives of love and service to humanity, demonstrating an active faith in God and in the prospect that "in a thousand thousand years" the power of the original ring will reveal itself, and a "wiser judge" will render a decision. The three rings, Nathan assures the Sultan, are paralleled by Christianity, Mohammedanism, and Judaism, and none can know which is "genuine." Increasingly impressed by Nathan's modest dignity and wisdom as the tale unfolds, and awed by the solemn grandeur of the vision with which the recital concludes, the Sultan humbly acknowledges his insignificance. He abandons his petty scheme and welcomes Nathan as a friend.

We then learn that the Sultan has spared the Templar because of his remarkable resemblance, in person and bearing, to Saladin's late brother, Assad. He now sends Nathan to summon the young man so that Sittah, too, may marvel at the likeness. When they meet, Nathan again turns aside the knight's now impassioned pleas for Recha's hand. Instead, he presses the Templar for details of his parentage and family history, much to the young man's confusion and frustration.

The servant Daja then finds occasion to reveal to the young knight that Recha is in fact a Christian—an orphan whom Nathan accepted in infancy after the death of her mother and the departure of her father on a long journey from which he did not return. Thereafter, Nathan has raised the child as his own. Confused and distraught by Nathan's apparent "treachery" in failing to reveal these facts to Recha, the young man turns for advice to the pompous, narrow-minded Patriarch of the local Christian community. The latter assures him that a Jew who has imposed apostasy upon a Christian merits death by fire. The Templar thereupon rushes to reveal his discovery to Saladin, who is seriously concerned by Nathan's apparent duplicity. However, he counsels restraint and will reserve judgment. The Templar is dispatched to bring Nathan for a final encounter and clarification of the manifold confusions. By the time the Templar reaches Nathan, however, he has reconsidered his impetuous conduct and regrets his over-hasty conclusions. He reconverts himself, as it were (as he has before, and as he will once again), from impulsive suspicion and mistrust of Nathan, the Jew, to well-considered faith and trust in Nathan, the upright human being (V.iii; V.v).

Nathan has meanwhile obtained the final proof of his long-felt presentiment regarding the parentage of the Templar and Recha. In a final confrontation of all principals, family records supplied, at long last, by the Friar who first brought the infant Recha to Nathan clearly reveal that the Templar and Recha are brother and sister. Their parents had long ago been friends of Nathan's; the mother a European and a Stauffen, the father a non-European whom Nathan knew as Wolf von Filneck. The Templar had been brought up in Europe as a von Filneck by a maternal uncle, and had used the name Stauffen in identifying himself to Nathan because of an instinctive mistrust.

The final revelation, long hinted at, can now be confirmed by Saladin, who identifies the handwriting of the records as that of his brother, Assad. The curtain may now descend on a scene of joyous familial reunion, in which Nathan, having conquered his sense of loss in surrendering his position as "real" father to Recha, can participate equally joyously in his new and hard-won role as "spiritual" father.[9]

From a fragmentary and unpublished "Preface" to *Nathan* one cannot deduce with certainty the author's position. Here he calls attention to the central importance of the parable as the "kernel, from which *Nathan* developed" in his mind, and it is worth noting that it comes at the exact center of the poem (III.vii). He also declares that "Nathan's disposition against *all* positive religion has been *my own* all along. But this is not the place to justify it." He would have little objection, he adds, if one wished to see in this work people from various races who have set themselves above all revealed religion and have nonetheless remained good people, and if one wished to detect here an intention to portray such people in a less reprehensible light than the one in which they are normally viewed by the "Christian herd." In the same breath he adds: "For a man can advocate these ideas and have this intention without himself completely discarding every revealed religion, not every one. I am not crafty enough to present myself as such a person: yet I am audacious enough not to pretend to be such a person."[10]

The last statement surely lends weight to the assumption that Lessing does indeed reject all revealed religions, and the parable is also sometimes invoked in evidence. Here, it has been said, the import is that *no* ring is genuine, and that Lessing "has thus to invest man with the ability of attaining the effect of the ring by his own efforts. . . . His plea for tolerance for virtuous conduct (justification by works) rather than acknowledgment of a positive creed (justification by faith) emerges clearly from this central passage."[11]

The value, indeed the necessity, of humanitarian works in Lessing's "system" is undeniable, and overzealous adherence to a particular creed at their expense is deplored. Yet it is worth noting that it is Nathan with whom Lessing identifies, rather than with the judge in the parable, who has suggested—probably only half-seriously—that all three sons have been duped by a false ring. Nathan sums up his "little story" by telling the Sultan that the "true ring could not be proved—it was almost as undemonstrable as the true faith is to us now" (III.vii). He does not say that they are all false. The "disposition" against positive religions, which Lessing shares with Nathan, is not a conviction that all are false, but rather an inclination to deplore the false pride that induces overzealous practitioners of one religion or another, in the face of insufficient evidence, to advance their own doctrines as demonstrably superior to all others.

This point is clearly made during the first meeting between Nathan and the Templar. What most attracts Nathan to the young knight, and what makes it possible for him to overlook or discount the latter's outbursts of scorn and mistrust, is his statement that the Jews alienate him, most of all, by their prideful boast that they possess the one true God: a hurtful pride that they have bequeathed to Christians and Moslems alike. Where and when in the world's history, the Templar asks in effect, has this "pious madness," this ambition of one sect to force its God upon the entire world, brought more harm to man than it has in this place and time? (He is referring, of course, to the bloodshed and suffering resulting from the misguided ambition that gave rise to the Crusades.) And in reply, Nathan exclaims: "Ha! You do not know how much closer I will now cling to you. Come, we must be friends, we must!" (II.v). Both can now rejoice in the discovery of a kindred spirit: one who places the claims of a shared humanity above the accidents of race and creed.

Or, turning again to the parable, it seems clear that within its framework, deeds alone are not enough to assure "the favor of God and man." The "lesson" of the parable is by no means solely a social ethic, for a mystic element is also postulated. The "magic power" of the ring is manifested only through those who have faith in it and who, animated by this faith, initiate positive, humane works for the benefit of their fellow men. The fundamental "mystery" is reflected also in the "open form" of the parable itself, beginning, as it does, with a ring whose origin is veiled in obscurity, and arching away at the conclusion into the reaches of an infinity.[12]

The visionary nature of the parable, as well as the elevated ethical plane upon which the action of the play attains its final resolution, are both reminiscent of the mystery and exaltation of Lessing's vision from the heights as he contemplates, in his prelude to the *Erziehung*, mankind's progressive development, and confirms, in its closing paragraphs, his faith in the ultimate realization of the vision.

When we seek to determine how this resolution is symbolically attained in the poem, we find, once more, the curious amalgam of rational and irrational elements that has more than once attracted our attention. It is Nathan who alerts us to the fact that beneficent deeds by both Saladin, who spares the life of the Templar, and the Templar himself, who rescues Recha, were necessary events in the chain which leads to the ultimate resolution of the conflict and the symbolic familial reunion.[13] What Nathan does not say, however, is equally important. For neither of these acts is consciously planned. Neither is the result of conflict culminating in a conscious act of will. Saladin responds to a mysterious dictate

originating in some other than a rational system; he responds to a
vague presentiment that links the unknown captive to the concept
of family on a temporal level (IV.iv). The motivation for the
Templar's deed is less restricted; it is more "humane" because a
less self-oriented act. In its origin, however, it is equally mysterious to the Templar himself. Confronted with Nathan's unwanted
gratitude, he at first attempts to belittle his rescue of Recha as a
mere automatic response to ingrained knightly training, or even
to ascribe it to a shattering despair at his "captive" state—a mood
that had become virtually suicidal. Both motives are irrational
enough, but Nathan will accept neither, sensing a "noble" impulse
for the deed behind the "detestable" façade which the Templar
attempts to erect. And when the young man later pauses and attempts to analyze his motives more carefully, he finds them un-
susceptible to rational investigation.[14]

Still another in the necessary chain of beneficent deeds is
revealed late in the play when Nathan recounts to the Friar his
own harrowing crisis of eighteen years before, when rampaging
Christians in Gath burned his wife and "seven promising sons"
to death. This monstrous act had shattered his faith and had cast
him into the outer darkness of despair. He had raged against his
fate and sworn undying hatred for all Christians. But reason had
gradually returned, saying:

> " '. . . und doch ist Gott!
> Doch war auch Gottes Ratschluss das! Wohlan!
> Komm! Übe, was du längst begriffen hast;
> Was sicherlich zu üben schwerer nicht,
> Als zu begreifen ist, wenn du nur willst.
> Steh auf!'—Ich stand! und rief zu Gott: Ich will!
> Willst du nur, dass ich will!—"

("'. . . yet God exists! This too was God's counsel. Forward! Come!
Carry out what you have long since understood; a course surely not
more difficult to follow than to grasp, if only it is your will. Arise!'—
I rose! and cried to God: I will! If only thou willt that I will" (IV.vii).

Here the voice of reason and the voice of God are inextricably
interwoven, and an act of will becomes indistinguishable from an
act of faith. In terms of the *Erziehung,* reason and revelation
coincide. At this crucial point in Nathan's spiritual development,
the Friar had arrived with the infant Recha. By accepting the
Christian child into his loving care and extending his love to all

fellow men, Nathan has "used the most negative experience to attain the most positive value accessible to man, to be his authentic self and to actualize the divine spirit within himself, not by mere resignation to an intolerable fate, like Job, but by an act of self-overcoming and self-transcending love in which morality becomes truly religious."[15]

The three deeds forming the mystic chain leading to the final resolution of the problem Lessing has set himself are alike in that all involve the preservation of human life, surely the noblest of good works. But clearly they markedly differ in the degree to which they represent consciously selfless acts. That of the Sultan is the more self-centered, associated, as it is, with the preservation of temporal family ties. That of the Templar is less so; but like the act of the Sultan, it is essentially involuntary, and the motive for it is obscure and is dimly perceived as a response to an amorphous "faith." Nathan, however, is clearly aware that faith is being confirmed by reason in the critical act which crowns his conscious decision to overcome selfish impulse in a deed of pure altruism. Here, too, Lessing demonstrates an affinity with the age of Idealism, where ethical will requires a hard decision to overcome personal inclination and respond to the dictates of a higher order.[16] The fact that Nathan must once more struggle to overcome the "selfish" impulse to retain Recha as his "real" daughter need not obscure the conscious selflessness of this purely humanitarian act. And his second struggle, we note, is also successful.

We may be reminded here of Lessing's earlier and repeated emphasis on the importance of acting with conscious intent—the kind of action which elevates man above the lesser creatures, and the kind of creative act that distinguishes the genius from lesser talents. Here the element of intent, which is central to Lessing's esthetic thought, is applied in the realm of human affairs to create in Nathan a genius in the art of living, and an artist in the area of human relations.

In these key situations, and in others, the interplay of the parable and the unfolding action of the work in which it is embedded is clear enough. The long-standing scholarly dispute regarding the correspondence of parable and dramatic plot in all their manifold details is less important for our purpose than the realization that they correspond to, and mutually reinforce, one another in their fundamental import.[17]

The three rings of the contending brothers, the three warring religions—each, in the fullness of time, will become dispensible, just as the ultimate goal of Freemasonry is to make "good deeds dispensible." Faith, tolerance, and love manifesting itself in humane action will restore the "magic power" of the ring, now inaccessible to the brothers who have neglected these fundamental duties in a self-centered struggle for power. Their rivalry will be dissolved in a restoration of mutual respect and love.

These same noble sentiments and actions, contending with the manifold obstacles generated by a narrow-minded sectarianism, with its inevitable corollary of mistrust of one's fellow man, eventually triumph in the poem, prefiguring Lessing's vision of a universal brotherhood. Both the parable and the dramatic poem affirm a faith in an ever-ascending progression, despite certain setbacks and digressions, that will ultimately transcend apparently unaccountable and undeserved suffering and evil, and lead to the re-establishment of the universal and loving family of man.[18] That the ultimate realization of this vision is lost in the unfathomable mists of the future did not blind Lessing to the necessity to strive endlessly for its fulfillment.

CHAPTER 13

A Lessing Perspective

IN summarizing an account from which much had necessarily to be omitted, it is possible only to recall, once again, the highest peaks of Lessing's accomplishments—those that elevated him so markedly above the eighteenth-century terrain, and still loom large on the present-day horizon as prominent heights toward which seekers for truth may continue to strive.[1]

No student of Lessing can fail to be impressed by the remarkable manner in which his earlier pronouncements and formulations so frequently foreshadow those dictated by his most mature thinking. The occasional shifts of emphasis—the alteration of an evaluation in the later years, the inconsistencies sometimes detectable in his criticism, or between the critical pronouncements and his own practice—need not obscure for us the essential unity (a conscious unity, surely, though Lessing in his later years ruefully admitted that he found it increasingly difficult to remain consistent) in his creative critical thinking. We may recall, for instance, his early realization that the artist in essence neither echoes nor imitates, but creates. The germ of this idea is apparent in *The Justifications of Horace*, and it is developed and elaborated in the critical masterpieces of the later years: the "Literaturbriefe," the *Laokoon*, and the *Hamburgische Dramaturgie*. And whether we examine the works of the early or the late Lessing, the ingredient in the creative process that elicits his most careful critical attention is invariably the element of conscious intent. Which is not to say that he accepts the prescriptive principles so widely advocated in his own age. With this view of artistic creation he seems never to have been in complete accord, even in the early years; and he moved farther away from it as his critical sense continued to develop. The inspirations of genius can be neither prescribed nor categorized. Lessing insists only that the gifted individuals to whom they are imparted be fully aware of what they are about; they need not be rationally cognizant of the *source* of their vision. There is, then, a gray area in Lessing's critical thinking which eludes rational analysis, just as the work of genius, in his view, cannot be encompassed by rational categories, although we instinctively recognize its rightness when the required conditions have been met.

For Lessing, these conditions, so frequently criticized as confining and often rejected by subsequent critics as outmoded, reassert the central importance of the attempt to view the world and all manifestations of human life in an objective manner, that is to say, as far as possible without preconceptions. To the notion of the central importance of the poet's own personality and attitude, later so markedly written into the German record by Goethe, and intensified in the Romantic era, Lessing opposes the objective view, placing the work itself in the central place and examining and judging it in its relation to the immutable laws of existence and its relevance for all men. It is this element of vitality in its fundamental sense—the relation to human life—that characterizes Lessing's critical attitude. The true work of art *affects* the viewer or the auditor in appropriate ways. This same spirit manifests itself also in those poetic works which justify our regarding Lessing not only as the creator of German literary criticism, but also as the creator of modern German literature.

In judging the products of Lessing's own genius, it appears that few would deny his creation of the modern German comedy. Far fewer students are inclined, however, to see a similar accomplishment in respect to tragedy. One may well be inclined to join them in the admission that *Miss Sara Sampson* possesses only historical interest, as a reflection of an important but transitory stage of sociological and theological development, and that stylistically it is now a museum piece. But such displays may have value, not only as fossilized remnants, summarizing the course already traversed, but also as signposts indicative of future developments. In this sense, Lessing's *Sara* still possesses a continuing validity and vitality.

Emilia Galotti exhibits this vitality more overtly, and in keeping with the intellectual development of its creator, the vital force

is manifested in a fashion at once more powerful and more controlled. The result is that the play has frequently been characterized as schematic in its inspiration, as coldly intellectualized in its
composition, and as repugnant in its dénouement—analyses which
fail, as the foregoing commentary has attempted to point out, to
take into account Lessing's acceptance of the limitations imposed
by man's existence in the dimension of time.

When this obstacle is symbolically removed in *Nathan der
Weise*, Lessing's vision achieves its ultimate poetic expression.
It is not without significance that *Sara, Emilia,* and *Nathan* may
still claim relevance in an inverse ratio to their rootedness in the
temporal dimension, and in direct proportion to their ability to
demonstrate the fundamental rightness of Lessing's principal
critical insight: that the work of art represents not the successful
demonstration of externally imposed prescriptions, but the instinctive realization of timeless laws embodying the noblest
potential of the human spirit when it is properly attuned to the
manifestations of the guiding spirit of the universe.

We have seen that a fundamental quality of Lessing's thought,
and of the style in which it was cast, is its clarity. In his own
efforts to establish rapport with the all-encompassing spirit, a
Lessing so constituted could not long remain on the stage represented by the youthful ode, wherein he had substituted a kind
of refuge in emotional awareness for the missing intellectual demonstration of God's existence. The later efforts increasingly stress
the reasoned approach. In the *Erziehung*, passages of which are
sometimes regarded as evidence of the recurrence of emotion in
mystic guise, or relegated to the realm of the exoteric, it seems
more appropriate to emphasize that the emergent clarity originates in flashes of intellectual rather than emotional awareness
and illumination. Upon his symbolic hilltop Lessing does not
dissolve in a mist of mystic feeling; he *sees*—and it is this figure
which, despite the evening haze, lends his vision a quality of
clarity which is enhanced by the symbolic presence of lingering
sunlight.

And if the element of feeling, sentimentality, and softly pleasurable suffering is by no means lacking in the earlier years, it is
more than offset by the astringence of Lessing's mature concept
of "Mitleid": the shared suffering whose purpose is not to melt
the heart, but to strengthen and, quite literally, enlighten it. Les-

sing's ever-present inclination to draw distinctions is especially productive in his speculation on the theory of tragedy, in that it creates a means by which man may experience suffering (the ultimate human riddle) in an esthetic guise not identical with its shattering and paralyzing effect in real life. Without "solving" the problem of suffering, Lessing has provided an avenue by which it may be intelligibly approached.

Just as the theory of tragedy provides the observer with a perspective in which suffering may be productively encompassed, so the historical perspective of the *Erziehung* removes the observer to heights upon which time-bound tragedy and the related temporal limitations of human existence can be surmounted. To Lessing, the view, despite its primitivism, and indeed in a measure because of it, represents not clouded superstition but the clarity of a pristine human reason unencumbered by preconceptions, and hence open and accessible to the manifestations of the transcendent spirit.

That Lessing assumes the existence of such a spirit is frequently denied. As we have seen, there are those who interpret his controversial theological pronouncements as indicative of such a denial. To these critics they represent Lessing's fundamental tendency and his contribution to the "secularization" of modern thought and attitudes, and the notion is widespread that he defended, even though cryptically, the assertion that human reason represents and encompasses the ultimate reality. Other critics, especially some of the more recent ones, espouse quite a different view by asserting that Lessing's ultimate position also includes the notion of a transcendent Being; a view which seems substantiated not only by the theological pronouncements but also by the fundamental thrust of his dramatic and critical activity.

But in consequence of the opposing interpretations, it is frequently maintained that in the realm of drama, esthetics, and theology Lessing represents merely the epitome of a highly questionable and, in any event, long outmoded philosophical optimism —an avoidance of the harsh realities of human existence by recourse to a theodicy, in virtue of which the essentially tragic configuration of human life is conveniently disposed of.

To this charge, one may reiterate that Lessing transcends that element of the philosophy of the Enlightenment which is frequently designated as an "easy" optimism; nor does his concept of determinism permit of the mechanistic interpretation which removes the burden of ethical responsibility from the individual. In the light of recorded history, it can never have been easy to maintain an optimistic attitude, although there were those in Lessing's time who minimized the difficulties. Lessing's critical and theological campaigns were devoted in good part to alerting them to their misconceptions. It was correspondingly easy for Voltaire in *Candide* to ridicule the superficial conclusions that such uncritical devotees could extract from the imperfectly represented Leibnizian optimism of a Christian Wolff.

How difficult, and yet how unavoidable it was to assert faith is demonstrated in Lessing. That it is possible to maintain it, despite the multitude of apparently rational objections to such a course, is the lesson that can be derived from his own reaction to vicissitudes and tragic blows, as well as from his recreations of the world as he observed it. From his accomplishments in both tragedy and comedy, we can extract the asurance that he ignored neither the ubiquitous threats to human fulfillment nor the possibility of human happiness which human life affords. He represents, in short, both the affective and rational views of human existence—a perfect amalgam of the notion that life is a tragedy to the man of feeling, and a comedy to the man of intellect.

In our own age, Hermann Hesse has assured us that all genuine artistic creation must convey some germ, some aspect of the artist's conviction that life is worth living. If he is to do this, it is clear that he will be obliged to transcend the shattering experiences and apparent demonstrations to the contrary he inevitably encounters in his collisions with what is called, for want of a better term, "reality." The would-be artist who cannot look beyond these temporal limitations, who cannot, in effect, live "beyond time," will not even survive his own in his works. Lessing is one of those to whom was granted the vision which could transcend the clearly demonstrable limitations of his age—including his own limits, which he certainly recognized—to perceive an order beyond the all-too-apparent chaos of human life.

It is this glimpse of an ultimate order—a unity in diversity— which Lessing attempted in all his best and most characteristic work to bequeath to those who followed, and which he urged them, by precept and example, to cultivate and embody in their own lives and works. In his poem "Das Göttliche" ("The Divine")

Goethe expresses the guarded hope that man's example may teach us to believe in the unknown higher Beings:

> Heil den unbekannten
> Höhern Wesen,
> Die wir ahnen!
> Ihnen gleiche der Mensch;
> Sein Beispiel lehr uns
> Jene glauben.

Lessing is a man who in his life and work sets such an example for us.

Notes and References

Preface

1. Immanuel Kant, *What is Enlightenment?* in: *Kant on History*, ed. L. W. Beck, trans. L. W. Beck et al. (Indianapolis, 1963), cited by Henry E. Allison, *Lessing and the Enlightenment* (Ann Arbor, 1966), p. 1.

2. See J. M. Creed and J. S. B. Smith, *Religious Thought in the Eighteenth Century* (Cambridge, Eng., 1934), p. 33: the selection from Matthew Tindal's *Christianity as Old as the Creation* (1730), which is designated "the culmination of the Deistic movement" (p. 31).

3. *Werke*, ed. P. Rilla, VIII, 488; the fragmentary essay, "Bibliolatrie."

4. Designations employed by A. C. M'Giffert, *Protestant Thought before Kant* (New York, 1911), esp. pp. 247–49, and Paul Wernle, *Der schweizerische Protestantismus im achtzeinten Jahrhundert*, 3 vols. (Tübingen, 1923–25), I, 468 ff. Cf. K. Aner, *Die Theologie der Lessingzeit* (Halle/Saale, 1929), p. 3; similarly Ernst Cassirer, *Die Philosophie der Aufklärung* (Tübingen, 1932), pp. 234 ff.

Chapter One

1. See Gerhard Stephan, *G. E. Lessing und seine Eltern . . .* (Kamenz, 1929), pp. 35–36.

2. Preface to *Schrifften*, III and IV (1754); see also C. G. Schumann, *Gotthold Ephraim Lessings Schuljahre* (Trier, 1884).

3. Letter to his mother, January 20, 1749; Rilla IX, 10.

4. Mylius is frequently called Lessing's cousin, but the relationship was technical and tenuous. See Gerhard Stephan, *Lessing*, p. 36. On Lessing in Leipzig, see also Heinrich Schneider, *Das Buch Lessing*, 2nd ed. (Berne/Munich, 1961), pp. 15–16.

5. Schneider, *op. cit.*, pp. 17–18, and B. Q. Morgan, "Lessing's Youthful Romance," *MLN*, LXVI (1951), 318–22.

6. Preface to *Schrifften*, III and IV (1754); Rilla, III, 673.

7. Paul Böckmann, *Formgeschichte der deutschen Dichtung*, 2nd ed., I, *Von der Sinnbildsprache zur Ausdruckssprache, . . .* (Hamburg, 1965) describes the inception (pp. 530–39) and later development (pp. 540–46) of this process.

8. A later (intentionally) satirical fragmentary comedy, *Weiber sind Weiber* (1749), ridicules even the "'sentimental' theme of the

loyal wife." See Paul P. Kies, "Lessing's Relation to Early English Sentimental Comedy," *PMLA,* XLVII (1932), 807–26, esp. p. 809. See also below, pp. 31 f.

9. Lessing's audience would recognize this touch of realism, for such a contest actually occurred in 1747.

10. See below, pp. 37, 77, 111, and 112.

11. See J. C. Gottsched, *Critische Dichtkunst,* 4th ed. (Leipzig, 1751), pp. 94–117, 650. Cf. B. Aikin-Sneath, *Comedy in Germany* . . . (Oxford, 1936), pp. 13, 16, 25–29.

12. Cf. Horst Steinmetz, *Die Komödie der Aufklärung* (Stuttgart, 1966), pp. 58–59.

13. On Lessing's debt to classical, French, German, and Italian sources, see Waldemar Oehlke, *Lessing und seine Zeit,* 2 vols., 2nd ed. (Munich, 1919), I, 115; on the English source materials see Paul P. Kies, "Lessing's Early Study of English Drama," *JEGP,* XXVIII (1929), 16–34, esp. pp. 18–22; 32–33, who argues for Lessing's early acquaintance with the work of Wycherley, Shadwell (*Bury Fair* an influence on *Damon*), Lansdowne, Congreve, and Etherege (and with Vanbrugh and Farquhar before the autumn of 1749), and for their influence on such unfinished plays as *Der Leichtgläubige; Die Witzlinge; Der gute Mann; Der Vater ein Affe, der Sohn ein Jeck;* and *Der Dorfjunker.* Lessing's general method for treating sources included simplification of plot lines, combination of materials from various sources, and the softening of objectionable elements.

14. Karl Holl, *Geschichte des deutschen Lustspiels* (Leipzig, 1923), p. 169, detects here and in the following play, as well as in *Damon,* traces of Latin, Greek, Danish, English, French, and Italian sources.

15. Cf. Hans Rempel, *Tragödie und Komödie im dramatischen Schaffen Lessings* (Darmstadt, 1967), p. 15.

16. Rilla, III, 652 ff.

17. E. Schmidt, *Lessing,* 3rd ed., I, 148.

18. See the contemporary review by Michaelis, *Göttingische Zeitung,* No. 65, 1755, pp. 599 f., and Julius W. Braun, *Lessing im Urtheile seiner Zeitgenossen* (Berlin, 1884–1897), I, 5, 60, 180–181, 183, 232, 326.

19. Johann Christoph Adelung, *Versuch eines vollständigen grammatisch-kritischen Wörterbuchs der hochdeutschen Mundart* (Leipzig, 1774–86), II, 290.

20. See E. Schmidt, *Lessing,* 1st ed., I, 131, 134; substantially unchanged in the later editions; a similar argument by F. J. Schmitz, *Lessings Stellung in der Entfaltung des Individualismus* (Berkeley, 1941), p. 46.

21. Gerhard Fricke also discounts the motive of jealousy, but ascribes Adrast's stress upon it in the key conversion scene to a slip on the part of the young playwright. The resulting overemphasis

serves to obscure the basic inner problem: to conquer by the exercise of selfless goodness Adrast's unjustified prejudices. Yet it would still seem that such exercise must await the injection of an intellectual note, intended perhaps as playfully satiric, in order to alert Adrast, and the audience, to its credibility. See below, p. 31. Fricke, "Bemerkungen zu Lessings *Freigeist* und *Miss Sara Sampson*" in: *Festschrift Josef Quint* (Bonn, 1964), pp. 83–120; *Der Freigeist*: pp. 83–96.

22. A number of critics have noted, without interpreting in this way, Theophan's angry outburst. See F. Andrew Brown, "The Conversion of Lessing's Freygeist," *JEGP*, LVI (1957), 186–202; esp. p. 198 and n. (Portions of this article have been used above by kind permission of the Board of Editors, *JEGP*.) To the number of critics mentioned, one may add Günter Wicke, *Die Struktur des deutschen Lustspiels . . .* (Bonn, 1965), p. 99. We should not overemphasize that in the play Theophan consciously "campaigns" for Adrast's acceptance; and that he plays an announced role. The part of a good-hearted, patient, and forgiving friend is, after all, completely in accord with his basic nature. If we reject this idea, and the corollary that his outburst represents a contrast to his fundamentally gentle character, we would be obliged to assume that he is by nature a thoroughly ill-tempered man who finally shows his true colors. It would seem more plausible to see in him a figure endowed not only with the noble qualities of Pastor Lessing and his colleagues, for whom the play was ostensibly written, but also with something of the father's "irascibility" to which Lessing later alludes. See below, p. 141. A differing view in Karl S. Guthke, *Der Stand der Lessing-Forschung . . .* (Stuttgart, 1965), p. 43.

23. See, for example, the comments on Wieland's "perfect" characters in "Literaturbriefe" No. 63; Rilla, IV, 293–94 (cf. below, p. 77), or on Weisse's *Richard der Dritte* in *Hamburgische Dramaturgie*, No. 74; Rilla, VI, 376–80.

24. Horst Steinmetz, *Die Komödie der Aufklärung*, p. 62.

Chapter Two

1. Rilla, III, 7.

2. Rilla, I, 199.

3. In the monthly literary supplement *Das Neueste aus dem Reiche des Witzes*, June, 1751; Rilla, III, 368.

4. Cf. Albert Malte Wagner, *Lessing: Das Erwachen des deutschen Geistes* (Leipzig/Berlin, 1931), p. 77.

5. *Discours . . . sur cette question . . . si la rétablissement des sciences et des Arts a contribué à épurer les moeurs;* Rilla, III, 331–48; 418.

6. Rilla, III, 163 ff.

7. Th. W. Danzel and G. E. Guhrauer, *Lessing*, 2 vols., 2nd ed. (Berlin, 1880–81), I, 178.

8. See above, Chapter 1, n. 13.

9. Rilla, III, 191, 206, 211 and n.

10. Rilla, III, 326–27. Cf. Hans Rempel, *Tragödie und Komödie*, p. 34.

11. Rilla, III, 328; published in *Schrifften*, V (1755). Lessing's interest in Plautus' themes and techniques is also evident in his scenario for a five-act comedy, *Justin*, a reworking of the *Pseudolus*, as well as in the fragment *Weiber sind Weiber*, a version of the *Stichus*. Sentimental and comic elements were to be interspersed also in the comedy *Die aufgebrachte Tugend*, a fragment based on William Burnaby's *The Modish Husband*. See Paul P. Kies, "Lessing and Burnaby," *MLN*, L (1935), 225–30.

12. Rilla, III, 663–65; a nearly identical discussion in the *Berlinische privilegierte Zeitung* for October 28, 1751. (LM IV, 364–65). Cf. Albert Köster, "Lessing und Gottsched," *Euphorion* I (1894), 64–70. Lessing's early admiration for Voltaire, and his friendly relation with the Frenchman, were permanently clouded when, in leaving Berlin for Wittenberg, he carried with him certain proof sheets of unpublished work by Voltaire. A misunderstanding ensued, and Voltaire complained to his royal patron, suspecting that Lessing planned to publish a pirated edition. Lessing's consistent failure to find preferment in the Prussian capital may well be traceable to this episode.

13. Huarte's work is still recognized as a pioneering effort in the experimental sciences of characterology and the psychology of the gifted. See Martin Franzbach, *Lessings Huarte–Uebersetzung...* (Hamburg, 1965).

14. Rilla, III, 671. "Part Two contains Letters. My readers will doubtless assume them to be love letters. But I must confess that I have not thus far had occasion to write such letters. To create imaginary feminine correspondents, and write to beautiful girls who don't exist, seemed to me in prose a little too poetic."

15. Rilla, III, 433–34.

16. Rilla, III, 560–61, 578, 580, 594.

17. Cf. Benno von Wiese, *Lessing* (Leipzig, 1931), pp. 23–24; Kurt May, *Lessings und Herders kunsttheoretische Gedanken* ... (Berlin, 1923), pp. 31–33.

18. Here the authors admittedly adopt the definition of Alexander Gottlieb Baumgarten, whose *Aesthetica* (1750–1758) is frequently regarded as the foundation for esthetics as a philosophical discipline. (Rilla, VII, 232.)

19. Rilla, VII, 236, 255, 272 and n. 22.

20. Rilla, III, 648, 649.

21. Otto G. Graf, "Lessing and the Art of Acting," *Papers of the Michigan Academy of Science, Arts, and Letters*, XL, Ann Arbor,

1955, pp. 293–301, esp. p. 299. Cf. Guthke, *Lessing-Forschung*, p. 72. Gerhard Piens, in his edition of *Francesco Riccoboni, "Die Schauspiel-kunst," übersetzt von G. E. Lessing* . . . (Berlin, 1954), finds Lessing to show a preference for Riccoboni's view. Victoria Pfeil concludes that Lessing's "final" position falls between the idealism of the French (cold beauty) and the realism of the English (raw truth). See "Lessing und die Schauspielkunst" (diss. Giessen, 1921), p. 37. Theodore Ziolkowski sees Lessing reaching for a "new naturalness" and striking a balance between the "visceral" style advocated by Sainte-Albine and the consciously controlled techniques recommended by Riccoboni. In *Miss Sara,* Lessing prescribes in the dialogue itself the desired movement, expression, and gesture, and thus begins a long and important development in which the latter will increasingly dominate language. See "Language and Mimetic Action in Lessing's *Miss Sara Sampson,*" GR, XL (1965), 261–76.

22. Curtis C. D. Vail, "Originality in Lessing's *Theatralische Bibliothek,*" GR, IX (1934), 96–101, esp. p. 99. Cf. Vail, *Lessing's Relation to the English Language and Literature* (New York, 1936), pp. 126–27.

23. LM, VI, 187–88, 190.

24. LM, VI, 197.

25. LM, VI, 197–98. Lessing once thought of dramatizing in these terms the tragic career of the seventeenth-century Neapolitan rebel leader Massaniello (Masaniello, or Tomaso Aniello). See the letter to his brother Karl, July 14, 1773; Rilla, IX, 581.

26. LM, VI, 190, 194.

Chapter Three

1. Cf. Emil Jenal, "Lessings *Samuel Henzi,*" *Schweizerische Monatshefte für Politik und Kultur,* IX (1929), 306–18.

2. K. Roald Bergethon, "Republicanism (?) and Revolution in G. E. Lessing's *Samuel Henzi,*" *Symposium,* I (1946), 60–72; the quotation from p. 65.

3. Hans Rempel, *Tragödie und Komödie,* p. 36.

4. *Ibid.,* pp. 37–38. For reasons given below, one might question Rempel's final criterion of similarity: the passivity of the central character, who provides merely the goal toward which all action tends.

5. See Paul P. Kies, "The Sources and Basic Model of Lessing's *Miss Sara Sampson,*" MP, XXIV (1926), 65–90, esp. pp. 66, 85 ff. Cf. Lawrence Marsden Price, *English Literature in Germany* (Berkeley and Los Angeles, 1953), pp. 154–58.

6. See Jakob Dusch in his *Vermischte kritische und satyrische Schriften* (1758); cf. Kies, *op. cit.,* p. 67, and below, p. 68.

7. On the matter of priority between Lessing's play and Christian Leberecht Martini's *Rhynsolt und Saphira*, a drama long regarded as an imitation of *Miss Sara*, see Richard Daunicht, *Die Entstehung des bürgerlichen Trauerspiels in Deutschland* (Berlin, 1963), p. 238, and Robert R. Heitner, *German Tragedy in the Age of Enlightenment* (Berkeley and Los Angeles, 1963), p. 170 and n. 5.

8. Oehlke, *Lessing*, I, 293.

9. For a discussion emphasizing economic and social aspects of the play, see Dietrich Sommer, "Die gesellschaftliche Problematik in Lessings bürgerlichem Trauerspiel, *Miss Sara Sampson*," *Wissenschaftliche Zeitschrift der Univ. Halle-Wittenberg; Gesellschafts- und sprachwissenschaftliche Reihe*, X (1961), 959–64, esp. p. 964.

10. Sara's deportment here is sometimes regarded as a contradiction of her essential passivity. Perhaps this is one of the "more essential perfections" for which, on occasion, Lessing would gladly sacrifice symmetry or regularity.

11. Hans Rempel, *Tragödie und Komödie*, p. 35; cf. Karl Holl, *Geschichte*, p. 180; E. Schmidt, *Lessing*, I, 266.

12. Fritz Brüggemann, "Lessings Bürgerdramen . . . ," *Jahrbuch des freien deutschen Hochstifts* (1926), p. 71; von Wiese, *Lessing*, pp. 32 ff.

13. The procedure here and elsewhere in *Sara* provides specific examples of the "renewal of the tragedy in form and content" as discussed by Otto Mann, *Geschichte des deutschen Dramas* (Stuttgart, 1963), pp. 156 ff., esp. p. 163. In *Sara*, the force of passion representing the un-godly or anti-godly element originates, according to Mann, in Mellefont and Marwood, and enmeshes an essentially passive Sara in catastrophe (p. 165). But Sara, too, admits complicity and acknowledges her susceptibility to the dark forces of overpowering emotional stimulus.

14. In the process of learning to accept forgiveness (here the key scene is III.iii, where Sara learns, through the servant Waitwell, of her father's continuing love for her), the theologian Heinrich Bornkamm finds the principal theme of Lessing's play. See "Die innere Handlung in Lessings *Miss Sara Sampson*," in: *Solange es "Heute" heisst: Festgabe für Rudolf Hermann* . . . (Berlin, 1957), pp. 42–51, esp. pp. 48–49. In this view, Sara's love for Mellefont must be discarded as a source of her strength— an interpretation which would seem to be contradicted in the play. Rilla, II, 85.

15. Cf. von Wiese, *Lessing*, pp. 34–35. The contention, therefore, that adherence to both social and religious laws prevents Sara from asserting the primacy of the subjective experience (von Wiese, pp. 36–37) appears to require modification.

16. Hans Rempel, *Tragödie und Komödie*, pp. 39–40.

17. Gerhard Fricke ("Bemerkungen," pp. 96–120) sees no hint of love's tragic power in the play, but views it rather as a vehicle in which Sara can reveal "virtue" ("love of the Good") ever more purely and completely. See esp. pp. 107–8.

18. Steven Brown, a relative of the author, suggests that Lessing ironically points up this parallel, despite the variant spelling, by endowing Sara with the surname Sampson. A less poetic explanation finds a source for the name in Congreve's Sir Sampson Legend (*Love for Love*). See Oehlke, *Lessing*, I, 292. Cf. also Richard Gerber, "Vom Geheimnis der Namen: Eine onomastische Studie über Lessings dramatisches Werk," *Neue Rundschau*, LXXVI (1965), 573–86, esp. p. 574.

19. Cf. von Wiese, *Lessing*, p. 49, who would limit this last analysis to Mellefont.

20. Emil Staiger, "Rasende Weiber in der deutschen Tragödie des achtzehnten Jahrhunderts; Ein Beitrag zum Problem des Stilwandels," *ZDP*, LXXX (1961), 364–404, esp. 382–83.

21. Cf. Brüggemann, "Lessings Bürgerdramen," p. 78.

22. See below, p. 59.

Chapter Four

1. See his letter from Berlin to his father, May 30, 1749; Rilla, IX, 22.

2. Rilla, I, 185.

3. Rilla, I, 201–12.

4. Rilla, I, 194. Cf. Johannes Schneider, *Lessings Stellung zur Theologie* . . . diss. Amsterdam, 1953 ('s-Gravenhage, n. d.), p. 59.

5. Lessing's approach has been compared to that of Giordano Bruno, but modern critics tend to find the mode of presentation and much of the content to be reminiscent of Leibniz, albeit a modified Leibniz. See Allison, *Lessing and the Enlightenment*, pp. 58–62, 179, n. 34, and Johannes Schneider, *Lessings Stellung* . . . , pp. 112–13.

6. Cf. Hans Leisegang, *Lessings Weltanschauung* (Leipzig, 1931), p. 63.

7. Oehlke, *Lessing*, I, 357; Garland, *Lessing*, p. 168. Johannes Schneider would distinguish, however, between Lessing's view and the Pantheism of a Spinoza (*Lessings Stelling* . . . , p. 113); a comparable distinction by Leisegang, *op. cit.*, p. 64, and Allison, *op. cit.*, pp. 59, 62–63.

8. Johannes Schneider, *Lessings Stellung* . . . , p. 115; a similar explanation by Christoph Schrempf, *Lessing als Philosoph*, 2nd ed. (Stuttgart, 1921), p. 33; cf. Allison, *op. cit.*, p. 61. Leisegang suggests a possible continuation in terms of Lessing's threefold classification of men (at the close of the fragment) in terms of their varying "perfections," their varying degrees of rational awareness of them, and

their differing ability to act in reponse to this awareness (*Lessings Weltanschauung,* pp. 104–107).

9. Leisegang, *Lessings Weltanschauung,* pp. 60–61.
10. Rilla, VII, 201–28. Cf. Kuno Fischer, *G. E. Lessing als Reformator der deutschen Literatur,* II, 5th ed. (Stuttgart/Berlin, 1905), pp. 43–46.
11. LM, V, 365–66.
12. *Schrifften,* II (1753); Rilla, III, 389–417.
13. Rilla, VII, 280–81.
14. Rilla, VII, 282–309. ·

Chapter Five

1. Rilla, III, 707, 734.
2. Rilla, VII, 273–79; the letters: Rilla, IX, 152, 162–163, 171. Lessing's jotted "Remarks on Burke" reveal a special interest in the psychological approach to esthetics.
3. Rilla, III, 699–705. Lessing's simile reminds one of Dryden's *Essay of Dramatick Poesie* (1668), where the beauties of French drama are equated with "the beauties of a statue, but not of a man, because not animated with the soul of poesie, which is imitation of humor and passions. . . ." Cf. Fred O. Nolte, "Lessing and the Bourgeois Drama," *JEGP,* XXXI (1932), 66–83; see esp. p. 68, n. 10. Lessing's translation of Dryden was not published until 1758, but he had mentioned him in the *Beiträge* (1749), and in December, 1756, he asked Mendelssohn for Cibber on Dryden.
4. See Robert Petsch, ed. *Lessings Briefwechsel mit Mendelssohn und Nicolai über das Trauerspiel,* Philosophische Bibliothek, No. 121 (Leipzig, 1910).
5. November, 1756; Rilla, IX, 75, 78. See Peter Michelsen, "Die Erregung des Mitleids durch die Tragödie . . ." *DVLG,* XL (1966), 548–566.
6. Rilla, IX, 79, 93–94.
7. Otto Mann, *Geschichte,* p. 165; cf. the same author's "*Miss Sara Sampson,*" in *Lessing: Sein und Leistung,* 2nd ed. (Hamburg, 1961), pp. 222–40, esp. p. 237.
8. Fred O. Nolte, "Lessing's Correspondence with Mendelssohn and Nicolai . . . ," *Harvard Studies and Notes in Philology and Literature,* XIII (1931), 309–32; see pp. 326–27.
9. February 2, 1757; Rilla, IX, 104–108.
10. See Folke Leander, *Lessing als ästhetischer Denker,* (Göteborg, 1942), p. 33. Paul Böckmann, "Lessings Begründung der klassischen Symbolform," *Zeitschrift für Deutschkunde,* L (1936), 413–28, traces this principle from its orgin through the seventeenth "Literaturbrief" and *Laokoon* to the *Hamburgische Dramaturgie.*

11. E. Schmidt, *Lessing*, I, 330–31. Paul P. Kies finds a principal source for the play in Nathaniel Lee's *Lucius Junius Brutus* (1681); see "Lessing and Lee," *JEGP*, XXVIII (1929), 402–409.

12. Carl Enders, "Der geistesgeschichtliche Standort von Lessings 'Horoskop,'" *Euphorion*, L (1956), 208–16, esp. 214–16, emphasizes the similarities in form and tone to *Nathan*. Cf. also the discussion of *Faust*, below, p. 71. The resemblance to subsequent "fate tragedies" is developed by Theodor Seelgen, *Lessings jambische Dramenfragmente* (Berlin, 1930), pp. 47–49.

13. Rilla, IX, 182, 185. Commentators nonetheless frequently view the work as a glorification of patriotism and love of fatherland. For a recent opinion survey, see H. H. J. de Leeuwe, "Lessings *Philotas*," *Neophilologus*, XXXXVII (1963), 34–40. Bernhard Ulmer's interesting study emphasizes the artistic maturity of *Philotas*, recognizes the tragic irony of the dénouement, but overemphasizes perhaps the heroic element. See "Another Look at Lessing's *Philotas*," in *Studies in Germanic Languages and Literatures* (St. Louis, 1963), pp. 35–42.

14. Rilla, IX, 61–62.

15. Cf. Robert Petsch, ed., *Lessings Faustdichtung*, Germanische Bibliothek, 2 Abt., IV (Heidelberg, 1911), pp. 13, 44–45.

16. Karl S. Guthke, "Problem und Problematik von Lessings Faust-Dichtung," *ZDP*, LXXIX (1960), 141–49. A similar warning reappears much later in Lessing's *Erziehung des Menschengeschlechts*.

17. Cf. Price, *English Literature in Germany*, p. 227; F. Andrew Brown, "Shakespeare in Germany: Dryden, Langbaine, and the *Acta Eruditorum*," *GR*, XL (1965), 87–95, and Brown, "Shakespeare and English Drama in German Popular Journals, 1717–1759," *KFLQ*, XII (1965), 113–27.

18. Robert Petsch, *Lessings Faustdichtung*, pp. 51–56, reproduces in part a contemporary criticism entitled *Briefe, die Einführung des englischen Geschmacks in Schauspielen betreffend* . . . (Frankfurt/Leipzig, 1760), perhaps by Mrs. Gottsched, which neatly establishes this point. For a sympathetic analysis, see Robert R. Heitner, "A Gottschedian Reply to Lessing's Seventeenth *Literaturbrief*," in *Studies in Germanic Languages and Literatures* . . . (St. Louis, 1963), pp. 43–58. On the other hand, Vail (*Lessing's Relation*, pp. 158–59) finds in the choice of the Faust theme and in the complexities of this excerpt a fulfillment of the requirements set forth in Lessing's letter.

19. Danzel-Guhrauer, *Lessing*, I, 438–439, 443; E. Schmidt, *Lessing*, I, 358–59.

20. Danzel-Guhrauer, *Lessing*, I, 387.

21. October 21, 1757; Rilla, IX, 148–49.

22. Cf. B. Rosenthal, *Der Geniebegriff des Aufklärungszeitalters* . . . (Berlin, 1933), pp. 165–66, 158.

23. Rilla, III, 713–18.

24. Rilla, IV, 45.

25. For a fruitful critique of Lessing's fable theory, and the relations (and contradictions) between theory and practice, see Karl August Ott, "Lessing und La Fontaine: Von dem Gebrauche der Tiere in der Fabel," *GRM*, XL (1959), 235–66.

26. Rilla, III, 719, 370 ff.; "Literaturbrief" No. 103; Rilla, IV, 372.

27. See Julius Petersen in *Lessings Werke*, eds. Julius Petersen and Waldemar von Olshausen (Berlin/Leipzig, etc., n. d.), XI, 11–12; and Robert R. Heitner, "Concerning Lessing's Indebtedness to Diderot," *MLN*, LXV (1950), 82–88; cf. Th. C. van Stockum, "Lessing und Diderot," *Neophilologus*, XXXIX (1955), 191–202. It is known that Diderot, in turn, admired *Miss Sara* and once planned to bring out a volume of translations that would have included this play. See Robert R. Heitner, "Diderot's Own *Miss Sara Sampson*," *CL*, V (1953), 40–49. For details of the translators who supplied Diderot with a French version of *Miss Sara*, see Edmund Heier, *L. H. Nicolay (1737–1820) and his Contemporaries*, Archives Internationales d'Histoire des Idées, IX (The Hague, 1965), esp. pp. 21–23.

Chapter Six

1. Letter of December 6, 1760; Rilla, IX, 206.

2. E. M. Butler, *The Tyranny of Greece over Germany* . . . (Cambridge, Eng., 1935), pp. 56–57, and note, p. 57. I follow in general the divisions suggested by Butler. An informative "Introduction" is found in Dorothy Reich, ed. *G. E. Lessing: Laokoon*, Clarendon German Series (London, 1965).

3. See H. A. Korff, "*Laokoon*—kurz und bündig," *Wissenschlaftliche Zeitschrift der Karl-Marx-Univ. Leipzig*, IV (1954–55); *Gesellschafts- und sprachwissenschaftliche Reihe*, Heft 1/2, pp. 125–27. For other suggested predecessors, see Hugo Blümner, ed. *Lessings "Laokoon,"* 2nd ed. (Berlin, 1880), "Einleitung," esp. pp. 39–50, 57–58, 61–67; William Guild Howard, ed. *Laokoon: Lessing, Herder, Goethe* (New York, 1910), "Introduction," esp. pp. i-xcviii; Rudolf Dikenmann, "Beiträge zum Thema Diderot und Lessing" (diss. Zurich, 1915); Butler, *op. cit.*, p. 58.

4. Rilla, V, 9–12. For an analysis of the similarities and differences between the approaches to art of Lessing and his principal chosen opponent, see Walther Rehm, "Winckelmann und Lessing," in *Götterstille und Göttertrauer; Aufsätze zur Deutsch-Antiken Begegnung* (Berne, 1951), pp. 183–201.

5. Chapters XI–XVI; Rilla, V, 93–123.

6. *Iliad* I.44–52. Reprinted from *The Iliad of Homer*, trans. Richmond Lattimore, by permission of the University of Chicago Press

(Chicago, 1951). Cf. Edward Allen McCormick, trans. *Laocoön,* (Indianapolis/New York, 1962), p. 206.

7. Butler, p. 65.

8. *Iliad* IV.116–118, 122–126; reprinted from *The Iliad of Homer,* trans. Richmond Lattimore, by permission of the University of Chicago Press (Chicago, 1951). Cf. McCormick, *op. cit.,* pp. 209–10.

9. E. Schmidt, *Lessing,* I, 490.

10. Henry Caraway Hatfield, *Winckelmann and his German Critics, 1755–1781* . . . (New York, 1943), pp. 52–53; Elida Maria Szarota, *Lessings "Laokoon"* . . . (Weimar, 1959), "Einleitung," pp. 10–12.

11. Cf. Butler, p. 47; Margarete Bieber, *Laocoon: The Influence of the Group since its Rediscovery* (New York, 1942), p. 19, explains that to seventeenth- and eighteenth-century observers, surrounded by highly exaggerated examples of baroque art, the group might have appeared tranquil by comparison.

12. Goethe, *Dichtung und Wahrheit,* II, VIII, in *Goethes Werke,* Hamburger Ausgabe, 14 vols., eds. Erich Trunz et al. (Hamburg, 1949–62), IX, 316.

13. Butler, p. 69; Korff, *"Laokoon,"* p. 127.

14. E. Schmidt, *Lessing,* I, 522; W. Kinkel, Lessings Lehre vom fruchtbaren Moment, historisch und systematisch betrachtet," *Archiv für Philosophie und Soziologie,* II. Abt.: *Archiv für systematische Philosophie und Soziologie,* N. F., XXXIII (1929), 259–280; see esp. p. 265. Cf. also Charlotte Ephraim, *Wandel des Griechenbildes im achtzehnten Jahrhundert* (*Winckelmann, Lessing, Herder*), Sprache und Dichtung, No. 61 (Berne/Leipzig, 1936), esp. pp. 138–39, 148. For a discussion of Lessing's altered intentions, see V. A. Rudowski, "Action as the Essence of Poetry: A Revaluation of Lessing's Argument," *PMLA,* LXXXII (1967), 333–41.

15. Korff, *"Laokoon,"* p. 127; E. H. Gombrich, "Lessing. A Lecture on a Master Mind," *Proceedings of the British Academy,* XLIII (1957) 133–56, esp. pp. 142–45.

16. *Ibid.,* pp. 144–45.

Chapter Seven

1. Letter of August 20, 1764; Rilla, IX, 237–38.

2. *Goethes Werke,* ed. cit., IX, 281 (= *Dichtung und Wahrheit,* II, VII).

3. Günter Wicke, *Die Struktur* . . . , p. 109.

4. Letter to Nicolai, May 25, 1777; Rilla, IX, 748.

5. Cf. Goethe in *Dichtung und Wahrheit* (*Goethes Werke,* ed. cit., IX, 281–82).

6. See Gerhard Fricke, "Lessings *Minna von Barnhelm,*" in: *Studien und Interpretationen* (Frankfurt/M., 1956), p. 29.

7. Ilse Appelbaum Graham, "The Currency of Love: A Reading of Lessing's *Minna von Barnhelm*," *GLL*, XVIII (1965), 270–78, see p. 271.

8. *Ibid.*, p. 272.

9. Brüggemann, "Lessings Bürgerdramen," pp. 82–83.

10. Raimund Belgardt, "Tellheim's Honor: Flaw or Virtue? A Reinterpretation," *GR*. XLII (1967), 16–29, esp. p. 29.

11. Garland, *Lessing*, pp. 129–30.

12. Wolfgang F. Michael, "Tellheim eine Lustspielfigur," *DVLG*, XXXIX (1965), 207–12, esp. pp. 211–12.

13. Emil Staiger, "*Minna von Barnhelm*," in *Die Kunst der Interpretation*, 2nd ed. (Zurich, 1957), pp. 88–89. Raimund Belgardt suggests that Minna's failure to convince Tellheim of the benevolence of Providence indicates that Lessing would reduce to absurdity this favorite Enlightenment tenet. See "Minna von Barnhelm als komischer Charakter," *Monatshefte*, LVIII (1966), 209–16. But if the Enlightenment's philosophy proves absurd on Minna's lips, so do the arguments of Tellheim when she turns them against him. See above, p. 96, and below, p. 100.

14. Karl Holl, *Geschichte*, p. 182.

15. Georg Lukács views the play in comparable terms as the depiction of the basic dilemma arising when general moral laws conflict with one another. Here Tellheim exemplifies the dilemma in attempting to maintain a "Stoical" attitude which leads to "inhuman" action. See "*Minna von Barnhelm*," *Akzente*, XI (1964), 176–91; esp. 179, 184, 188. Cf. also Emil Staiger's view, expressed in fundamentally theological terms, below, n. 21.

16. The presence of completely integrated elements of comedy and tragedy, arising from the same source, are said to qualify *Minna von Barnhelm* as a tragicomedy—a classification which makes it possible to account logically for the intermingled comic and serious elements, long a puzzle to commentators. See Karl S. Guthke, *Geschichte und Poetik der deutschen Tragikomödie* (Göttingen, 1961), pp. 32–43, esp. pp. 35, 37–39.

17. Price, *English Literature in Germany*, p. 91.

18. See esp. Guthke, *op. cit.*, p. 38; Otto Mann, "*Minna von Barnhelm*," in *Das deutsche Drama*, ed. Benno von Wiese (Düsseldorf, n. d.), I, 91; Horst Steinmetz, *Die Komödie der Aufklärung*, p. 67; Belgardt, "Tellheim's Honor," p. 21.

19. Steinmetz, *Die Komödie*, pp. 67–68.

20. Lessing to his brother Karl, February 10, 1772 (Rilla, IX, 498–99). Karl had objected that in the earlier acts of the play Emilia Galotti appeared only "pious and obedient." Despite Lessing's announced distate for philosophical heroines, the remainder of his reply

makes it clear that he did not share his brother's view that Emilia is devoid of spirit. Lessing, of course, knew how the play ended, while his brother, at that time, did not.

21. Emil Staiger draws a parallel between the King's noble gesture in putting aside the obstacles and misunderstandings created by venal officials, and the majesty of God in whom all human evils and confusions are resolved. (*Die Kunst der Interpretation*, pp. 90–91.)

Chapter Eight

1. Heinrich Schneider, "Leben und Werk," in Karl S. Guthke and Heinrich Schneider, *Gotthold Ephraim Lessing* (Stuttgart, 1967), pp. 38–39.

2. An exhaustive study of Lessing's relation to other critics may be found in J. G. Robertson, *Lessing's Dramatic Theory . . .*, ed. Edna Purdie (Cambridge, Eng., 1939).

3. See Eugen Lerch, "Lessing, Goethe, Schiller und die französische Klassik," *Mainzer Universitäts-Reden*, Heft 11/12 (Mainz, 1948), pp. 1–34, esp. pp. 20–22.

4. For a historical sketch and an analysis of the chief interpretations, see Otto Mann, ed. *G. E. Lessings "Hamburgische Dramaturgie,"* 2nd ed. (Stuttgart, 1963), pp. 460–63.

5. Oskar Walzel, "Lessings Begriff des Tragischen," in *Vom Geistesleben alter und neuer Zeit* (Leipzig, 1922), pp. 232–61, esp. pp. 256–57, 259–60; cf. E. L. Stahl, ed. *Lessing: "Emilia Galotti"* (Oxford, 1958), "Introduction," p. xv.

6. Max Kommerell, *Lessing und Aristoteles: Untersuchung über die Theorie der Tragödie*, 3rd ed. (Frankfurt/M., 1960), pp. 93–94, 106–107. But cf. also Wolf-Hartmut Friedrich, "Sophokles, Aristoteles und Lessing," *Euphorion*, LVII (1963), 4–27; for catharsis see esp. pp. 20–22. See the fruitful analysis of contending views by Hans Mayer, "Lessing und Aristoteles," in *Festschrift für Bernhard Blume . . .*, eds. Egon Schwarz et al. (Göttingen: Vandenhoeck and Ruprecht, 1967), pp. 61–75.

7. Hugo Friedrich, "Lessings Kritik und Missverständnis der französischen Klassik," *Zeitschrift für deutsche Bildung*, VII (1931), 601–11, esp. 601–603, 611.

8. Eugen Lerch, "Lessing, Goethe, Schiller," pp. 14–15, 18.

9. Cf. Folke Leander, *Lessing*, pp. 34–35.

10. Cf. Hugo Friedrich, "Lessings Kritik," pp. 602–603. The likelihood of such a critical sense in the creative genius is sometimes questioned.

11. *Ibid.*, p. 601. For a differing view, see Robert R. Heitner, "The Effect of the *Hamburgische Dramaturgie*," *GR*, XXXI (1956), 23–34.

12. See Garland, *Lessing*, pp. 69–71; Eugen Lerch, "Lessing, Goethe, Schiller," p. 33.

13. Preface to *Schrifften* III and IV (1754); Rilla, III, 675. Cf. also Lessing's warning in the final number, below, p. 113.

14. Price, *English Literature in Germany*, pp. 231–34.

15. Cf. Heitner, "Lessing's Indebtedness," p. 84. Further criticism of Diderot appears in Nos. 86–88.

16. Dated April 19, 1768, but written, as he said, "almost a year later," Nos. 101–104; Rilla, VI, 503–19, 515.

Chapter Nine

1. On Lessing in Hamburg, see Heinrich Schneider, "Leben und Werk," in Guthke-Schneider, *Lessing*, p. 40. For Lessing on problems of copyright and publishing, see the fragmentary proposals under the title, *Leben und leben lassen* (*Live and Let Live*)—Rilla, VI, 537–43. Lessing's waning interest in the theater may well account for his failure to complete a number of projected plays, including *Der Schlaftrunk* (*The Sleeping Potion*)—an attempted demonstration of his old contention that the same material could be employed in a comedy or a tragedy—*Die Matrone von Ephesus*—his fragmentary attempt to motivate in modern terms and, as he said, to soften the biting satire on the subject of marital fidelity in this ancient comedy—or his anti-tyrannical fragment of a *Spartacus* play. Cf. Rilla, II, 569–72, IX, 398. On the first play, see Konrad Zwierzina, " 'Der Schlaftrunk' von Lessing," in *Festschrift für Bernhard Seuffert* (Leipzig/Vienna, 1923 [*Euphorion*, Ergänzungsheft No. 16, pp. 63–72]); on *Matrone*, see Th. C. van Stockum, "Lessings Dramenentwurf 'Die Matrone von Ephesus,' " *Neophilologus*, XXXXVI (1962), 125–34.

2. Letter to Nicolai, January 21, 1758; Rilla, IX, 157.

3. Letter of February 10, 1772; Rilla, IX, 497–98.

4. For a detailed discussion of Lessing-Schiller parallels, particularly stylistic similarities, see Edward Dvoretzky, "Lessing in Schiller's *Kabale und Liebe*," *MP*, LXIII (May, 1966), 311–18. Paul Rilla's politically oriented commentary (Emilia a "sacrifice" to courtly vice and oppression) may be regarded as a model for many contemporary East German critics; Rilla, II, 574, X, 273–80.

5. See Brüggemann, "Lessings Bürgerdramen," pp. 96–106; Elise Dosenheimer finds Lessing anticipating Hebbel's theory that milieu may appear as the alternate for ancient fate, in *Das deutsche soziale Drama von Lessing bis Sternheim* (Konstanz, 1949), pp. 23–31, esp. pp. 24, 27.

6. Wolfgang Martini, "Die grosse Episode in Lessings dramatischer Technik," *Neue Jahrbücher für das klassische Altertum, Geschichte,*

und deutsche Literatur und für Pädagogik, XLV (1920), 341–55; on Orsina, see pp. 346–47.

7. Staiger, "Rasende Weiber," pp. 382–83, 393–95.

8. Robert R. Heitner, *"Emilia Galotti*: An Indictment of Bourgeois Passivity," *JEGP*, LII (1953), 480–90; the quotations are at pp. 488–89.

9. See Rilla, IX, 489, 497–500; E. L. Stahl's essay, *"Emilia Galotti,"* in *Das deutsche Drama*, ed. Benno von Wiese, (Düsseldorf, n. d.), I, 101–12, and the same author's edition of *Emilia Galotti* (Oxford, 1958), "Introduction," pp. xii–xiii, xix, xxxii. For an opposing view, see Hermann Hettner, *Geschichte der deutschen Literatur im 18. Jahrhundert*, ed. Georg Witkowski (Leipzig, 1929), II, 318–20. Edward Dvoretzky has surveyed the reactions to the play expressed by German, Swiss, and Austrian writers of the eighteenth and nine-teenth centuries in *The Enigma of "Emilia Galotti"* (The Hague, 1963). See also his study of "Modern German Writers' Views of Lessing's *Emilia Galotti*," *The South Central Bulletin*, XXIII, 4 (1963), 51–59.

10. E. L. Stahl, ed. *Emilia Galotti*, "Introduction," p. xviii.

11. Max Kommerell, *Lessing und Aristoteles*, 2nd ed. (Frankfurt/ M., 1947), pp. 128–29, cited by Stahl in his *"Emilia Galotti," Das deutsche Drama*, p. 108.

12. Hermann J. Weigand, "Warum stirbt Emilia Galotti?" *JEGP*, XXVIII (1929), 467–81.

13. Harry Steinhauer, "The Guilt of Emilia Galotti," *JEGP*, XLVIII (1949), 175–85, esp. pp. 173, 177, 184. A similar explanation by Hugo Göring, ed. *Lessings sämtliche Werke* (Stuttgart, n. d.), IV, 10, "Einleitung."

14. Steinhauer, *op. cit.*, p. 184. Cf. F. W. Kaufmann, "Zu Lessings *Emilia Galotti*," *Monatshefte*, XXVII (1935), 50–53, who describes a similar character development from heteronomy (respect for authority) to autonomy (independent recognition of her duty to act in accord with reason and virtue). He invites comparison with the three-stage progression described in Lessing's *Christentum der Vernunft* (see above p. 61, and Chapter Four, n. 8).

15. Long ago Max Winkler objected in these terms to Düntzer's similar postulation of an Emilia overawed by the Prince. See Winkler's edition of *Emilia Galotti* (Boston, 1895), "Introduction," p. xxiii, and Heinrich Düntzer, *Erläuterungen zu den deutschen Klassikern*, 6. Abt.: *Erläuterungen zu Lessings Werken*, IV, *Emilia Galotti* (Leipzig, 1873), pp. 68–69.

16. Henry Hatfield, "Emilia's Guilt Once More," *MLN*, LXXI (1956), 287–96.

17. Heinrich Schneider, "Emilia Galotti's Tragic Guilt," *MLN*,

LXXI (1956), 353–55. Schneider invites comparison to Günther Müller, *Geschichte der deutschen Seele* (Freiburg, 1939), pp. 269–70.

18. F. J. Lamport, "'Eine bürgerliche Virginia,'" *GLL* XVII (1964), 304–12; quoting Dilthey, *Das Erlebnis und die Dichtung*, 1907 ed., p. 66. See esp. Lamport, pp. 309, 310, 311. R. K. Angress makes an interesting and expanded application of the theme of failure. In the play, the younger generation vainly looks for a source of viable leadership. The dénouement suggests "that behind the failure of men is God's own failure to guide their affairs." See "The Generations in *Emilia Galotti*," *GR*, XLIII (1968), 15–23. But in the presence of such a thorough failure, it is difficult to grant Angress' contention that Emilia is the counterpart of Philotas, "a child who dies to prove himself worthy of his father."

19. Vail, *Lessing's Relation . . .* , pp. 186–87, finds that the frequently criticized "aphoristic" quality of the dialogue, that "almost approaches wit," even in highly tragic scenes, is derived from Lessing's preoccupation with "English criticism and tragedy."

20. Otto Mann, *Lessing: Sein und Leistung*, 2nd ed. (Hamburg, 1961), p. 266, notes this element but finds Emilia's tragic flaw rather in her great beauty, as the Greeks in the instance of Helen, or Hebbel in *Agnes Bernauer*.

21. Benno von Wiese sees in Emilia's final attitude that of the martyr, whose death is an avoidance of the essentially tragic. It is rather Odoardo who embodies the tragic conflict of an individual opposed to a fallible world order. See *Die deutsche Tragödie von Lessing bis Hebbel*, 3rd ed. (Hamburg, 1955), p. 41. It might be argued that Emilia generates the necessary tragic pity and fear on the temporal level, while Odoardo provides the required "silhouette" of the universe. Cf. Guthke, *Lessing-Forschung*, pp. 50–51, 53, for whom the tragic conflict lies in the religious plane of an Odoardo whose religious principles prevent his killing the Prince, but whose "ethical autonomy" dictates the murder of his child. For an interesting examination of the fateful quality of time, with extended applications not attempted above, see Ilse Appelbaum Graham, "Minds Without Medium: Reflections on *Emilia Galotti* and *Werthers Leiden*," *Euphorion*, LVI (1962), 3–24, and the discussion by Edward Dvoretzky, "Goethe's *Werther* and Lessing's *Emilia Galotti*," *GLL*, XVI (1962), 23–26, who finds the play symbolizing winter and death and suggesting to Werther a solution to the problem of passion.

22. Fred O. Nolte, "Lessing's *Emilia Galotti* in the Light of his *Hamburgische Dramaturgie*," *Harvard Studies and Notes in Philology and Literature*, XIX (1937), 175–97, esp. pp. 193, 195. Nolte finds no direct relation between the play and the critical principles of the *Dramaturgie*, which Lessing would invoke only for the greatest tragic

dramatists, like Shakespeare or Sophocles, not for the work of lesser mortals. But Vail (*Lessing's Relation* . . . , p. 187) points out that Lessing's contemporaries agreed that *Emilia Galotti* satisfied the demands of the *Dramaturgie* "in that it united Greek simplicity with the Shakespearean spirit." Yet Vail rejects as inane the suggestion of Lessing's contemporary Eschenburg that Emilia's search for a "Haarnadel" stems from Hamlet's reference to the bodkin.

Chapter Ten

1. Rilla, V, 623.
2. Rilla, V, 674.
3. Rilla, V, 677, 723.
4. *Goethes Werke*, ed. cit., IX, 317 (= *Dichtung und Wahrheit*, II, viii). Cf. Oehlke, *Lessing*, II, 94; Garland, *Lessing*, pp. 89–90. Hatfield sees here a thinly veiled criticism of the then-current superstitious view of death as an evil—a position which Lessing characterized as "misunderstood religion." See *Aesthetic Paganism in German Literature* . . . (Cambridge, 1964), pp. 27–28.
5. See the "Beiträge zu einem deutschen Glossarium" and the "Grammatisch-Kritische Anmerkungen über einige Dichter" (Rilla, VII, 141–80); for Scultetus: LM, XI, 165–73; *Zerstreute Anmerkungen über das Epigramm* . . . (1771); Rilla, VII, 7–140. See Eric A. Blackall's informative discussion of Lessing's own language and style in *The Emergence of German as a Literary Language, 1700–1775* (Cambridge, Eng., 1959), pp. 351–71. Lessing's emphasis on clarity and the resultant beauty is stressed: "Clear conciseness is Lessing's sovereign stylistic ideal. It is also his sole stylistic ideal" (p. 362). His own language is "both rhetorical and vivid"; his style "dramatic, verbal [and] dynamic" (p. 371).
6. LM, XII, 159–97.
7. LM, XI, 380–94; the quotation from p. 393.
8. See Heinrich Schneider, *Lessing und Wolfenbüttel* (Wolfenbüttel, 1924), pp. 17–22, and the same author's essay, "Lessings bibliothekarische Arbeit," in *Lessing: Zwölf biographische Studien* (Berne, 1951), pp. 74–93.
9. LM, XV, 125–423.
10. Rilla, VII, 310–477.
11. Garland, *Lessing*, p. 155; letter of October 25, 1770; Rilla, IX, 382–83.
12. The positive portion, attempting to establish a "natural" religion based exclusively on rational grounds, had been published in Reimarus' lifetime under the title *Abhandlung von den vornehmsten Wahrheiten der natürlichen Religion* (*Treatise on the Principal Truths of Natural Religion*, 1754).

13. Rilla, VII, 670–71; Lessing's emphases.

14. Rilla, VII, 813.

15. Rilla, VII, 818–19.

16. Rilla, VIII, 12. Lessing's emphasis. In a posthumously published essay, *Neue Hypothese über die Evangelisten als bloss menschliche Geschichtsschreiber betrachtet* (*A New Hypothesis on the Evangelists Regarded as Merely Human Historians*), Lessing on the basis of a historically oriented philological examination of the four Gospels, works out a theory, since rejected by Biblical scholars, that they were all based on a lost common Gospel. Cf. Garland, *Lessing*, p. 159; Andrew Brown, "John Locke and the Religious Aufklärung," *Review of Religion*, XIII (1949), 126–54, see esp. pp. 143–50, on the Neologians. (Portions of this article have been used by kind permission of Columbia Univ. Press; see Chapter 11, n. 2; 4; 7.)

17. Rilla, VIII, 14–15.

18. Rilla, VIII, 16, 19–20.

19. Rilla, VIII, 27.

20. Rilla, VIII, 25; Lessing's emphasis.

21. Rilla, VIII, 195.

22. Rilla, VIII, 256.

23. Rilla, VIII, 407–408.

24. Rilla, VIII, 418. Lessing adds that Goeze is wrong in saying that all Christian sects accept the Bible as the sole basis for the Christian religion. The Catholics, for example, do not. And to Elise Reimarus he wrote that what he "understood" by the Christian religion was not necessarily synonymous with what he "believed" of it. Rilla, IX, 795–96.

Chapter Eleven

1. Rilla, VIII, 590–615.

2. Cf. Brown, "John Locke," pp. 129–30.

3. See Martha Waller, *Lessings "Erziehung des Menschengeschlechts,"*. . . Germanische Studien, No. 160 (Berlin, 1935), pp. 17 ff, cf. below, p. 144–45.

4. *Ibid.*, pp. 35–37, 93; cf. Brown, "John Locke," pp. 129, 131–32.

5. These are dealt with by Heinrich Schneider in "Lessings letzte Prosaschrift," *Lessing: Zwölf biographische Studien* (Berne, 1951), pp. 222–230.

6. Helmut Thielicke, *Offenbarung, Vernunft und Existenz: Studien zur Religionsphilosophie Lessings*, 4th ed. (Gütersloh, 1957), esp. pp. 63–68, 134–35. Allison, *Lessing and the Enlightenment*, pp. 158–59, would resolve the dilemma in Platonic-Leibnizian terms, equating § 4 with the "logical structure" of the truths in question and § 77 with the "psychological conditions for their apprehension."

7. Cf. Arthur von Arx, *Lessing und die geschichtliche Welt* (Frauenfeld/Leipzig, 1944), pp. 125–39, esp. pp. 131–32; Brown, "John Locke," pp. 151–54.

8. Cf. Allison, *op. cit.*, p. 60.

9. M. Waller, *Lessings "Erziehung . . . ,"* p. 193.

10. Lessing refers approvingly to "certain mystics of the thirteenth and fourteenth century" (§§ 87–90). Both Thielicke (pp. 135–36) and Johannes Schneider (p. 231) warn against the inclination to find ultimate "answers" in Lessing's theological speculation. Martha Waller devotes Part Three of her book (pp. 166–87) to distinguishing the extent and limits of the irrationalistic element in the work.

11. Rilla, VII, 524, 533–34. In another essay, *Leibniz von den ewigen Strafen* (*Leibniz on Eternal Punishment*) in the *Beiträge*, 1773, Lessing again urges retention of a tenet easier to defend, he said, than to refute (Rilla, VII, 479–83).

12. Rilla, IX, 596–98.

13. Cf. Rilla, VII, 870; Heinrich Kofink, *Lessings Anschauungen über die Unsterblichkeit und Seelenwanderung* (Strassburg, 1912), pp. 87–106.

14. Rilla, VII, 579.

15. Rilla, VII, 567; Lessing's emphasis. In Wolfenbüttel Lessing had known and admired the young Jerusalem, whose subsequent suicide triggered the composition of Goethe's early novel *Die Leiden des jungen Werthers* (1774). Lessing wished to offset the impression that his young friend had been, in fact, the sort of "enthusiast" represented by Goethe's central character, and once sketched the first scene of a play, *Werther der Bessere* (*The Better Werther*), intending to satirize Goethe's theme.

16. Rilla, VIII, 619.

17. Rilla, VII, 305–308; cf. Johannes Schneider, *Lessings Stellung . . . ,* pp. 146–47.

18. Th. C. van Stockum, in his "Spinoza-Jacobi-Lessing . . ." (diss. Groningen, 1916), discusses many Lessing-Spinoza parallels, but concludes (see esp. p. 99) that Lessing was no thorough-going "Spinozist," and especially not in his interpretation of determinism. Cf. also Gottfried Fittbogen, *Die Religion Lessings* (Leipzig, 1923), pp. 231–40, and Julius Petersen, "Goethe und Lessing," *Euphorion*, XXX (1929), 175–88, esp. p. 183. M. Waller (*Lessings "Erziehung . . . ,"* pp. 192–93) sees the "interest" in Spinoza—not Spinozism—as a particularly close link between Lessing and the coming age of Idealism. In her view, the teachings of Spinoza, modified by the Leibnizian concepts of individuality and evolutionary development, provided both Lessing and his successors with a means of "liberation" from the anthropomorphism of the Deists. Hans Butzmann, "Lessings bürgerliches

Trauerspiel 'Tonsine'. . . ." *Jahrbuch des freien deutschen Hochstifts,* 1966, pp. 109–18, in treating the recently rediscovered sketch of this projected bourgeois tragedy, advances the theory that Lessing planned to portray the trials and fate of an enlightened Japanese heroine transported to Europe, and to demonstrate the exalted heights of ethical development and noble self-sacrifice attainable within the framework of her philosophical system—a form of Buddhism with strong parallels to the teachings of Spinoza.

19. Rilla, VIII, 533–39.

20. Henry Chadwick nonetheless finds Lessing's theological speculation to have exerted a "pervasive" influence on nineteenth- and twentieth-century religious thought. See *Lessing's Theological Writings,* trans. Henry Chadwick (Stanford, 1957), "Introduction," esp. pp. 48–49.

Chapter Twelve

1. Rilla, VIII, 547–89; Nos. 1–3 published in 1778; Nos. 4–5 in 1780, quite possibly without Lessing's consent; cf. Rilla, VIII, 647–48. For details see Heinrich Schneider, "Lessing und die Freimaurer," in: *Lessing,* pp. 166–97; on the publication of Nos. 4 and 5, see esp. p. 194.

2. Rilla, VIII, 549–50, 554, 556, 562–63.

3. Cf. Allison, *Lessing and the Enlightenment,* pp. 137–39.

4. Rilla, IX, 747, 749, II, 321, 575. See Peter Demetz, ed. *Nathan der Weise* (Frankfurt/M./Berlin, 1966): text, with useful documents, analysis, and bibliography.

5. Hans Rempel, *Tragödie und Komödie,* p. 105; Warren R. Maurer, "The Integration of the Ring Parable in Lessing's *Nathan der Weise,*" *Monatshefte,* LIV (1962), 49–57, esp. p. 50; Stuart Atkins, "The Parable of the Rings in Lessing's *Nathan der Weise,*" *GR,* XXVI (1951), 259–67. According to Atkins the dramatic action takes precedence, and the parable represents only "a function of the all-important family plot, which symbolizes the brotherhood of man. . . ." Richard M. Meyer has described the several ways in which the characters, themes, and action in *Nathan* have been elevated above the milieu reflected in *Die Juden.* See "Zwei Dramen Lessings," in *Aufsätze literarhistorischen und biographischen Inhalts,* I (Berlin, 1911), 146–63.

6. Cf. von Wiese, *Die deutsche Tragödie,* p. 43.

7. For a discussion of these and other "triadic" elements of composition, see F. W. Kaufmann, "Nathan's Crisis," *Monatshefte,* XLVIII (1956), 277–80; cf. Maurer, "Integration," pp. 50, 55.

8. Cf. H. Schneider, *Das Buch Lessing,* p. 238.

9. See Christoph E. Schweitzer, "Die Erziehung Nathans," *Monatshefte*, LIII (1961), 277–84. Horst S. Daemmrich criticizes Recha's acceptance of the Templar as brother and the latter's rapid shift from desire for marriage to acceptance of Recha as sister. See "The Incest Motif in Lessing's *Nathan der Weise* and Schiller's *Braut von Messina*," *GR*, XLII (1967), 184–96.

10. Rilla, II, 322–23; Lessing's emphases.

11. Garland, *Lessing*, p. 182.

12. Helen Adolf, "Wesen und Art des Rings: Lessings Parabel, nach mittelalterlichen Quellen gedeutet," *GQ*, XXXIV (1961), 228–34, esp. p. 230; and Heinz Politzer, "Lessings Parabel von den drei Ringen," *GQ*, XXXI (1958), 161–77.

13. E.g. II.vii; III.vii; Rilla, II, 380–81, 409–10.

14. II.v; Rilla, II, 375; soliloquy in III.viii; Rilla, II, 410–11.

15. F. W. Kaufmann, "Nathan's Crisis," pp. 278–79.

16. M. Waller, *Lessings "Erziehung . . . ,"* p. 192.

17. See Günter Rohrmoser, *"Nathan der Weise,"* in *Das deutsche Drama*, ed. Benno von Wiese (Düsseldorf, n. d.), I, 113–26.

18. For Meno Spann, the differences resolved in Lessing's drama in the realm of reason must appear irreconcilable to modern man, conditioned as he is by the teachings of Romanticism, and inclined to an essentially tragic view of life.

Harold Lenz would oppose to the thought categories of Romanticism the humanistic Idealism of Nathan; a faith in the existence of an absolute truth.

Fred L. Fehling could extract from the reviews of a New York production of *Nathan* in 1942 the assurance that the play still commands attention and elicits favorable, though not uncritical, comment on the continuing viability of its central message. See Meno Spann, "Der 'Nathan' im heutigen Literaturunterricht," *GQ*, XII, 3 (1939), 153–59; see also XIV, 4 (1941), 211–16; Harold Lenz, "Der Deutschlehrer und Lessings 'Nathan,'" *GQ*, XIV, 2 (1941),121–27; XIV, 3 (1941), 170–75; see also XIV, 4 (1941), 216–17; Fred L. Fehling, "Epilogue to 'Nathan,'" *GQ*, XVIII, 3 (1945), 149–53.

Chapter Thirteen

1. In relation to the summary, see esp. Christoph Schrempf, *Lessing als Philosoph*, pp. 190–91; Horst Stephan, "Lessing und die Gegenwart," *Zeitschrift für Theologie und Kirche*, N. F., X (1929), 401–34; Cassirer, *Die Philosophie der Aufklärung*, pp. 254–57; Otto Mann, "Lessing in der modernen Wissenschaft," *Der Deutschunterricht*, VIII (1956), 68–86.

Selected Bibliography

I. Lessing's Works

Schrifften, 6 vols. (Berlin: Voss, 1753–55). The first collected edition, selected and arranged, with prefaces, by Lessing himself.

Werke, 23 vols., eds. R. Boxberger et al. (Berlin: Hempel, 1868–79). The first edition containing scholarly commentary; still useful.

Sämtliche Werke, 20 vols., ed. Hugo Göring (Stuttgart: Cotta, n. d.). Contains explanatory introductions.

Sämtliche Schriften, 23 vols., ed. Karl Lachmann, 3rd ed., ed. Franz Muncker (Stuttgart/Leipzig: G. J. Göschen'sche Verlagsbuchhandlung, 1886–1924). The most complete scholarly standard edition; omits most of Lessing's translations; includes available correspondence to and from Lessing. (Photomechanical reprint, 1968.)

Werke. Vollständige Ausgabe in fünfundzwanzig Teilen, eds. Julius Petersen and Waldemar von Olshausen, etc. (Berlin/Leipzig, etc.: Bong [1925–35]). A scholarly edition, and a companion to Lachmann-Muncker; detailed introductions and annotations; includes some of Lessing's translations, but omits the correspondence.

Gesammelte Werke, 10 vols., ed. Paul Rilla (Berlin: Aufbau-Verlag, 1954–58). The most useful of the newer editions; contains succinct annotations and commentary and a detailed index of names. Rilla's long essay, "Lessing und sein Zeitalter" ("Lessing and his Era") resounds with strongly political overtones. (X, 11–450)

Werke, 3 vols., ed. Walter Hoyer (Leipzig: VEB Bibliographisches Institut, 1962). A useful selection, especially for students; much of Lessing's critical-theoretical writing arranged under subject headings; helpful introductions, annotation, and indices.

Werke, auf Grund der von Julius Petersen und Waldemar von Olshausen besorgten Ausgabe, 6 vols., ed. Fritz Fischer (Zurich/Frankfurt, etc.: Stauffacher-Verlag, 1965). Excerpts the Petersen-Olshausen edition.

Gesammelte Werke, 2 vols., ed. Otto Mann (Gütersloh: Siegbert Mohn, 1966). Vol. I (pp. 5–32) contains a useful introduction, surveying Lessing's accomplishments; no further annotation.

Werke, 3 vols., ed. Kurt Wölfel (Frankfurt/M.: Insel-Verlag, 1967). A selection containing introductory essays and explanatory notes by Karlmann Beyschlag and Bodo Lecke. (See also Kurt Wölfel,

189

Renate Klar, and Bodo Lecke, eds. *Lessings Leben und Werk in Daten und Bildern* [Frankfurt/M.: Insel-Verlag, 1967].)

English Translations

The Dramatic Works of G. E. Lessing, trans. from the German, 2 vols., ed. Ernest Bell. Bohn's Standard Library (London: G. Bell and Sons, 1895); I: Tragedies; II: Comedies.

The Education of the Human Race, trans. F. W. Robertson, in The Harvard Classics, ed. Charles W. Eliot: XXXII (New York: Collier, 1910), pp. 194–217.

Emilia Galotti. A Tragedy in Five Acts, trans. Edward Dvoretzky (New York: Ungar, 1962). Contains a brief, informative Introduction, sketching Lessing's accomplishments as critic, theologian, and dramatist. Notes that public attention reverts to *Emilia Galotti* "especially at times when the basic integrity of the political and social structure is threatened."

Hamburg Dramaturgy, trans. Helen Zimmern. With a new Introduction by Victor Lange (New York: Dover Publications, 1962).

Laocoön. An Essay on the Limits of Painting and Poetry, trans. Edward Allen McCormick. The Library of Liberal Arts, No. 78 (Indianapolis/New York: Bobbs-Merrill, 1962). Contains an introductory sketch of Lessing's career and explanatory notes.

Laocoön, Nathan the Wise, Minna von Barnhelm, trans. with an Introduction by William A. Steel, in Everyman's Library, No. 843 (London: Dent; New York: Dutton, 1930).

Lessing's Masonic Dialogues (Ernst und Falk), trans. with Introduction and annotations by A. Cohen (London: Baskerville Press, 1927).

Minna von Barnhelm; or The Soldier's Fortune, trans. Ernest Bell in The Harvard Classics, ed. Charles W. Eliot, XXVI (New York: Collier, 1908–10), pp. 287–366.

Nathan the Wise; a Dramatic Poem in Five Acts, trans. (into English verse) by Bayard Quincy Morgan (New York: Ungar, 1955).

Selected Prose Works of G. E. Lessing, trans. E. C. Beasley and Helen Zimmern, ed. Edward Bell, Bohn's Standard Library (London: G. Bell, 1879). [*Laocoön; How the Ancients Represented Death; Dramatic Notes.*]

Lessing's Theological Writings; Selections in Translation with an Introductory Essay by Henry Chadwick, A Library of Modern Religious Thought (Stanford: Stanford Univ. Press, 1957). Informative introduction, pp. 9–49; emphasizes ambiguities in Lessing's religious position; views indications of Lessing's belief in transcendent revelation exoterically; Lessing a "pervasive" influence in subsequent nineteenth- and twentieth-century religious thought.

II. SECONDARY SOURCES

(The significance of items unannotated below is discussed in the preceding text and notes.)

AIKIN-SNEATH, BETSY, *Comedy in Germany in the First Half of the Eighteenth Century*, Oxford Studies in Modern Languages and Literature, ed. H. G. Fiedler (Oxford: The Clarendon Press, 1936). No discussion of Lessing's plays. Outlines the triumph of popular comedy, which sought only to amuse, over the satirical drama, sponsored by a minority of reformers bent on moral uplift. Appendices on theory of comedy, translations of foreign comedies, and original German comedies.

ALLISON, HENRY E., *Lessing and the Enlightenment: His Philosophy of Religion and its Relation to Eighteenth-Century Thought* (Ann Arbor: Univ. of Michigan Press, 1966).

ANER, KARL, *Die Theologie der Lessingzeit* (Hildesheim: Georg Olms, 1964) = repr. of Halle ed., 1929. Lessing the founder of Rationalism; or, more precisely, the first rationalist, in a third stage of development, following Wolffianism and Neology.

ARX, ARTHUR VON, *Lessing und die geschichtliche Welt*, Wege zur Dichtung, ed. Emil Ermatinger, XLIII (Frauenfeld/Leipzig: Huber and Co., 1944). History for Lessing a qualitative development rooted in the nature of man, encompassing the attainment of ever-higher levels in the religious, ethical, political, and cultural realms.

BERGETHON, K. ROALD, "Republicanism (?) and Revolution in G. E. Lessing's *Samuel Henzi*," *Symposium*, I (1946), 60–72.

BIEBER, MARGARETE, *Laocoon: The Influence of the Group Since its Rediscovery* (New York: Columbia Univ. Press, 1942). Sketches various reactions to the sculpture, e.g. Winckelmann: moral; Lessing: formal and antiquarian; Goethe: human. Describes nineteenth-century aversion to the group and present-day historical evaluation as an example of late Hellenistic baroque in transition toward late Republican and Augustan "classicizing tendencies."

BLACKALL, ERIC A., *The Emergence of German as a Literary Language, 1700–1775* (Cambridge: The University Press, 1959).

BLUEMNER, HUGO, ed. *Lessings "Laokoon*," 2nd ed. (Berlin: Weidmannsche Buchhandlung, 1880). The standard edition. Contains also earlier drafts and L.'s sketches and notes for the projected continuation.

BOECKMANN, PAUL, "Lessings Begründung der klassischen Symbolform," *Zeitschrift für Deutschkunde*, L (1936), 413–28.

————, *Formgeschichte der deutschen Dichtung*, 2nd ed., I, *Von der Sinnbildsprache zur Ausdruckssprache*, ... (Hamburg: Hoffmann and Campe, 1965).

BORNKAMM, HEINRICH, "Die innere Handlung in Lessings *Miss Sara Sampson*," in *Solange es "Heute" heisst. Festgabe für Rudolf Hermann* . . . (Berlin: Evangel. Verlagsanstalt, 1957), pp. 42–51.

BRAUN, JULIUS W., *Lessing im Urtheile seiner Zeitgenossen*, 3 vols. (Berlin, 1884–97).

BROWN, F. ANDREW, "The Conversion of Lessing's Freygeist," *JEGP*, LVI (1957), 186–202.

————, "Shakespeare in Germany: Dryden, Langbaine, and the *Acta Eruditorum*," *GR*, XL (1965), 87–95. Discusses Dryden's role in disseminating knowledge of Shakespeare in Germany at the beginning of the eighteenth century.

————, "Shakespeare and English Drama in German Popular Journals, 1717–1759," *KFLQ*, XII (1965), 113–27. Survey of Lessing's journalistic predecessors in fostering interest in and appreciation of Shakespeare and English drama before the seventeenth "Literaturbrief."

BRUEGGEMANN, FRITZ, "Lessings Bürgerdramen und der Subjektivismus als Problem: Psychogenetische Untersuchung," *Jahrbuch des freien deutschen Hochstifts* (1926), pp. 69–110.

BUTLER, E. M., *The Tyranny of Greece over Germany: A Study of the Influence Exercised by Greek Art and Poetry over the Great German Writers of the Eighteenth, Nineteenth, and Twentieth Centuries* (Cambridge: Cambridge Univ. Press, 1935). Lively and entertaining study, deploring (but overemphasizing) the pejorative effect on German literature of its preoccupation with classical forms and themes.

CASSIRER, ERNST, *Die Philosophie der Aufklärung*, Grundriss der philosophischen Wissenschaft, ed. Fritz Medicus (Tübingen: J. C. B. Mohr [Paul Siebeck], 1932). Enlightenment philosophy differs from the systematized philosophy of the preceding age, not primarily in its discovery of novel abstractions, but in the breakthrough to novel applications, by no longer emphasizing thought content, but rather an expanded area of discourse for philosophic speculation, in which it becomes a productive force in the whole spectrum of thought: political, scientific, theological, and esthetic. Includes English and French, as well as German contributions.

CREED, JOHN MARTIN, and JOHN SANDWITH BOYS SMITH, *Religious Thought in the Eighteenth Century: Illustrated from Writers of the Period* (Cambridge: The University Press, 1934). Selections, with brief individual commentaries, from writers on religion, chiefly English, from Locke to Kant and William Paley, primarily on the relation of reason and revelation.

DANZEL, TH. W., and G. E. GUHRAUER, *Gotthold Ephraim Lessing: Sein Leben und seine Werke*, 2 vols., 2nd ed., eds. W. von

Maltzahn and R. Boxberger (Berlin: Theodor Hofmann, 1880–81). Detailed, useful account. Much background material.

DAUNICHT, RICHARD, *Die Entstehung des bürgerlichen Trauerspiels in Deutschland*, Quellen und Forschungen zur Sprach- und Kulturgeschichte der germanischen Völker, N. F. VIII (Berlin: De Gruyter, 1963).

DEMETZ, PETER, ed. *Gotthold Ephraim Lessing: "Nathan der Weise,"* Dichtung und Wirklichkeit, (Frankfurt/M./Berlin: Ullstein, 1966).

DIKENMANN, RUDOLF, "Beiträge zum Thema Diderot und Lessing" (diss. Zürich, 1915). Lists many parallels, especially regarding art, the Laokoön problem, etc., but concludes that no direct influence of Direot on Lessing can be proved.

DUENTZER, HEINRICH, *Erläuterungen zu den deutschen Klassikern*, 6. Abteilung: *Erläuterungen zu Lessings Werken*, IV, *Emilia Galotti* (Leipzig: Wartig, 1873).

DVORETZKY, EDWARD, *The Enigma of "Emilia Galotti"* (The Hague: Nijhoff, 1963).

――――, "Lessing in Schiller's *Kabale und Liebe*," *MP*, LXIII (1966), 311–18.

――――, "Modern German Writers' Views of Lessing's *Emilia Galotti*," *The South Central Bulletin*, XXIII, 4 (1963), 51–59.

ENDERS, CARL, "Der geistesgeschichtliche Standort von Lessings 'Horoskop,'" *Euphorion*, L (1956), 208–16.

FISCHER, KUNO, *G. E. Lessing als Reformator der deutschen Literatur*, 1. Theil, 2nd ed., 2. Theil, 5th ed. (Stuttgart/Berlin: Cotta, 1904–1905).

FITTBOGEN, GOTTFRIED, *Die Religion Lessings*, Paluestra, No. 141 (Leipzig: Mayer and Müller, 1923).

FRICKE, GERHARD, "Bemerkungen zu Lessings *Freigeist* und *Miss Sara Sampson*," in *Festschrift Josef Quint*, eds. Hugo Moser et al. (Bonn: Semmel, 1964), pp. 83–120.

――――, "Lessings *Minna von Barnhelm*," in *Studien und Interpretationen* (Frankfurt/M.: Mencke, 1956).

FRIEDRICH, HUGO, "Lessings Kritik und Missverständnis der französischen Klassik," *Zeitschrift für deutsche Bildung*, VII (1931), 601–11.

GARLAND, H. B., *Lessing: The Founder of Modern German Literature*, 2nd ed. (London: Macmillan, 1962). The most recent, and most useful, full-length discussion of Lessing in English. The works primarily of historical importance only; Lessing's integrity of character as his principal legacy.

GOMBRICH, E. H., "Lessing: A Lecture on a Master Mind," *Proceedings of the British Academy*, XLIII (1957), 133–56.

GRAF, OTTO G., "Lessing and the Art of Acting," *Papers of the Michigan Academy of Science, Arts, and Letters,* XL (Ann Arbor, 1955), 293–301.

GRAHAM, ILSE APPELBAUM, "The Currency of Love: A Reading of Lessing's *Minna von Barnhelm,*" *GLL,* XVIII (1965), 270–78.

GUTHKE, KARL S., *Geschichte und Poetik der deutschen Tragikomödie* (Göttingen: Vandenhoeck und Ruprecht, 1961).

————, "Problem und Problematik von Lessings Faust-Dichtung," *ZDP,* LXXIX (1960), 141–49.

————, "Der Stand der Lessing-Forschung: Ein Bericht über die Literatur von 1932–1962," *DVLG,* XXXVIII (1964), Sonderheft (also Sonderdruck [Stuttgart: Metzler, 1965]). Valuable survey, with analysis of Lessing scholarship in the period 1932–62.

GUTHKE, KARL S., and HEINRICH SCHNEIDER, *Gotthold Ephraim Lessing,* Sammlung Metzler, No. 65 (Stuttgart: Metzler, 1967). Extremely useful biographical and bibliographical survey.

HATFIELD, HENRY, *Aesthetic Paganism in German Literature; From Winckelmann to the Death of Goethe* (Cambridge: Harvard Univ., Press, 1964). A study of the tension between Christian and non-Christian ("this-worldly") forces in the work of Lessing, Wieland, Schiller, some Romanticists (e.g. Novalis, a "crypto-pagan"), transcended in Goethe's all-encompassing and by no means unambiguous concept of love at the close of *Faust,* Part II.

————, *Winckelmann and his German Critics, 1755–1781: A Prelude to the Classical Age,* Columbia Univ. Germanic Studies, N. S. XV (New York: King's Crown Press, 1943). Examines Winckelmann's contribution to the establishment of a favorable attitude toward Greek art and culture, particularly through influence on such writers and editors as C. F. Weisse, Nicolai, Klotz, and Christian Gottlob Heyne.

HEITNER, ROBERT R., "Concerning Lessing's Indebtedness to Diderot," *MLN,* LXV (1950), 82–88. Discusses the several parallels in theory and practice, but demonstrates that chronology and other considerations preclude the assumption of a definite influence of Diderot on Lessing. The precise nature of the "indebtedness" a mystery.

————, "*Emilia Galotti:* An Indictment of Bourgeois Passivity," *JEGP,* LII (1953), 480–90.

————, *German Tragedy in the Age of Enlightenment: A Study in the Development of Original Tragedies, 1724–1768* (Berkeley and Los Angeles: Univ. of California Press, 1963).

HETTNER, HERMANN, *Geschichte der deutschen Literatur im acht-zehnten Jahrhundert,* 4 vols., ed. Georg Witkowski (Leipzig: Paul List, 1929).

HOLL, KARL, *Geschichte des deutschen Lustspiels* (Leipzig: J. J. Weber, 1923).

HOWARD, WILLIAM GUILD, ed. *Laokoon: Lessing, Herder, Goethe* (New York: Holt, 1910). Excerpts on the subject of Laocoön; the Introduction contains detailed background discussion.

KAUFMANN, F. W., "Nathan's Crisis," *Monatshefte*, XLVIII (1956), 277–80.

————, "Zu Lessings *Emilia Galotti*," *Monatshefte*, XXVII (1935), 50–53.

KIES, PAUL P., Lessing's Early Study of English Drama," *JEGP*, XXVIII (1929), 16–34.

————, "Lessing's Relation to Early English Sentimental Comedy," *PMLA*, XLVII (1932), 807–26.

————, "The Sources and Basic Model of Lessing's *Miss Sara Sampson*," *MP*, XXIV (1926), 65–90.

KOFINK, HEINRICH, *Lessings Anschauungen über die Unsterblichkeit und Seelenwanderung* (Strassburg: Trübner, 1912). Detailed analysis of Lessing's views, with suggested sources and parallels for his theorizing on the questions of immortality and transmigration of souls.

KOMMERELL, MAX, *Lessing und Aristoteles: Untersuchung über die Theorie der Tragödie*, 3rd ed. (Frankfurt/M.: Klostermann, 1960).

KORFF, H. A., "*Laokoon*—kurz und bündig," *Wissenschaftliche Zeitschrift der Karl-Marx Univ. Leipzig*, IV (1954–1955), Gesellschafts-und sprachwissenschaftliche Reihe, Heft 1/2, pp. 125–27. Brief outline of content and effect, stressing the later importance of motion in literature (e.g. in Schiller and Goethe) and relating the argument of *Laokoon* to the anti-French campaign in the *Hamburgische Dramaturgie*.

LEANDER, FOLKE, *Lessing als ästhetischer Denker*, Göteborgs Högskolas Årsskrift, XLVIII, 3 (1942). (Göteborg, 1942).

LEEUWE, H. H. J. DE, "Lessings *Philotas*," *Neophilologus*, XXXXVII (1963), 34–40. Takes issue with those who identify Lessing's view with that of his youthful hero.

LEISEGANG, HANS, *Lessings Weltanschauung* (Leipzig: Felix Meiner, 1931).

LENZ, HAROLD, "Der Deutschlehrer und Lessings 'Nathan,'" *GQ*, XIV (1941), 121–27, 170–75; see also XIV (1941), 216–17.

LERCH, EUGEN, "Lessing, Goethe, Schiller und die französische Klassik," *Mainzer Universitäts-Reden*, Heft 11/12 (Mainz, 1948), pp. 1–34.

LUKÁCS, GEORG, "*Minna von Barnhelm*," *Akzente*, XI (1964), 176–91.

MANN, OTTO, *Geschichte des deutschen Dramas* (Stuttgart: Kröner, 1963).

————, ed. *G. E. Lessing*: *"Hamburgische Dramaturgie,"* 2nd ed. (Stuttgart: Kröner, 1963).

————, "Lessing in der modernen Wissenschaft," *Der Deutschunter- richt*, VIII, 5 (1956), 68–86.

————, *Lessing*: *Sein und Leistung*, 2nd ed. (Hamburg: Marion von Schröder, 1961): *"Miss Sara Sampson,"* pp. 220–40; *"Emilia Galotti,"* pp. 240–68.

————, *"Minna von Barnhelm,"* in *Das deutsche Drama*, ed. Benno von Wiese (Düsseldorf: August Bagel, n.d.), I, 79–100.

MARTINI, WOLFGANG, "Die grosse Episode in Lessings dramatischer Technik," *Neue Jahrbücher für das klassische Altertum, Ge- schichte, und deutsche Literatur und für Pädagogik*, XLV (1920), 341–55.

MAY, KURT, *Lessings und Herders kunsttheoretische Gedanken in ihrem Zusammenhang*, Germanische Studien, No. 25 (Berlin, 1923).

MICHELSEN, PETER, "Die Erregung des Mitleids durch die Tragödie: Zu Lessings Ansichten über das Trauerspiel im Briefwechsel mit Mendelssohn und Nicolai," *DVLG*, XL (1966), 548–66.

NOLTE, FRED O., *The Early Middle-Class Drama (1696–1774)* (Lan- caster, Pa.: Lancaster Press, 1935).

————, "Lessing and the Bourgeois Drama," *JEGP*, XXXI (1932), 66–83.

————, "Lessing's Correspondence with Mendelssohn and Nicolai, August 31, 1756 to May 14, 1757," *Harvard Studies and Notes in Philology and Literature*, XIII (1931), 309–32.

————, "Lessing's *Emilia Galotti* in the Light of his *Hamburgische Dramaturgie*," *Harvard Studies and Notes in Philology and Liter- ature*, XIX (1937), 175–97.

OEHLKE, WALDEMAR, *Lessing und seine Zeit*, 2 vols., 2nd ed. (Munich: Beck, 1919). Detailed biography with special atten- tion to the literary milieu for the works of Lessing.

OTT, KARL AUGUST, "Lessing und La Fontaine: Von dem Gebrauche der Tiere in der Fabel," *GRM*, XL (1959), 235–66.

PETERSEN, JULIUS, "Goethe und Lessing," *Euphorion*, XXX (1929), 175–88.

————, in *Lessings Werke*, Petersen-Olshausen ed., XI (= *Das Theater des Herrn Diderot*, "Einleitung.") Lessing owes to Diderot no "settled truths," and derives from him only encour- agement to explore potential avenues to truth.

PETSCH, ROBERT, ed. *Lessings Briefwechsel mit Mendelssohn und Nicolai über das Trauerspiel*, Philosophische Bibliothek, No. 121 (Leipzig, 1910).

————, ed. *Lessings Faustdichtung*, Germanische Bibliothek, 2. Abteilung, IV (Heidelberg, 1911).

PIENS, GERHARD, ed. *Francesco Riccoboni, "Die Schauspielkunst,"* *übersetzt von G. E. Lessing* . . . (Berlin: Henschel, 1954). Reproduces Lessing's translation of Riccoboni's treatise; introductory commentary (pp. 5–49) argues for Lessing's adherence to Riccoboni's views of the art of acting.

POLITZER, HEINZ, "Lessings Parabel von den drei Ringen," *GQ*, XXXI (1958), 161–77.

PRICE, LAWRENCE MARSDEN, *English Literature in Germany* (Berkeley and Los Angeles: Univ. of California Press, 1953 = Univ. of Calif. Pubs. In Modern Philol., XXXVII, 1–548).

REMPEL, HANS, *Tragödie und Komödie im dramatischen Schaffen Lessings,* Sonderausgabe, Reihe "Libelli," CCXX (Darmstadt: Wissenschaftliche Buchgesellschaft, 1967) = repr. of Neue Forschung, No. 26 (Berlin: Junker und Dünnhaupt, 1935.

ROBERTSON, J. G., *Lessing's Dramatic Theory, Being an Introduction to and Commentary on his "Hamburgische Dramaturgie,"* ed. Edna Purdie (Cambridge: Cambridge Univ. Press, 1939). Exhaustive study, particularly of Lessing's "debt" to predecessors and contemporaries.

ROHRMOSER, GUENTER, *"Nathan der Weise"* in *Das deutsche Drama,* ed. Benno von Wiese (Düsseldorf: August Bagel, n.d), I, 113–26.

ROSENTHAL, B., *Der Geniebegriff des Aufklärungszeitalters (Lessing und die Popularphilosophen),* Germanische Studien, No. 138 (Berlin, 1933).

SCHMIDT, ERICH, *Lessing. Geschichte seines Lebens und seiner Schriften,* 2 vols. (Berlin: Weidmannsche Buchhandlung), 1st ed., 1884–92; 2nd ed., 1899; 3rd ed., 1909; 4th ed., 1923. The standard Lessing biography. Unless otherwise indicated, all references above are to the 4th ed.

SCHMITZ, FRIEDRICH JOSEPH, *Lessings Stellung in der Entfaltung des Individualismus,* Univ. of Calif. Pubs. in Mod. Philol., XXIII (Berkeley: Univ. of Calif. Press, 1941). The element of rationalism, i.e. the invocation of abstract norms imposed "despotically" from above, has been overstressed by Lessing scholarship. He seeks to preserve the unique, individualistic, irrational element in human accomplishment, while relating it to fundamental laws of human life; forerunner of Storm and Stress, Classicism, and Romanticism.

SCHNEIDER, HEINRICH, "Emilia Galotti's Tragic Guilt," *MLN*, LXXI (1956), 353–55.

—————, *Das Buch Lessing: Ein Lebensbild in Briefen, Schriften, Berichten,* 2nd ed. (Berne/Munich: Francke, 1961).

—————, *Lessing. Zwölf biographische Studien* (Berne: A. Francke, 1951). Contains previously unrecorded Lessing correspondence,

Lessing utterances, and essays on his work and associates, especially in the Wolfenbüttel period.

SCHNEIDER, JOHANNES, *Lessings Stellung zur Theologie vor der Herausgabe der Wolfenbüttler Fragmente* (diss. Amsterdam, 1953; 's-Gravenhage: Excelsior, n.d.). Lessing's religious position transcends both the orthodox and the rationalistic wing of the Enlightenment but rejects mysticism; God the highest manifestation of Reason, worthy of veneration because it encompasses a universal harmony. Lessing embodies the duty to strive to comprehend rationally the irrational elements only dimly perceived in the religion of revelation.

SCHREMPF, CHRISTOPH, *Lessing als Philosoph*, 2nd ed. (Stuttgart: Fromann, 1921). Emphasizes Lessing's "intuition" in matters of speculation, and the close relation between his esthetic and religious-philosophical thought.

SCHWEITZER, CHRISTOPH E., "Die Erziehung Nathans," *Monatshefte*, LIII (1961), 277–84.

SPANN, MENO, "Der *Nathan* im heutigen Literaturunterricht," *GQ*, XII (1939), 153–59; see also XIV (1941), 211–16.

STAHL, E. L., "*Emilia Galotti*," in *Das deutsche Drama*, ed. Benno von Wiese (Düsseldorf: August Bagel, n.d.), I, 101–12.

————, ed. *Lessing: Emilia Galotti* (Oxford: Basil Blackwell, 1958), "Introduction."

STAIGER, EMIL, "*Minna von Barnhelm*," in *Die Kunst der Interpretation*, 2nd ed. (Zurich: Atlantis, 1957), pp. 75–96.

————, "Rasende Weiber in der deutschen Tragödie des achtzehnten Jahrhunderts: Ein Beitrag zum Problem des Stilwandels," *ZDP*, LXXX (1961), 364–404.

STEINHAUER, HARRY, "The Guilt of Emilia Galotti," *JEGP*, XLVIII (1949), 173–85.

STEINMETZ, HORST, *Die Komödie der Aufklärung*, Sammlung Metzler, No. 47 (Stuttgart: Metzler, 1966).

STEPHAN, GERHARD, *Gotthold Ephraim Lessing und seine Eltern in ihren Beziehungen zu Kamenz . . . als Jahrbuch 1929 des Geschichts- und Altertumsvereins Kamenz . . .* (Kamenz: Im Selbstverlag des Vereins, 1929). Reprints, with commentary, documents from municipal and church archives relating to Lessing and his forebears.

STEPHAN, HORST, "Lessing und die Gegenwart," *Zeitschrift für Theologie und Kirche*, N. F., X (1929), 401–34.

STOCKUM, TH. C. VAN, "Lessing und Diderot," *Neophilologus*, XXXIX (1955), 191–202. Asserts, on questionable grounds, an influence of Diderot on Lessing's ideas regarding desirability of "nature and truth" in drama and an ethical aim for tragedy.

―――, "Lessings Dramenentwurf 'Die Matrone von Ephesus,' " *Neophilologus*, XXXXVI (1962), 125–34. Concludes that Lessing found it impossible to devise a noble motive for the widow's decision to give up her melancholy vigil and "return" to life with the officer.

―――, "Spinoza-Jacobi-Lessing: Ein Beitrag zur Geschichte der deutschen Literatur und Philosophie im 18. Jahrhundert" (diss. Groningen, 1916).

SZAROTA, ELIDA MARIA, *Lessings "Laokoon," eine Kampfschrift für eine realistische Kunst und Poesie*, Beiträge zur deutschen Klassik, ... Abhandlungen, IX (Weimar: Arion-Verlag, 1959). Contains the most detailed analysis of Lessing's views on plastic art and literature, including comparisons with predecessors and contemporaries. Poltical overtones.

THIELICKE, HELMUT, *Offenbarung, Vernunft und Existenz: Studien zur Religionsphilosophie Lessings*, 4th ed. (Gütersloh: Bertelsmann, 1957).

ULMER, BERNHARD, "Another Look at Lessing's *Philotas*," in *Studies in Germanic Languages and Literatures in Memory of Fred O. Nolte*, eds. Erich Hofacker and Liselotte Dieckmann (St. Louis: Washington University Press, 1963), pp. 35–42.

VAIL, CURTIS C. D., "Originality in Lessing's *Theatralische Bibliothek*," *GR*, IX (1934), 96–101. The critical comments largely derivative; only the analysis of Seneca demonstrates an original critical position.

―――, *Lessing's Relation to the English Language and Literature*, Columbia Univ. Germanic Studies, N. S., No. 3 (New York: Columbia Univ. Press, 1936). Lessing a masterful translator, with a complete command of English; English influence decisive in the criticism from 1759–60 onward; *Emilia Galotti* a synthesis of Aristotle and Shakespeare; *Nathan* a culmination of the influence of English dramatic freedoms; the introduction of blank verse ascribed to English influence alone.

WAGNER, ALBERT MALTE, *Lessing: Das Erwachen des deutschen Geistes* (Leipzig/Berlin: Horen-Verlag, 1931). Stresses the artistic, hence unsystematic, non-rational and non-intellectual elements as central to Lessing's activity; he embodies a "vital force" and practices a "productive criticsm," intending not to analyze and "explain," but to "improve and alter."

WALLER, MARTHA, *Lessings "Erziehung des Menschengeschlechts"; Interpretation und Darstellung ihres rationalen und irrationalen Gehaltes; eine Auseinandersetzung mit der Lessingforschung*, Germanische Studien, No. 160 (Berlin, 1935). Carefully delineates extent and limits of rational and irrational aspects of

Lessing's thought. Exhaustive analysis of the pertinent scholarship.

WALZEL, OSKAR, "Lessings Begriff des Tragischen," in *Vom Geistesleben alter und neuer Zeit* (Leipzig: Insel, 1922), pp. 232–61.

WEIGAND, HERMANN J., "Warum stirbt Emilia Galotti?" *JEGP*, XXVIII
(1929), 467–81.

WERNLE, PAUL, *Der schweizerische Protestantismus im achtzehnten
Jahrhundert*, 3 vols. (Tübingen, 1923–25).

WICKE, GUENTER, *Die Struktur des deutschen Lustpiels der Aufklärung: Versuch einer Typologie*, Abhandlungen zur Kunst- Musik-
und Literaturwissenschaft, XXVI (Bonn: Bouvier, 1965).

WIESE, BENNO VON, *Die deutsche Tragödie von Lessing bis Hebbel*,
3rd ed. (Hamburg: Hoffmann und Campe, 1955).

—————, ed. *Das deutsche Drama vom Barock bis zur Gegenwart*,
2 vols. (Düsseldorf: August Bagel Verlag, n.d. [11.–14. Tausend
= 1962]).

—————, *Lessing: Dichtung, Aesthetik, Philosophie*, Das wissenschaftliche Weltbild, ed. P. Hinneberg (Leipzig, 1931). Finds a unify-
ing element in Lessing's accomplishments in drama, esthetics,
and theology-philosophy in the primacy of his ethical sense: a
"moral subjectivism" which supplies the organizing principle for
his threefold attempt to arrive at a rationally acceptable view of
the world.

ZIOLKOWSKI, THEODORE, "Language and Mimetic Action in Lessing's
Miss Sara Sampson," *GR*, XL (1965), 261–76.

Index

(Includes investigators when the cited work does not appear in the Selected Bibliography.)